Exam Ref MS-102
Microsoft 365
Administrator

Orin Thomas

Exam Ref MS-102 Microsoft 365 Administrator

Published with the authorization of Microsoft Corporation by:
Pearson Education, Inc.

ISBN-13: 978-0-13-819946-3
ISBN-10: 0-13-819946-9

Library of Congress Control Number: 2023944921

1 2023

TRADEMARKS

WARNING AND DISCLAIMER

SPECIAL SALES

For information about buying this title in bulk quantities or for special sales opportunities (which may include electronic versions; custom cover designs; and content particular to your business, training goals, marketing focus, or branding interests), please contact our corporate sales department at *corpsales@pearsoned.com* or (800) 382-3419.

For government sales inquiries, please contact *governmentsales@pearsoned.com*.

For questions about sales outside the U.S., please contact *intlcs@pearson.com*.

EDITOR-IN-CHIEF
Brett Bartow

EXECUTIVE EDITOR
Loretta Yates

ASSOCIATE EDITOR
Shourav Bose

DEVELOPMENT EDITOR
Rick Kughen

MANAGING EDITOR
Sandra Schroeder

SENIOR PROJECT EDITOR
Tracey Croom

PRODUCTION EDITOR
Dan Foster

COPY EDITOR
Rick Kughen

INDEXER
Valerie Haynes Perry

PROOFREADER
Dan Foster

TECHNICAL EDITOR
Ed Fisher

EDITORIAL ASSISTANT
Cindy Teeters

COVER DESIGNER
Twist Creative, Seattle

COMPOSITOR
Danielle Foster

Pearson's commitment to diversity, equity, and inclusion

Pearson is dedicated to creating bias-free content that reflects the diversity of all learners. We embrace the many dimensions of diversity, including but not limited to race, ethnicity, gender, socioeconomic status, ability, age, sexual orientation, and religious or political beliefs.

Education is a powerful force for equity and change in our world. It has the potential to deliver opportunities that improve lives and enable economic mobility. As we work with authors to create content for every product and service, we acknowledge our responsibility to demonstrate inclusivity and incorporate diverse scholarship so that everyone can achieve their potential through learning. As the world's leading learning company, we have a duty to help drive change and live up to our purpose to help more people create a better life for themselves and to create a better world.

Our ambition is to purposefully contribute to a world where:

- Everyone has an equitable and lifelong opportunity to succeed through learning.
- Our educational products and services are inclusive and represent the rich diversity of learners.
- Our educational content accurately reflects the histories and experiences of the learners we serve.
- Our educational content prompts deeper discussions with learners and motivates them to expand their own learning (and worldview).

While we work hard to present unbiased content, we want to hear from you about any concerns or needs with this Pearson product so that we can investigate and address them.

Please contact us with concerns about any potential bias at
https://www.pearson.com/report-bias.html.

Contents

Chapter 2   Managing M365 users, groups, and identity synchronization   53

**Chapter 5   Manage security and threats using
              Microsoft 365 Defender   177**

Acknowledgments

I'd like to thank Loretta Yates, Shourav Bose, Ed Fisher, Dan Foster, and Rick Kughen for all the work they did getting this book to print.

About the author

Orin Thomas is a Principal Hybrid Cloud Advocate at Microsoft and has written more than 40 books for Microsoft Press on topics including Windows Server, Windows Client, Azure, Hybrid Cloud, Microsoft 365, Office 365, System Center, Exchange Server, Security, and SQL Server. You can connect with him at *aka.ms/orin*.

Introduction

The MS-102 exam deals with advanced topics, requiring candidates to have an excellent working knowledge of Microsoft 365 administration. Some of the exam comprises topics that even experienced Microsoft 365 administrators may rarely encounter unless they work across all elements of a Microsoft 365 tenancies regularly. To pass this exam, candidates need to understand how to deploy and manage Microsoft 365 tenancies and integrate Microsoft 365 with an on-premises Active Directory environment, manage security and threats, and implement the compliance technologies in Microsoft Purview. They also need to keep up to date with new developments with Microsoft 365, including new features and changes to the interface.

Candidates for this exam are Information Technology (IT) Professionals who want to validate their advanced skills as an administrator of Microsoft 365. To pass, candidates must have a thorough theoretical understanding and meaningful, practical experience implementing technologies, including Microsoft Entra, Microsoft 365 Defender, Microsoft Purview, and Microsoft 365 tenancy configuration.

This edition of this book covers Microsoft 365 and the MS 102 exam objectives circa mid-2023. As the Microsoft 365 suite evolves, so do the Microsoft 365 exam objectives, so you should check carefully if any changes have occurred since this edition of the book was authored and study accordingly.

This book covers every major topic area on the exam but does not cover every exam question. Only the Microsoft exam team has access to the exam questions, and Microsoft regularly adds new questions to the exam, making it impossible to cover specific questions. You should consider this book a supplement to your relevant real-world experience and other study materials. If you encounter a topic in this book that you do not feel completely comfortable with, use the "Need more review?" links you'll find in the text to find more information and take the time to research and study the topic. Great information is available on *learn.microsoft.com* and in blogs and forums.

Organization of this book

This book is organized by the "Skills measured" list published for the exam. The "Skills measured" list is available for each exam on the Microsoft Learn website: *microsoft.com/learn*. Each chapter in this book corresponds to a major topic area in the list, and the technical tasks in each topic area determine a chapter's organization. For example, if an exam covers six major topic areas, the book will contain six chapters.

Preparing for the exam

Microsoft certification exams are a great way to build your résumé and let the world know about your level of expertise. Certification exams validate your on-the-job experience and product knowledge. Although there is no substitute for on-the-job experience, preparation through study and hands-on practice can help you prepare for the exam. This book is *not* designed to teach you new skills.

We recommend augmenting your exam preparation plan by using a combination of available study materials and courses. For example, you might use the *Exam Ref* and another study guide for your at-home preparation and take a Microsoft Official Curriculum course for the classroom experience. Choose the combination that you think works best for you. Learn more about available classroom training, online courses, and live events at *microsoft.com/learn*.

Note that this *Exam Ref* is based on publicly available information about the exam and the author's experience. To safeguard the integrity of the exam, authors do not have access to the live exam.

Microsoft certifications

Microsoft certifications distinguish you by proving your command of a broad set of skills and experience with current Microsoft products and technologies. The exams and corresponding certifications are developed to validate your mastery of critical competencies as you design and develop, or implement and support, solutions with Microsoft products and technologies both on-premises and in the cloud. Certification brings a variety of benefits to the individual and to employers and organizations.

> **MORE INFO ALL MICROSOFT CERTIFICATIONS**
>
> For information about Microsoft certifications, including a full list of available certifications, go to *microsoft.com/learn*.

Access the exam updates chapter and online references

The final chapter of this book, "MS-102 Microsoft 365 Administrator exam updates," will be used to provide information about new content per new exam topics, content that has been removed from the exam objectives, and revised mapping of exam objectives to chapter content. The chapter will be made available from the link below as exam updates are released.

Throughout this book are addresses to webpages that the author has recommended you visit for more information. Some of these links can be very long and painstaking to type, so we've shortened them for you to make them easier to visit. We've also compiled them into a single list that readers of the print edition can refer to while they read.

The URLs are organized by chapter and heading. Every time you come across a URL in the book, find the hyperlink in the list to go directly to the webpage.

Download the Exam Updates chapter and the URL list at

MicrosoftPressStore.com/ERMS102/downloads

Errata, updates, and book support

We've made every effort to ensure the accuracy of this book and its companion content. You can access updates to this book—in the form of a list of submitted errata and their related corrections—at:

MicrosoftPressStore.com/ERMS102/errata

If you discover an error that is not already listed, please submit it to us at the same page.

For additional book support and information, please visit *MicrosoftPressStore.com/Support*.

Please note that product support for Microsoft software and hardware is not offered through the previous addresses. For help with Microsoft software or hardware, go to *support.microsoft.com*.

Stay in touch

Let's keep the conversation going! We're on Twitter: *twitter.com/MicrosoftPress*.

CHAPTER 1

Deploy and configure Microsoft 365 tenants

The old saying goes, "Measure twice; cut once." When it comes to Microsoft 365, it's better to understand the decisions you must make and choose the appropriate path before deploying Microsoft 365 than to realize you've made an unsuitable choice after your organization is already using the service. In this chapter, you'll learn about the decisions you must make when deploying a Microsoft 365 tenancy, how to integrate DNS domain names into Microsoft 365, how to manage organizational settings, how to monitor subscription health, and how to determine how the people in your organization use Microsoft 365 services.

Skills in this chapter:

- Skill 1.1: Deploy a Microsoft 365 tenant
- Skill 1.2: Manage Microsoft 365 DNS domains
- Skill 1.3: Manage Microsoft 365 organizational settings
- Skill 1.4: Manage Microsoft 365 subscription and tenant health
- Skill 1.5: Monitor adoption and usage

> **IMPORTANT   REBRANDING TO MICROSOFT ENTRA ID**
>
> In August 2023, Microsoft announced that it was rebranding Azure Active Directory (Azure AD) to Microsoft Entra ID. In addition, products such as Azure AD Connect, Azure AD Connect Cloud Sync, and Azure Active Directory Domain Services were renamed. The actual functionality of these products has not been changed, and it is also likely that it will be some time before UI elements in various administrative portals and Microsoft's official documentation is updated to use the new brand guidelines. Practice tests and study materials that use the original names will still provide you with relevant information about functionality. However, for the foreseeable future, multiple names will be used to label the same product or service.

Skill 1.1: Deploy a Microsoft 365 tenant

The first step when adopting Microsoft 365 is deploying a Microsoft 365 tenant. To do this successfully, you'll need to plan your tenancy and understand the relationship between tenancies, organizations, and subscriptions.

> **This section covers the following topics:**
> - Plan and create a tenant
> - Plan and create subscriptions

Plan and create a tenant

When planning a Microsoft 365 tenant, you must understand the difference between these three terms:

- **Organization** A group such as a business, an institution, or a government agency that will use Microsoft 365 or another Microsoft cloud offering. Organizations are usually identified by one or more public domain names, such as *tailwindtraders.com*. An organization can have multiple subscriptions.

- **Subscription** An agreement with Microsoft for one or more services. In the case of Microsoft 365, charges accrue to subscriptions based on per-user license fees. A subscription can only be associated with one Azure AD tenant.

- **Tenant** A regional location that houses the infrastructure that provides cloud services. An Azure AD tenant is an individual instance of Azure AD hosting user accounts or groups. Microsoft 365 subscriptions are associated with an Azure AD tenant. Multiple Microsoft cloud-offering subscriptions can be associated with the same Azure AD tenant. You often do this so that your organization can use a single identity provider across multiple services.

> **MORE INFO** **ORGANIZATIONS, SUBSCRIPTIONS, AND TENANTS**
>
> You can learn more about organizations, subscriptions, and tenants at *https://learn. microsoft.com/microsoft-365/enterprise/subscriptions-licenses-accounts-and-tenants-for-microsoft-cloud-offerings*.

The most important initial decisions you will make about your Microsoft 365 tenancy will be the tenant's name and region. When you create a Microsoft 365 subscription, the subscription tenancy is automatically assigned a custom *onmicrosoft.com* domain. The tenant name is in the *name.onmicrosoft.com* format, where *name* is the name you want to assign to your organization's tenancy. This name must be unique; no two organizations can share the same tenant name. When creating the tenancy, a check is performed against your proposed name. You must select an alternative if a tenant with that name already exists.

Although you're unlikely to actually use the *onmicrosoft.com* domain name after you have fully configured your organization's tenancy, it is important to note that *you cannot change the tenant name after you configure your Microsoft 365 subscription*. The tenant name chosen at setup remains with the subscription throughout the subscription's existence and cannot be removed. Resist the temptation to assign an amusing name because your organization will be stuck with it even if it isn't the primary domain name used.

The tenant region determines the following:

- Which Microsoft 365 services will be available to the subscription
- The taxes that will be included in the subscription fee
- The billing currency for the subscription
- The Microsoft data center that will host the resources allocated to the subscription

For example, if you select the United States as the tenant region, your organization's Microsoft 365 tenancy will be allocated resources in a US data center. Selecting Australia means your organization's Microsoft 365 tenancy will be allocated resources in a data center in Australia.

Unlike with other Microsoft 365 settings, you cannot change the tenant region after you have selected it. The only way to alter a tenant region is to cancel your existing subscription and create a new one. It is possible to migrate tenant data to a new region, but this is not a simple operation.

Selecting the correct tenant is important from a compliance perspective. There are many stories of consultants in countries outside the United States setting up US tenancies, only to find out later that they must re-create the tenancy because customer data is stored outside the associated organization's national borders.

> **MORE INFO** **WHERE TENANCY DATA IS STORED**
>
> You can learn more about where tenancy data is stored at *https://learn.microsoft.com/microsoft-365/enterprise/o365-data-locations*.

Multi-geo functionality

Although you cannot change your tenancy region, Microsoft offers multi-geo capability. This functionality enables an organization to expand Microsoft 365 services across multiple geographic regions, allowing specific data generated by a multinational organization to be stored in specific locations to meet legal requirements for data residency. To enable multi-geo functionality for a Microsoft 365 tenancy, the organization's account team must request it.

Moving tenant data

Microsoft allows customers to move an existing tenant's data to a new region if a new data center opens in that region. For example, before 2015, Australian customers had their data stored in the Asia/Pacific data center. When the Australian data center became available, Microsoft offered customers with existing tenancies in the Asia/Pacific data center the option of migrating to the Australian one. However, if an Australian customer deployed a new tenancy today in a data center other than the one in Australia, they would not be able to request a migration because they already had the option of deploying to an Australian data center.

Plan and create subscriptions

A subscription is an agreement with Microsoft to obtain one or more services. There are many Microsoft 365 subscription options. Before purchasing a subscription, you should assess your users' needs to determine the most suitable one. You may have several different groups of users in your organization who have separate needs. Because Microsoft 365 allows you to associate multiple subscriptions with a single tenancy, you can add subscriptions as necessary to a tenancy and assign licenses to users as appropriate.

You add subscriptions to a tenancy on the **Purchase Services** page. To access this page, select **Purchase Services** under **Billing** in the left pane of the Microsoft 365 admin center, as shown in Figure 1-1.

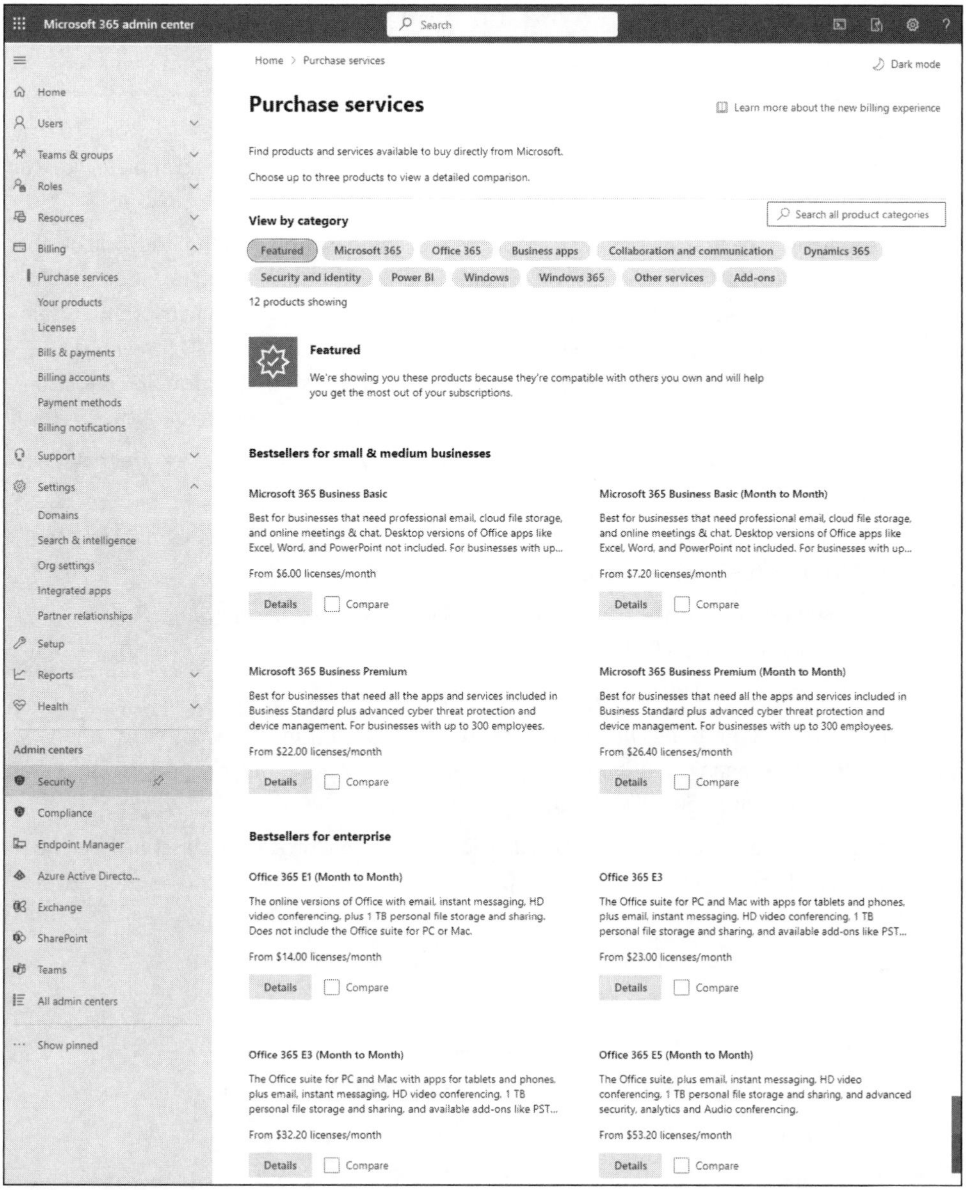

FIGURE 1-1 Purchase Services page

Evaluate Microsoft 365 for an organization

Organizations considering adopting Microsoft 365 can create a trial subscription, which is available to existing Office 365 subscribers. A trial subscription enables the organization to create and use a Microsoft 365 tenancy and the associated Microsoft 365 services for a 30-day evaluation period. The trial period allows 25 licenses. After the trial period is complete, you can convert a trial to a traditional Microsoft 365 subscription.

Before initiating the trial, an organization should do some planning so that they will be able to use the 30-day evaluation period for maximum benefit. Although the organization should approach the trial as a pilot that could eventually evolve into an ongoing subscription, certain actions, such as integrating the on-premises directory with Microsoft Entra ID (previously Azure AD), should not be taken until the organization is satisfied that Microsoft 365 is appropriate and that it will indeed obtain an ongoing subscription.

Specifically, before initiating a Microsoft 365 trial, an organization should ensure that it has done the following:

- Identify 25 users who are ready to participate in the trial. These users should represent how Microsoft 365 will be used in your organization.

- Provide these users with separate computers with trial versions of Windows 10 Enterprise edition installed.

- Identify meaningful workloads to be run during the trial.

It is important to determine whether Microsoft 365 is appropriate for your organization during the trial. This means identifying any potential hurdles during the trial period rather than after Microsoft 365 has been fully adopted.

Creating a test plan or use case involves developing a formal process to describe how the pilot will proceed and how the results of the pilot will be assessed. The test plan should involve the following general phases:

- Deploying the Microsoft 365 tenancy that will be used for the pilot

- Creating user accounts for pilot users

- Configuring active use of email for pilot users

- Deploying Microsoft 365 Apps for enterprise software

- Enabling pilot user access to Microsoft 365 services

- Soliciting pilot user feedback about the experience

> **NOTE ONE SIZE DOES NOT FIT ALL**
>
> Each organization's plans will be slightly different.

You must record pilot user feedback so you can use it when evaluating how decisions made in the planning phase stack up against real-world outcomes. Doing so will enable you to make adjustments during the deployment phase.

You can migrate the email accounts of a small number of users from your on-premises environment to Microsoft 365 while keeping the majority of your existing mailboxes in the on-premises mail solution. This is called *simple domain sharing* for SMTP email addresses.

For example, consider this scenario:

- Your organization has provisioned the *contoso.microsoftonline.com* Office 365 tenancy.
- Your organization has its own on-premises mail solution, which uses the *contoso.com* email suffix.
- Your organization hosts its own DNS records on servers: *dns1.contoso.com* and *dns2. contoso.com*.
- An MX record in the *contoso.com* zone points to the *mailserver.adatum.com* host with a priority of 10.
- An SPF record in the contoso.com DNS zone has the value *v=spf1 mx include:contoso.com -all*.

Take the following steps to configure Office 365 so that some pilot users can receive email through Microsoft 365 while others still use the on-premises solution:

1. Update the SPF record to *v=spf1 mx include:contoso.com include:spf.protection.outlook. com -all*.

2. Confirm ownership within Microsoft 365 of the *contoso.com* DNS zone by configuring the appropriate TXT record.

3. Mark the domain as shared in Exchange Online. You do this on the **Mail Flow** page in the Exchange admin center. (To access the Exchange admin center from the Microsoft 365 admin center, select **Admin** in the pane on the left and then select **Exchange**.)

4. Set the domain as an **Internal Relay** domain.

5. Configure the on-premises mail solution to forward mail for each pilot user account to the *contoso.microsoftonline.com* mail domain. For example, the on-premises mailbox for the *don.funk@contoso.com* email account should forward all incoming email to *don.funk@contoso.microsoftonline.com*.

6. Configure each pilot user's account in Microsoft 365 to use the on-premises DNS zone mail domain. For example, Don Funk's Microsoft 365 user account should be configured with a reply-to address of *don.funk@contoso.com*.

7. Use the Exchange admin center to migrate the contents of the pilot users' on-premises mailboxes.

MORE INFO **TRIAL MICROSOFT 365**

You can learn more about using the Microsoft 365 trial edition if you have an existing Office 365 subscription at *https://learn.microsoft.com/microsoft-365/commerce/ try-or-buy-microsoft-365*.

Upgrade existing subscriptions to Microsoft 365

An organization that already has Office 365 subscriptions for its users can upgrade those subscriptions to Microsoft 365. Similarly, an organization with Office 365 and EMS subscriptions can upgrade them to include Microsoft 365 licenses.

You purchase additional services on the **Purchase Services** page. To access this page, select **Billing** in the left pane in the Microsoft 365 admin center and then select **Purchase Services**. After you purchase the appropriate licenses, you can assign them to users.

> **NOTE** Microsoft's FastTrack for Microsoft 365 service provides information and advice on upgrading an existing deployment or performing a new deployment.

Manage tenant subscriptions

You can manage Microsoft 365 tenant subscriptions from the **Your Products** page. To access this page, select **Billing** in the left pane in the Microsoft 365 admin center and then select **Your Products** (see Figure 1-2).

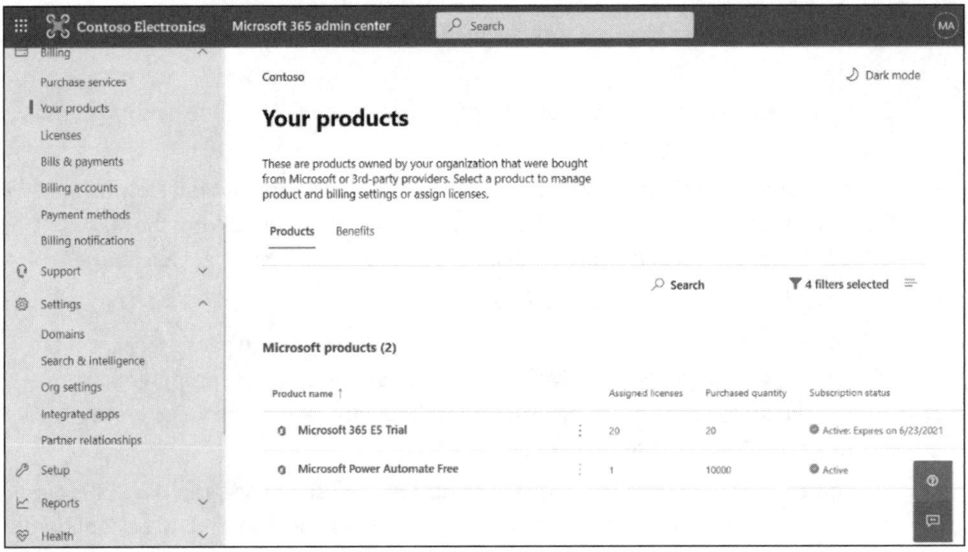

FIGURE 1-2 Your Products page

Clicking each product allows you to see the details of the subscription associated with that product. Figure 1-3 shows the properties of an Enterprise Mobility + Security E5 Demo Trial subscription.

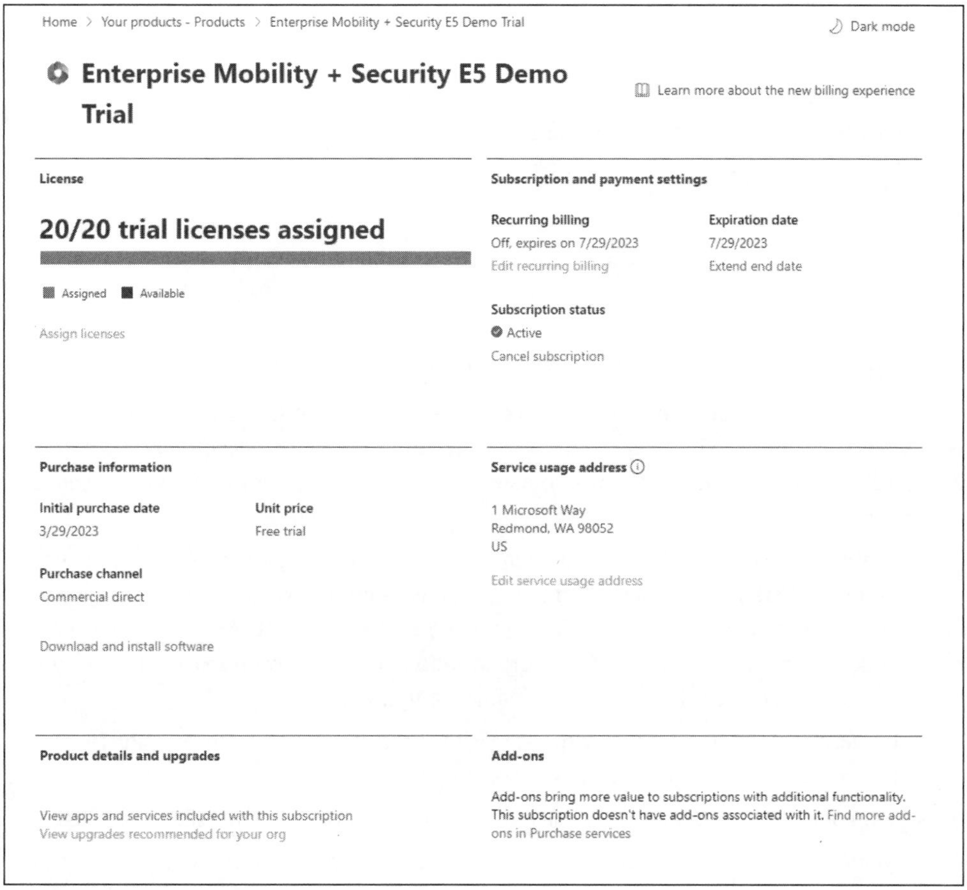

Home > Your products - Products > Enterprise Mobility + Security E5 Demo Trial   🌙 Dark mode

⊙ Enterprise Mobility + Security E5 Demo Trial

📖 Learn more about the new billing experience

License

20/20 trial licenses assigned

▇▇▇▇▇▇▇▇▇▇▇▇▇▇▇▇▇▇▇▇▇

■ Assigned   ■ Available

Assign licenses

Subscription and payment settings

Recurring billing	**Expiration date**
Off, expires on 7/29/2023	7/29/2023
Edit recurring billing	Extend end date

Subscription status

✓ Active

Cancel subscription

Purchase information

Initial purchase date	**Unit price**
3/29/2023	Free trial

Purchase channel

Commercial direct

Download and install software

Service usage address ⓘ

1 Microsoft Way
Redmond, WA 98052
US

Edit service usage address

Product details and upgrades

View apps and services included with this subscription
View upgrades recommended for your org

Add-ons

Add-ons bring more value to subscriptions with additional functionality. This subscription doesn't have add-ons associated with it. Find more add-ons in Purchase services

FIGURE 1-3   Subscription properties

EXAM TIP

Ensure that you understand the difference between a subscription and a tenancy.

Skill 1.2: Manage Microsoft 365 DNS domains

By configuring DNS records, Microsoft 365 makes it relatively simple to associate a DNS domain name with a subscription. Depending on your organization's needs, you can associate many DNS names with a single subscription or just use a single name.

> **This section covers the following topics:**
> - Implement a domain name strategy
> - Manage domains
> - Configure workloads for a new domain name

Implement a domain name strategy

Microsoft 365 supports adding as many as 900 domains to a single subscription. You can use separate domain names with a subscription, such as *contoso.com* or *tailwindtraders.com*, and you can also associate subdomains of a domain name, such as *partners.tailwindtraders.com* or *australia.contoso.com*.

Being able to associate as many as 900 domain names with a single subscription gives your organization a substantial number of options for implementing a domain name strategy. For example, you could configure each service associated with a Microsoft 365 subscription with a different domain name. In this case, if your organization owned the *contoso.com* domain, you might choose to have the following domain name configuration:

- *Contoso.com*   Domain name associated with Exchange Online. Each user signs in to Microsoft 365 using an account with a *contoso.com* UPN suffix.
- *sharepoint.contoso.com*   Subdomain name associated with the SharePoint services.
- *Mdm.contoso.com*   Subdomain name associated with mobile device management functionality for Microsoft 365.

You might also configure separate subdomains and provide them as alternate email domains with secondary addresses for Exchange Online mailboxes. For example, you could use *adele.vance@contoso.com* as the primary email address for a mailbox but configure *adele.vance@tailwindtraders.com* as a proxy address. A single Adele Vance mailbox could then receive emails addressed to multiple addresses.

Manage domains

You can assign the tenant a domain name that you own so that you don't have to use the tenant name regularly. For example, you might sign up for a Microsoft 365 subscription with the *contoso.onmicrosoft.com* tenant name. Any account you create will use the *contoso.onmicrosoft.com* email suffix for the account's Office 365 Exchange mailbox.

However, after you set up Microsoft 365, you can assign a custom domain name and use it as the primary email suffix. For example, assuming you owned the *contoso.com* domain name, you could configure your tenancy to use the custom *contoso.com* domain name with the *contoso.onmicrosoft.com* tenancy.

Acquire a domain name

If your organization wants to use a new domain name with its Microsoft 365 tenancy, it can procure one with a registrar. When you do this, you can choose to have the registrar host the name server records for the domain or select your own name server records.

Most organizations will have already procured a domain name and hosted it with a specific domain registrar, their ISP, or even on their own DNS servers. To use a domain with Microsoft 365, the DNS servers used as name servers for the domain must support the following record types:

- **CNAME records** To fully support Microsoft Teams, the name server DNS servers must be able to support multiple CNAME records in a DNS zone.
- **SPF/TXT records** These records enable you to configure sender protection framework records, which can be used to combat unsolicited commercial email. TXT records are also a way to verify domain ownership.
- **SRV records** SRV records are used to identify the domain name of the service that is responsible for handling Microsoft Teams discovery.
- **MX records** These records are used to route mail to Exchange Online mail servers.

Purchase a domain through Microsoft 365

In some regions, you can purchase a custom domain name from within Microsoft 365. When you do this, you're limited to the following top-level domains:

- .biz
- .com
- .info
- .me
- .mobi
- .net
- .org
- .tv
- .co.uk
- .org.uk

Purchasing a domain through Microsoft 365 can be advantageous because most DNS-related operations will be performed automatically for you. However, you shouldn't choose this option if your organization will continue to use email services outside Microsoft 365 because you won't be able to modify the appropriate MX records.

Configure a custom domain name

To configure Microsoft 365 to use a custom domain name, you must add the custom domain name to Microsoft 365. The account used to perform this action must be a Global Administrator of a business or enterprise plan.

To add a custom domain to Microsoft 365, perform the following steps:

1. In the left pane of the Microsoft 365 admin center, under **Settings**, select **Domains** (see Figure 1-4).

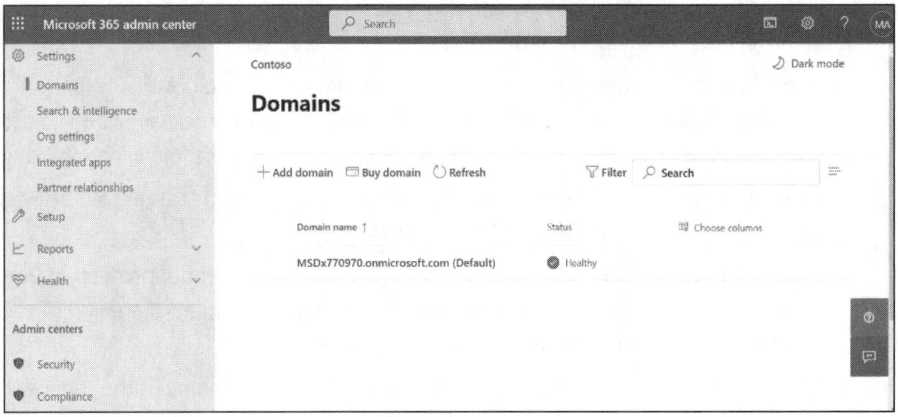

FIGURE 1-4 The Domains page

2. If your organization already has a domain, select **Add Domain**.

> **NOTE SUPPORTED REGISTRARS**
>
> You can also buy a domain through Office 365 and GoDaddy. To do so, select the Buy Domain button on the Domains page. When you buy a domain through GoDaddy, the entire process of assigning a custom domain to Microsoft 365 occurs automatically. However, if your organization's domain is already hosted elsewhere, you will have to confirm ownership of that domain by configuring special TXT or MX records that the setup process can check.

3. The **New Domain** page opens.

4. In the **Domain Name** box, type the name of the existing domain you want to configure and select **Use This Domain** (see Figure 1-5).

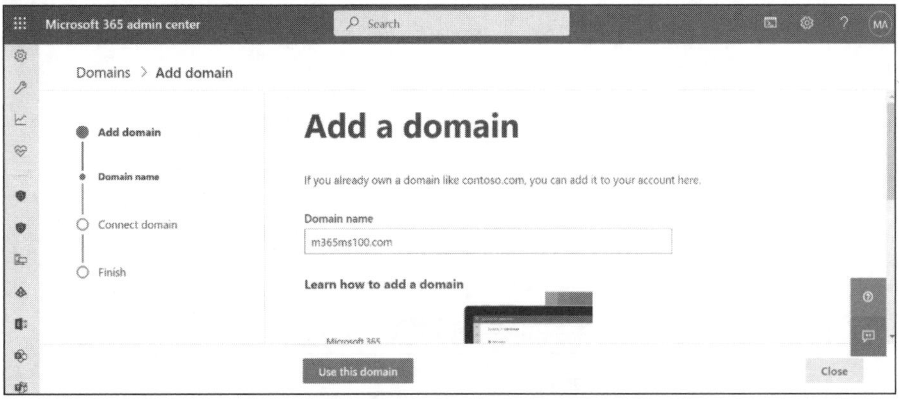

FIGURE 1-5   Adding an existing domain in Microsoft 365

This begins the process of adding the domain. You will need to confirm ownership before you can use the domain. See the next section for instructions.

Verify a custom domain

You can only use a custom domain name with Microsoft 365 if your organization owns that domain name. Microsoft requires you to perform a series of DNS configuration changes to the domain name to prove that your organization owns and controls the domain. After you specify the domain you want to add, you verify it on the **Domain Verification** page, which opens automatically when you select **Use This Domain**.

To confirm ownership of your organization's domain, follow these steps:

1. On the **Domain Verification** page (see Figure 1-6), you can choose one of the following options:

   ■ **Add A TXT Record To The Domain's DNS Records**

   ■ **If You Can't Add A TXT Record, Add An MX Record To The Domain's DNS Records**

   ■ **Add A Text File To The Domain's Website**

2. For this example, choose **Add A TXT Record To The Domain's DNS Records** and select **Continue**.

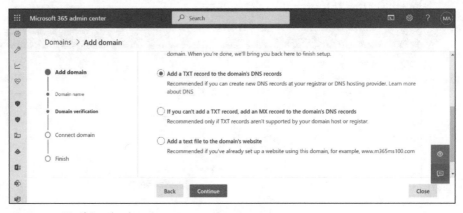

FIGURE 1-6 Verifying the domain

3. On the page that appears, follow the step-by-step instructions to add a TXT record to the domain to verify domain ownership (see Figure 1-7).

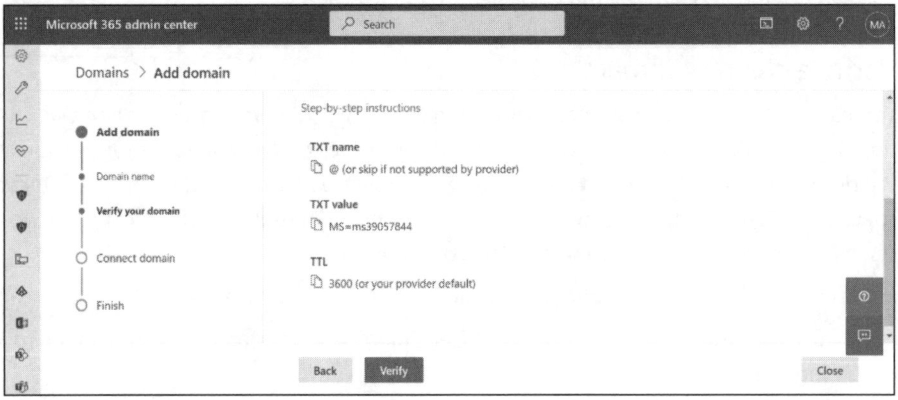

FIGURE 1-7 TXT record details

4. Select **Verify**.

5. Microsoft 365 will attempt to confirm the presence of the record. Depending on how the DNS is configured, the verification process may take as long as 15 minutes to complete.

> **NOTE** **THE SIMPLE OPTION**
> If you use GoDaddy as your DNS hosting provider, the Microsoft 365 setup process can add all the necessary Microsoft 365 services. Alternatively, you can perform the steps manually, as outlined later in this chapter.

> ***MORE INFO*** **ADDING A DOMAIN TO MICROSOFT 365**
>
> **You can learn more about this topic at *https://learn.microsoft.com/microsoft-365/admin/setup/add-domain*.**

Verify DNS settings

You can check DNS settings at any time. To do so, select the Microsoft 365 admin center domain, select **Refresh**, and note whether the domain status is listed as **Healthy** (see Figure 1-8). Microsoft 365 determines whether a domain is healthy by performing a query against the records required for the services you have chosen and validating that the results returned by the query match those required by Microsoft 365.

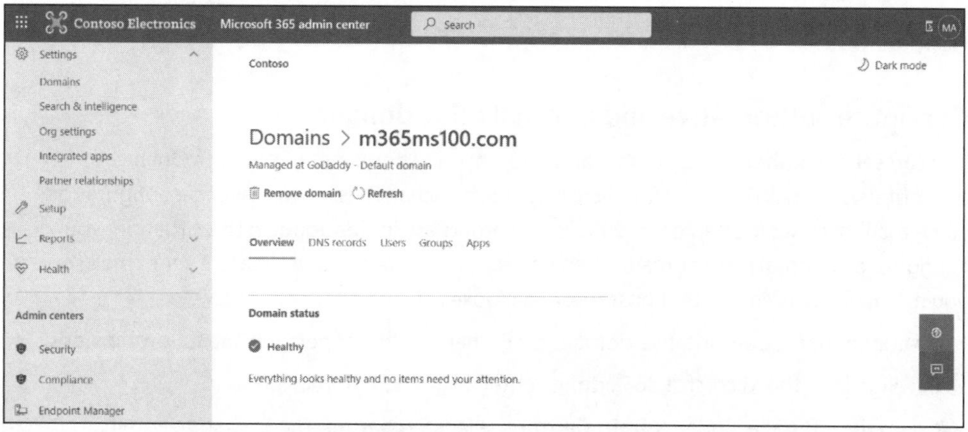

FIGURE 1-8 TXT record in Azure DNS

> ***MORE INFO*** **MICROSOFT 365 DOMAINS FAQ**
>
> **You can learn more about configuring domains for Microsoft 365 at *https://learn.microsoft.com/microsoft-365/admin/setup/domains-faq*.**

Set the default domain

Setting the default domain specifies which domain suffix will automatically be used with Microsoft 365 user accounts. You can select a default domain only if you have configured Microsoft 365 with at least one custom domain.

Follow these steps to set the default domain:

1. Sign in to the Microsoft 365 admin center as a Global Administrator.
2. In the left pane, under **Settings**, select **Domains**.
3. Select the domain that you want to set as the default domain.

4. On the **Domains** page shown in Figure 1-9, select **Set As Default**.

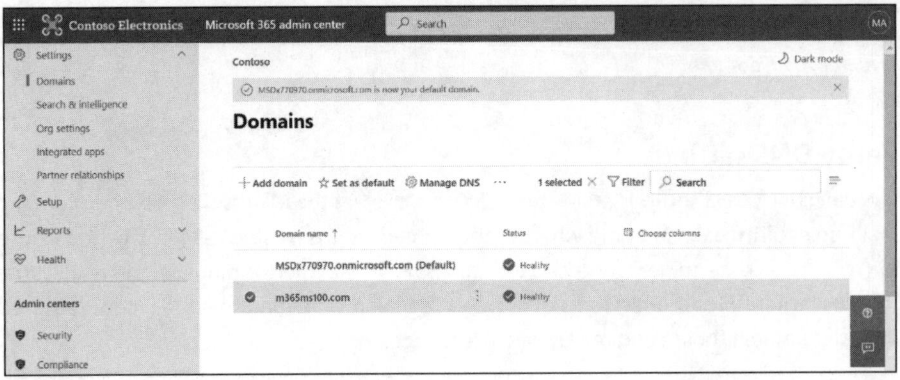

FIGURE 1-9 Listing of domains

Configure authoritative and internal relay domains

You can set the authoritative domain and internal relay domains in Exchange Online. An authoritative domain is used with Microsoft 365. If Exchange is set to a hybrid configuration, some mailboxes are located on-premises and others are in the cloud. In this situation, you configure an internal relay domain when you have a connector to a separate set of mail servers you maintain on-premises that host these mailboxes.

To configure the authoritative domain for Exchange Online, perform the following steps:

1. Sign in to the Microsoft 365 admin center as a Global Administrator.
2. In the left pane, under **Admin Centers**, select **Exchange**. The Exchange admin center opens.
3. Under **Mail Flow**, select **Accepted Domains**.
4. A list of **Accepted Domains** appears (see Figure 1-10).

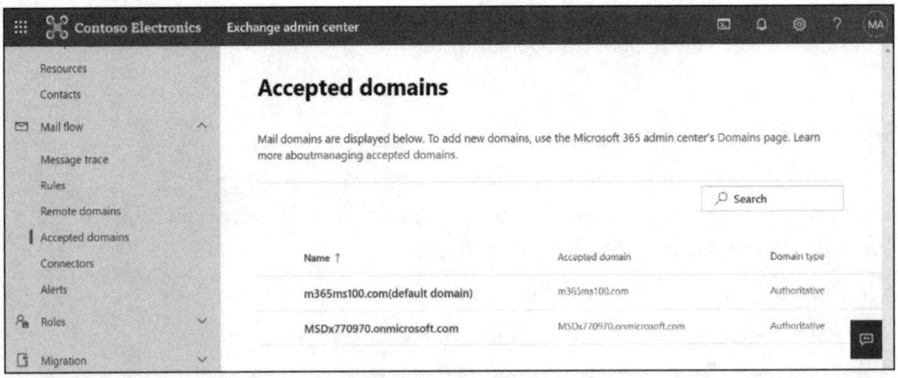

FIGURE 1-10 Accepted domains in Exchange admin center

5. Select the domain you want to configure.

6. On the **Accepted Domain** page, ensure that the **Authoritative** option is selected (see Figure 1-11).

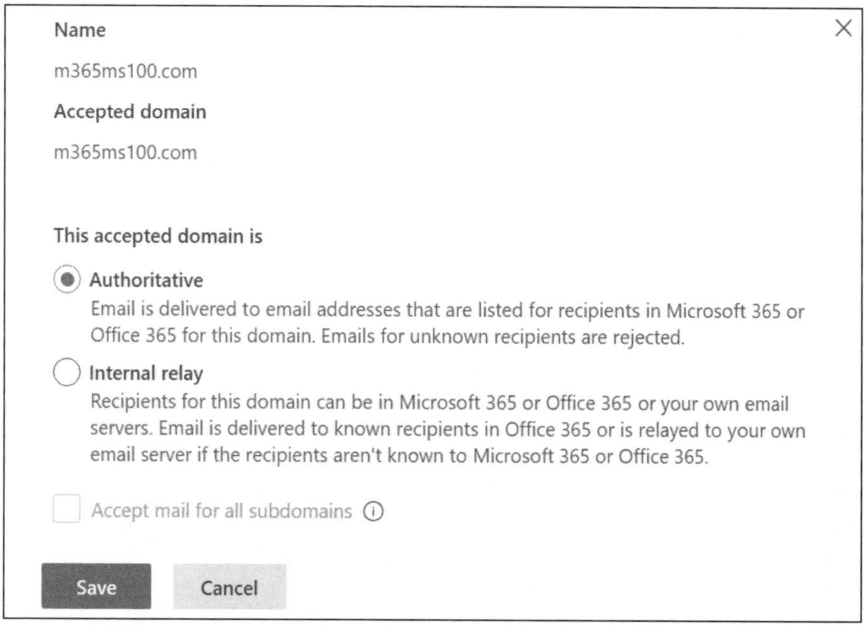

Name	×
m365ms100.com	

Accepted domain

m365ms100.com

This accepted domain is

◉ **Authoritative**
  Email is delivered to email addresses that are listed for recipients in Microsoft 365 or Office 365 for this domain. Emails for unknown recipients are rejected.

○ **Internal relay**
  Recipients for this domain can be in Microsoft 365 or Office 365 or your own email servers. Email is delivered to known recipients in Office 365 or is relayed to your own email server if the recipients aren't known to Microsoft 365 or Office 365.

☐ Accept mail for all subdomains ⓘ

[Save] [Cancel]

FIGURE 1-11 Configuring the authoritative domain

MORE INFO   ACCEPTED DOMAINS IN EXCHANGE ONLINE

You can learn more about configuring accepted domains for Exchange Online at *https:// learn.microsoft.com/exchange/mail-flow-best-practices/manage-accepted-domains/ manage-accepted-domains*.

Configure user identities for new the domain name

When your Microsoft 365 organization adopts a new custom domain name, you will need to determine what steps you should take to allow users to leverage that domain name. For example,

- Should all newly created user accounts be assigned that domain name for email and the UPN sign-in?

- Should existing user accounts be modified so that they use the new domain name for email and UPN sign-in?

- Should the new domain name simply be added as an alternative domain suffix to the existing organization email address?

In this section, you will learn what steps you can take to modify the primary address so that it uses a new domain name.

Manage email addresses

The default address—also known as the primary address and reply-to address—is the address users employ to sign in to Microsoft 365 resources, including Office 365, and to which recipients reply when they receive an email message from a user. You can view a user's primary email address in the Microsoft 365 admin center on the user's properties page (see Figure 1-12).

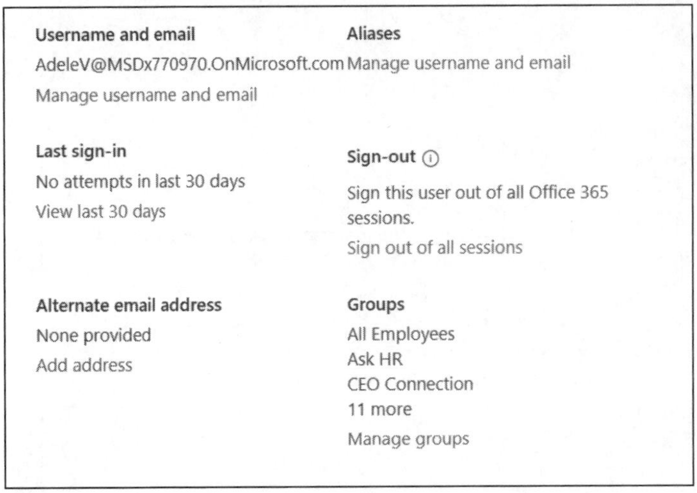

Username and email
AdeleV@MSDx770970.OnMicrosoft.com
Manage username and email

Aliases
Manage username and email

Last sign-in
No attempts in last 30 days
View last 30 days

Sign-out ⓘ
Sign this user out of all Office 365 sessions.
Sign out of all sessions

Alternate email address
None provided
Add address

Groups
All Employees
Ask HR
CEO Connection
11 more
Manage groups

FIGURE 1-12 Locating a user's primary email address

You can change the primary email address if you add another email address to a Microsoft 365 user account (see Figure 1-13). Be aware that changing the primary email address also changes the username.

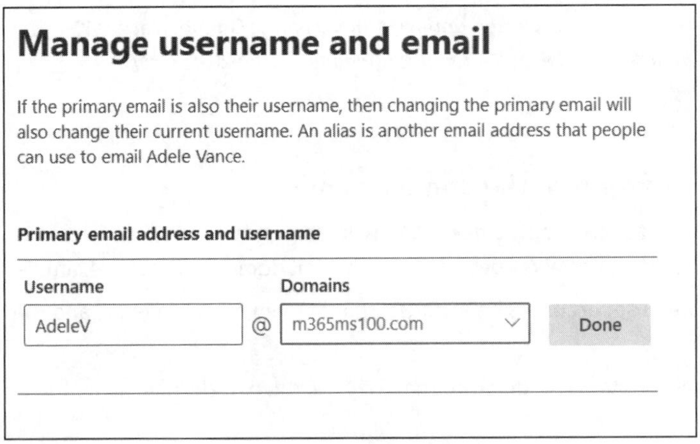

Manage username and email

If the primary email is also their username, then changing the primary email will also change their current username. An alias is another email address that people can use to email Adele Vance.

Primary email address and username

Username	Domains	
AdeleV	@ m365ms100.com ⌄	Done

FIGURE 1-13 Changing a user account's primary email address

> **NOTE CONFIGURE ACCEPTED DOMAIN**
>
> The email suffix for the primary address must be configured as an accepted domain for the Office 365 tenancy.

To perform a bulk email address update, you can use PowerShell. You might do this if, for example, the name of the organization changes. This step should be taken with extreme care. Supporting a small number of users through a transition to a new email and login address is relatively simple, but supporting every user in the organization through such a transition is what might politely be termed "logistically intensive."

To update the email and login domains of multiple users, perform the following steps:

1. In the left pane of the Microsoft 365 admin center, under **Users**, select **Active Users**.

2. On the **Active Users** page, select all the users whose email and login domains you want to update (see Figure 1-14).

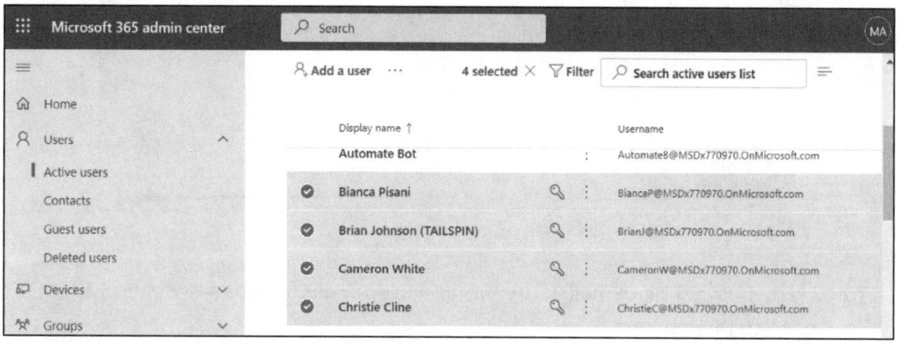

FIGURE 1-14 Selecting multiple users

3. Open the **More** dropdown and select **Change Domains**.

4. In the **Change Domains** panel, open the **Change Domains** dropdown, select one of the domains added to Microsoft 365, and select **Save Changes** (see Figure 1-15).

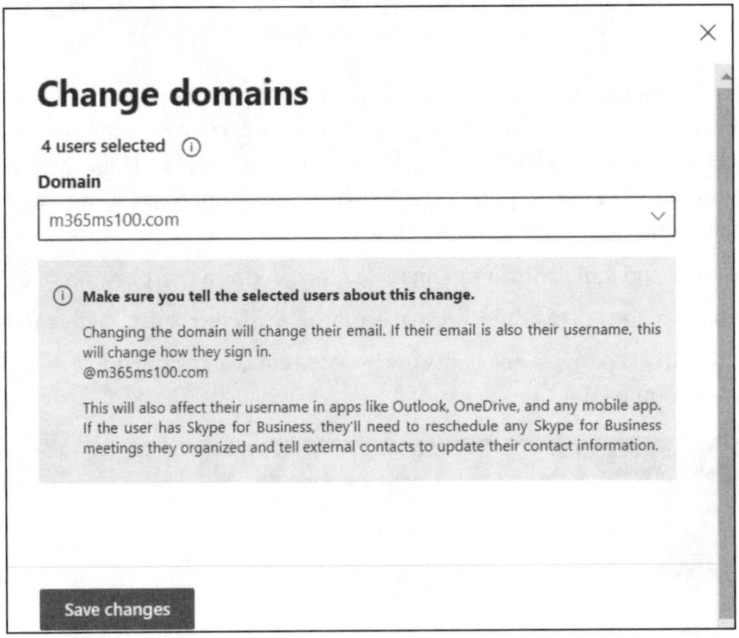

FIGURE 1-15 Select multiple users

You will be notified that email addresses and usernames in apps associated with Microsoft 365 will need to be updated.

Set up additional email addresses

Having additional email addresses enables mailboxes to receive messages from multiple addresses. Also known as proxy or secondary addresses, they can take any format and use any domain name associated with the organization's Microsoft 365 tenancy. For example, Adele Vance's user account could have the primary username and address as *AdeleV@contoso.com*, but it could also have the following addresses associated with the same Exchange mailbox:

- *adele.vance@contoso.com*
- *adele.vance@tailwindtraders.com*
- *adeleV@fabrikam.com*
- *feedback@contoso.com*
- *suggestions@contoso.com*

You can set up additional email addresses for an Office 365 account's Exchange Online mailbox using a variety of methods. To set up an additional email address for an Exchange Online mailbox using the Exchange admin center, perform the following steps:

1. Sign in to the Microsoft 365 admin center with a user account with Tenant Administrator permissions.

2. In the left pane, under **Admin Centers**, select **Exchange**.

3. In the Exchange admin center, select **Recipients** > **Mailboxes**.

4. Select the recipient for whom you want to set up an additional email address. In Figure 1-16, the entry for Adele Vance is selected.

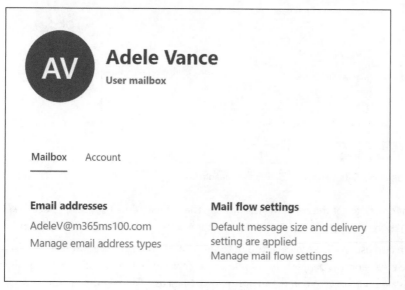

FIGURE 1-16 Selecting a recipient for an additional email address

5. On the **User Mailbox** properties page, select **Manage Email Address Types**, as shown in Figure 1-17.

FIGURE 1-17 The User Mailbox properties page

6. Select **Add Email Address Type**.

7. On the **New Email Address** page, ensure that **SMTP** is selected and enter the new email address. You can also specify the new email address as the default reply-to address.

To set up an additional email address for an Exchange Online mailbox using the Microsoft 365 admin center, perform the following steps:

1. In the left pane of the Microsoft 365 admin center, under **Users**, select **Active Users**.

2. Select the user for which you want to configure the additional email address. The user account's properties page opens.

3. Under **Aliases**, select **Manage Username And Email**.

4. On the **Manage Username And Email** page, under **Aliases**, type the new email address in the **Username** and **Domains** boxes, and select **Save Changes** (see Figure 1-18).

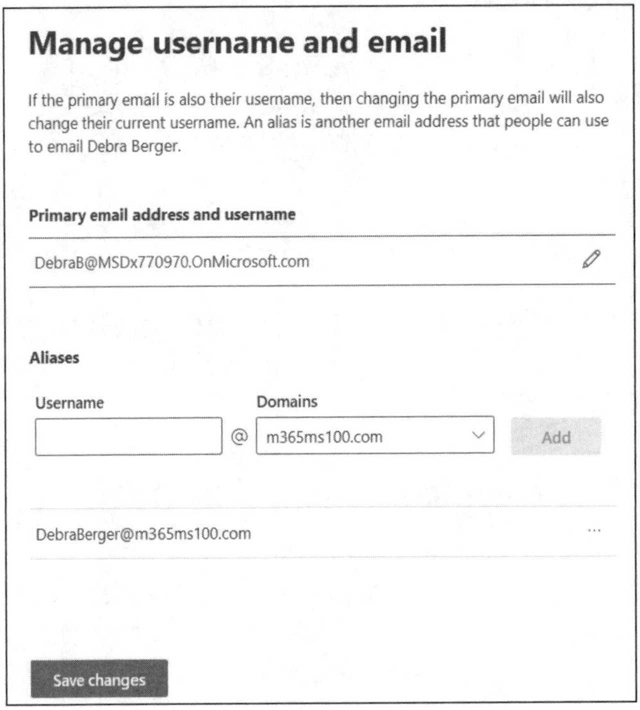

Manage username and email

If the primary email is also their username, then changing the primary email will also change their current username. An alias is another email address that people can use to email Debra Berger.

Primary email address and username

DebraB@MSDx770970.OnMicrosoft.com

Aliases

Username	Domains
	@ m365ms100.com ⌄ Add

DebraBerger@m365ms100.com ...

Save changes

FIGURE 1-18 Setting up an additional email address

5. Optionally, to set the new email address as the primary email address, select the ellipsis (**...**) to the right of the email address and then select **Change To Primary Email**.

You can also use the *Set-Mailbox* cmdlet to set up additional email addresses. For example, to add the email address *berger.debra@m365ms100.com* to Debra Berger's Exchange Online mailbox, issue the following command using PowerShell as a Global Administrator:

```
Set-Mailbox"" "Debra Berger""" -EmailAddresses @{Add=berger.debra@m365ms100.com}
```

Configure workloads for a new domain name

By configuring a custom domain's purpose, you can choose how it will be used with a variety of Microsoft 365 services. For example, you might want to use one custom domain as an email suffix, another custom domain with SharePoint, and another for Microsoft Teams. You can only configure a domain's purpose after you have verified the DNS zone.

Exchange Online–related DNS records

When you provision Microsoft 365 for your organization, Microsoft ensures that the DNS records for your organization's tenant domain (the *onmicrosoft.com* domain) are configured properly so that email addresses using the tenant domain as an email domain suffix have mail routed properly.

For example, if you provision a Microsoft 365 tenant with the *contoso.onmicrosoft.com* tenant domain, then emails sent to users at this email domain—such as an email sent to *don. funk@contoso.onmicrosoft.com*—will arrive at the correct location because Microsoft 365 will provision the appropriate DNS records automatically when the tenancy is provisioned.

When you add a custom domain to Microsoft 365, you must configure an appropriate set of DNS records to ensure that mail flows properly to Exchange Online mailboxes that use the custom domain. For example, if your custom domain is *tailspintoys.com*, you must configure DNS so that email will function properly for Exchange Online mailboxes configured to use the *tailspintoys.com* email domain. When properly configured, the user associated with the *don. funk@tailspintoys.com* Exchange Online mailbox will receive emails sent from other hosts on the internet.

If your custom DNS zone is hosted by GoDaddy, Microsoft 365 can configure the appropriate DNS records for you automatically. If another DNS hosting provider hosts your custom DNS zone, you must manually configure DNS records. Specifically, you must configure the following DNS records:

- The Autodiscover CNAME record for Autodiscover service
- An MX record for mail routing
- A Sender Policy Framework (SPF) record to verify the identity of the mail server

These records are listed in Table 1-1. The specifics of records will be provided for you by the Microsoft DNS setup wizard. The MX record takes the form *<customdnsname>.mail.protection. outlook.com* and will vary depending on the custom domain name being registered.

TABLE 1-1 Microsoft 365 Exchange DNS records

Type	Priority	Host name	Value	TTL
MX	0	@	<customdnsname>.mail.protection.outlook.com	1 hour
TXT	-	@	v=spf1 include:spf.protection.outlook.com -all	1 hour
CNAME	-	autodiscover	autodiscover.outlook.com	1 hour

MX records

You must configure an MX record in your custom domain to point to an Office 365 target mail server. The address of this target mail server will depend on the name of the custom domain and is described in the documentation as being in the *<mx token>.mail.protection.outlook.com* form. You can review the value for an MX record by performing the following steps:

1. In the left pane of the Microsoft 365 admin center, under **Settings**, select **Domains**.
2. Select the custom domain you created.
3. The **Domain Properties** page opens. Locate the MX record (see Figure 1-19).

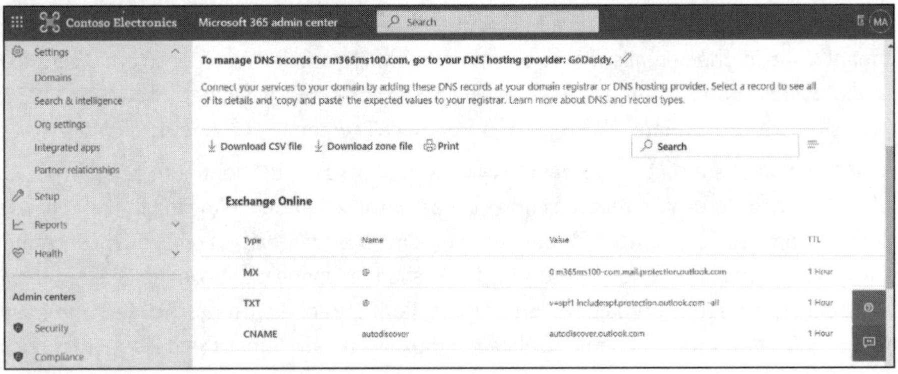

FIGURE 1-19 DNS record information

To ensure that mail routes properly, you must configure the MX priority for the record to be a lower value than any other MX records configured for the custom domain. When mail is routed, a check is performed to determine which MX record has the lowest value for the priority field. For example, an MX record with a priority of 10 will be chosen as a destination for mail routing over an MX record with a priority of 20.

SPF records

The Sender Policy Framework (SPF) record is a special TXT record that reduces the possibility of malicious third parties using the custom domain to send spam or other types of unwanted email. An SPF record is used to validate which email servers are authorized to send messages on behalf of the custom domain. The SPF record must be a TXT record, and the TXT value must include the following:

```
v=spf1 include:spf.protection.outlook.com -all
```

The record should also be set with a TTL value of 3600. Only one TXT record for an SPF should exist within a specific zone. If an SPF record is already present, append the Microsoft 365 values to the existing record rather than creating a new one.

Autodiscover CNAME records

You must create a CNAME record that uses the autodiscover alias to point to the host name *autodiscover.outlook.com* so that Outlook clients' settings are automatically provisioned for Exchange Online. For example, if the custom domain you assigned to Microsoft 365 was *tailspintoys.com*, you would need to create the *autodiscover.tailspintoys.com* CNAME record and have it point to *autodiscover.outlook.com*.

Exchange federation TXT records

When configuring federation between an on-premises Exchange deployment and Exchange Online, you must create two special TXT records, including a custom-generated domain-proof hash text.

The first record will include the custom domain name and the hash text, such as *tailspintoys.com* and *Y96nu89138789315669824*, respectively. The second record will include the *exchangedelegation* name with the custom domain name and custom-generated domain-proof hash text like *exchangedelegation.tailspintoys.com* and *Y3259071352452626169*.

Exchange federation CNAME records

If you are configuring federation, you need an additional CNAME record to support federation with Office 365. This CNAME record will need the *autodiscover.service* alias and should also point to *autodiscover.outlook.com*.

> **MORE INFO   MICROSOFT 365 DNS RECORDS**
>
> You can learn more about DNS records for Microsoft 365 at *https://learn.microsoft.com/microsoft-365/enterprise/external-domain-name-system-records*.

Microsoft Teams DNS records

Microsoft Teams requires the DNS records listed in Table 1-2 if you use Skype for Business Online Phones for Microsoft Teams or if you are using PowerShell cmdlets that use Skype for Business Online infrastructure for management. This will only be necessary if your organization has migrated from Skype for Business or Lync.

TABLE 1-2   Microsoft 365 Teams DNS records

Type	Host name	Value
SRV (Federation)	<domain>	Domain: <domain> Service: sipfederationtls Protocol: TCP Priority: 100 Weight: 1 Port: 5061 Target: sipfed.online.lync.com
SRV (SIP)	<domain>	Domain: <domain> Service: sip Protocol: TLS Priority: 100 Weight: 1 Port: 443 Target: sipdir.online.lync.com
CNAME	Lyncdiscover.<domain>	Target: *webdir.online.lync.com*

Mobile Device Management for Microsoft 365 DNS records

If you are using mobile device management (MDM) for Microsoft 365, you must create two CNAME records, also known as aliases, so that devices can find the appropriate location to register. These two records are listed in Table 1-3.

TABLE 1-3   Microsoft 365 Mobile Device Management DNS records

Type	Host name	Value	TTL
CNAME	enterpriseregistration	enterpriseregistration.windows.net	1 hour
CNAME	enterpriseenrollment	enterpriseenrollment.manage.microsoft.com	1 hour

---

EXAM TIP

Remember the types of DNS records that you can configure to verify ownership of a specific custom domain name.

Skill 1.3: Manage Microsoft 365 organizational settings

After deploying Microsoft 365, you'll want to configure organizational settings. This includes setting up the organizational profile with settings such as password policies and settings related to sharing organizational data.

This section covers the following topics:

- Configure organizational settings
- Complete the organizational profile
- Add a Microsoft partner or work with Microsoft FastTrack
- Complete the subscription setup wizard
- Edit an organizational profile

Configure organizational settings

To configure the organizational settings, select **Settings** in the left pane of the Microsoft 365 admin center, and then select **Org Settings**. This opens the **Org Settings** page. This page has three tabs: **Services**, **Security & Privacy**, and **Organization Profile**. The **Services** tab enables you to configure the settings shown in Figure 1-20.

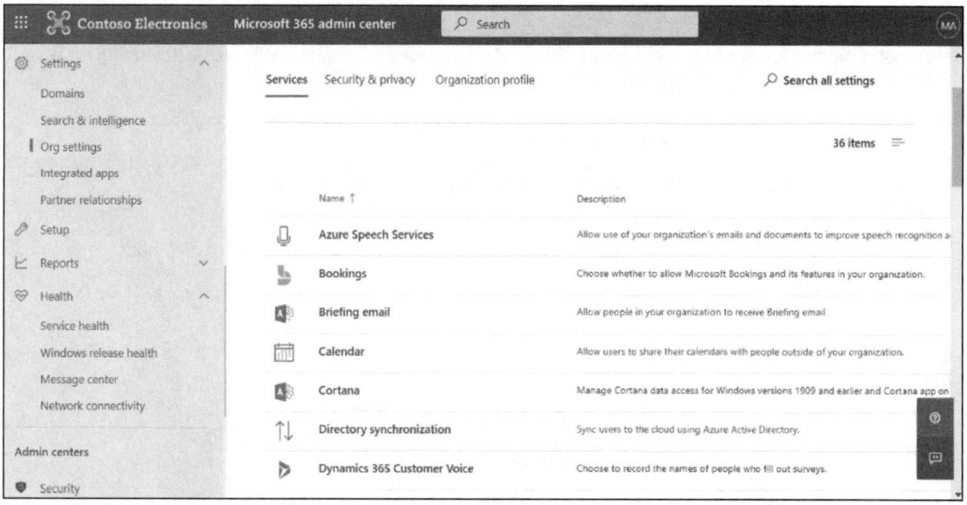

FIGURE 1-20 The Services tab of the Org Settings page

These services are listed in Table 1-4.

TABLE 1-4 Organizational settings

Setting	Description
Azure Speech Services	Allow your organization's emails and documents to be used to improve speech-recognition accuracy.
Bookings	Enable Microsoft Bookings (a scheduling tool) and its features.
Briefing Email	Specify whether people receive Briefing emails. These are generated by Outlook, which looks for actionable tasks and includes them in the email.
Calendar	Configure calendar-sharing for people outside your organization.
Cortana	Manage Cortana data access for Windows 10 versions 1909 and earlier.
Directory Synchronization	Configure Azure AD synchronization.
Dynamics 365 Customer Coice	Specify whether people who fill out customer surveys will have their names stored.
Dynamics 365 Sales Insights–Analytics	Specify whether Dynamics 365 can generate insights based on user data.
Dynamics 365 Sales Insights–Connection Graph	Manage connection graph settings for Dynamics 365 Sales Insights.
Dynamics CRM	Manage organization Dynamics CRM settings.
Mail	Configure auditing, message tracking, and spam and malware protection for email.
Microsoft 365 groups	Manage external sharing settings.
Microsoft Azure Information Protection	Configure Azure Information Protection settings.
Microsoft Communication To Users	Configure whether users in your organization will receive marketing messages from Microsoft.
Microsoft Forms	Manage whether the names of organization users who fill out forms will be shared externally.
Microsoft Graph Data Connect	Manage Microsoft Graph data connection settings.
Microsoft Planner	Configure whether users can publish plans and tasks to iCalendar.
Microsoft Rewards	Specify whether users can connect their Azure AD and Microsoft Rewards accounts.
Microsoft Search In Bing Home Page	Customize the Bing. com page for signed-in users.
Microsoft Teams	Configure Microsoft Teams settings.
Microsoft To Do	Configure Microsoft To Do settings.
Modern Authentication	Configure Exchange Online authentication settings at the organization level.
Multi-Factor Authentication	Configure multifactor authentication settings for users.
MyAnalytics	Configure MyAnalytics settings.
News	Configure how organization news is sent and displayed.

Office Installation Options	Specify how often users receive feature updates and which Office apps users can install.
Office on the web	Specify whether users can employ third-party storage services with Office on the web.
Office Scripts	Configure automation settings for Office on the Web.
Productivity Score	Configure privacy controls for Productivity Score.
Reports	Manage privacy controls for reports in Microsoft 365 admin center.
Sharepoint	Configure external sharing settings for SharePoint.
Sway	Specify sharing and content sources that can be configured for Sway.
User Consent To Apps	Set the level of consent that users can provide to allow apps access to organization data.
User-Owned Apps And Services	Configure user access to Office Store and Office 365 trials.
What's New In Office	Specify whether users will be notified about new Office features.
Whiteboard	Configure access to Microsoft Whiteboard and shared whiteboard collaboration settings.

The **Security & Privacy** tab shown in Figure 1-21 allows you to configure the settings shown in Table 1-5.

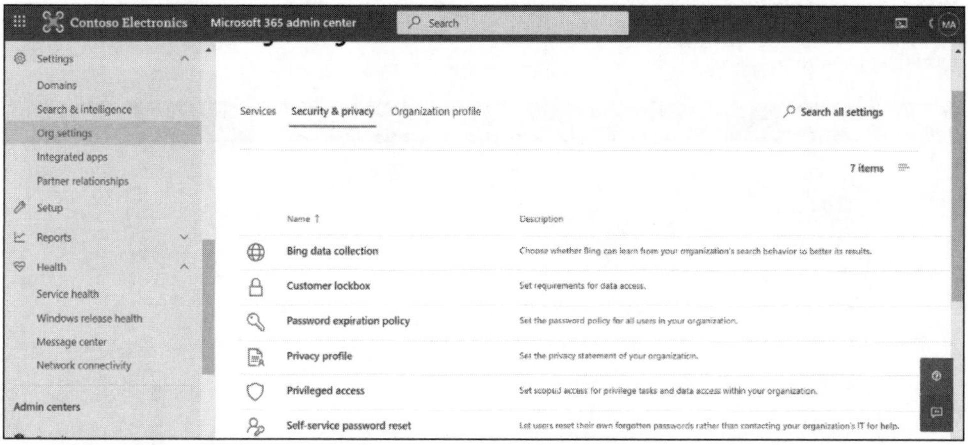

FIGURE 1-21 The Security & Privacy tab of the Org Settings page

TABLE 1-5 Security & Privacy settings

Setting	Description
Bing Data Collection	Specify whether Bing can use organization search behavior to improve results.
Customer Lockbox	Configure requirements for data access.
Password Expiration Policy	Configure the organization's password policy.
Privacy Profile	Set the organization's privacy statement.
Privileged Access	Configure scoped access for privileged tasks and data access.
Self-Service Password Reset	Configure self-service password reset settings.
Sharing	Configure settings related to external access to organization data.

MORE INFO   **MICROSOFT 365 ADMIN CENTER**

You can learn more about the different areas of the Microsoft 365 admin center that you can use to configure organizational settings at *https://learn.microsoft.com/microsoft-365/ admin/admin-overview/admin-center-overview.*

Complete the organization profile

The **Organization Profile** tab, shown in Figure 1-22, allows you to configure the settings shown in Table 1-6.

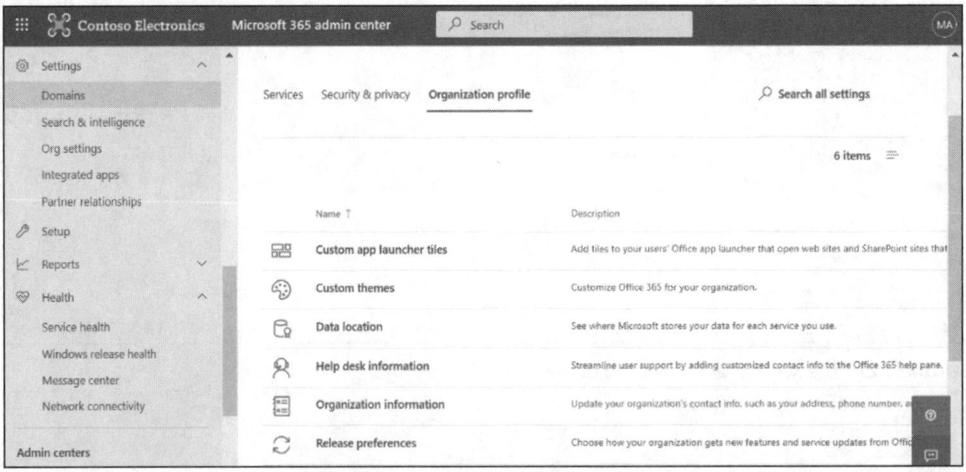

FIGURE 1-22   The Organization Profile tab of the Org Settings page

TABLE 1-6 Organization Profile settings

Setting	Description
Custom App Launcher Tiles	Configure tiles for the Office App launcher to enable users to easily access web and SharePoint sites.
Custom Themes	Configure themes for Office 365.
Data Location	Specify where data is stored for each Microsoft 365 service used by your organization.
Help Desk Information	Enter customized contact information for the Office 365 Help pane.
Organization Information	Enter organization information, including phone number and address.
Release Preferences	Specify how the organization will consume new features and service updates.

> *MORE INFO* **MICROSOFT 365 ORGANIZATIONAL PROFILE**
>
> You can learn more about configuring the organizational profile at *https://learn.microsoft.com/microsoft-365/admin/manage/change-address-contact-and-more.*

Add a Microsoft partner or work with Microsoft FastTrack

The Microsoft FastTrack program assists organizations in deploying and migrating to Microsoft 365. FastTrack can aid in the following areas:

- Core onboarding
- Microsoft 365 Apps
- Network health
- Azure Active Directory and Azure AD Premium
- Azure Information Protection
- Discover & Respond
- Insider Risk Management
- Microsoft 365 Defender
- Microsoft Cloud App Security
- Microsoft Defender for Endpoint
- Microsoft Defender for Identity
- Microsoft Defender for Office 365
- Microsoft Information Governance
- Microsoft Information Protection
- Microsoft Intune
- Exchange Online
- Microsoft Teams

- Outlook for iOS and Android
- Power BI
- Project Online
- SharePoint Online
- OneDrive
- Yammer Enterprise
- Windows 11
- Windows Virtual Desktop
- App Assure

> **MORE INFO   FASTTRACK FOR MICROSOFT 365**
>
> You can learn more about Microsoft FastTrack at *https://learn.microsoft.com/fasttrack/products-and-capabilities*.

Microsoft partners enable you to delegate control of parts of your tenancy to people outside your organization. You might want to do this when you outsource support to a third party. To configure partner access, the partner must send an email request to a Microsoft 365 administrator for partner status, and the Microsoft 365 administrator must accept the invitation in the Microsoft 365 admin center. The administrator does this from the **Partner Relationships** page shown in Figure 1-23. (To access this page, select **Settings** in the left pane of the Microsoft 365 admin center and then select **Partner Relationships**.) This page also describes the relationship type and the roles assigned to the partner and allows you to remove partners and partner roles from your organization's tenancy.

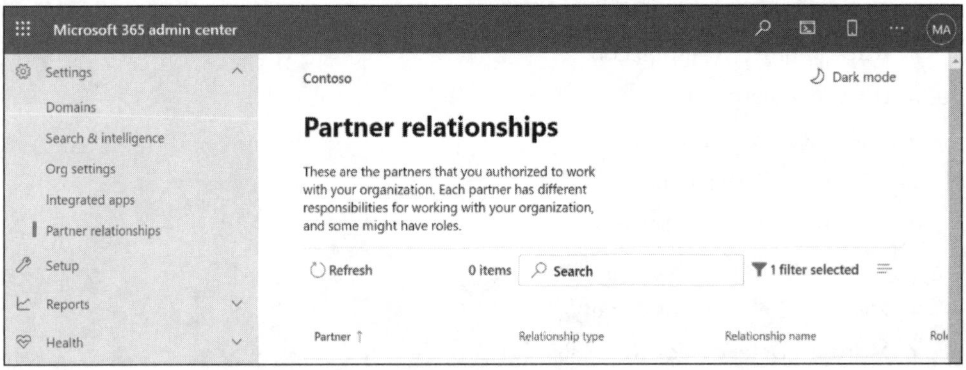

FIGURE 1-23   The Partner Relationships page in the Microsoft 365 admin center

Microsoft 365 supports the partner types shown in Table 1-7.

TABLE 1-7 Partner types

Partner types	Description
Reseller	Resells Microsoft products to organizations.
Delegated Administrator	Manages products and services for organizations. This type of partner is assigned the Global Administrator role in Azure AD for your tenancy and can create user accounts, assign and manage licenses, and perform password resets.
Reseller and Delegated Administrator	A combination of the reseller and delegated administrator partner types.
Partner	Is given a user account in your organization's tenancy and can be delegated rights.
Advisor	Can perform password resets and handle support incidents.
Line-of-Business (LOB) Partner	Can develop, submit, and manage LOB apps for your organization.

> **MORE INFO**   **MANAGE MICROSOFT 365 PARTNERS**
>
> You can learn more about managing partner relationships at *https://learn.microsoft.com/microsoft-365/commerce/manage-partners.*

Edit an organizational profile

You must have Global Administrator rights to the subscription to update your organization's name, address, phone, and technical contact information. To make these modifications to the organization profile, perform the following steps:

1. In the left pane of the Microsoft 365 admin center, under **Settings**, select **Org Settings**.
2. Select the **Organization Profile** tab.
3. Select **Organization Information**.

4.   The **Organization Information** pane opens (see Figure 1-24).

Organization information

This info will be displayed in places like sign-in pages and bills to your organization.

Learn more about editing your organization's info

Name *

| Contoso |

Street address *   Apartment or suite

City *   State or province *

ZIP or postal code *   Country or region

United States

FIGURE 1-24   The Organization Information pane

5.   Provide the following information:

- Name
- Street Address
- Apartment Or Suite
- City
- State Or Province
- ZIP Or Postal Code
- Country Or Region
- Phone
- Technical Contact
- Preferred Language

> **MORE INFO**   **EDIT ORGANIZATION INFORMATION**
>
> You can learn more about editing organization information at *https://learn.microsoft.com/en-us/microsoft-365/admin/manage/change-address-contact-and-more*.

EXAM TIP

Remember what tool to use to allow a partner to have delegated administrator rights to your Microsoft 365 tenancy.

Skill 1.4: Manage Microsoft 365 subscription and tenant health

This section deals with managing subscription and tenant health for a Microsoft 365 deployment. To master this skill, you will need to understand options when it comes to managing service health, creating and managing service requests, creating a health response plan, and monitoring service health.

> **This section covers the following topics:**
> - Manage service health alerts
> - Create an internal service health response plan
> - Monitor service health

Manage service health alerts

The Service Health dashboard shows you the health status of all services related to your organization's Microsoft 365 subscription. For example, the **Service Health** dashboard shown in Figure 1-25 shows that several services are in a healthy state, and others are listed with advisories. To open this dashboard, select **Health** in the left pane of the Microsoft 365 admin center and then select **Service Health**.

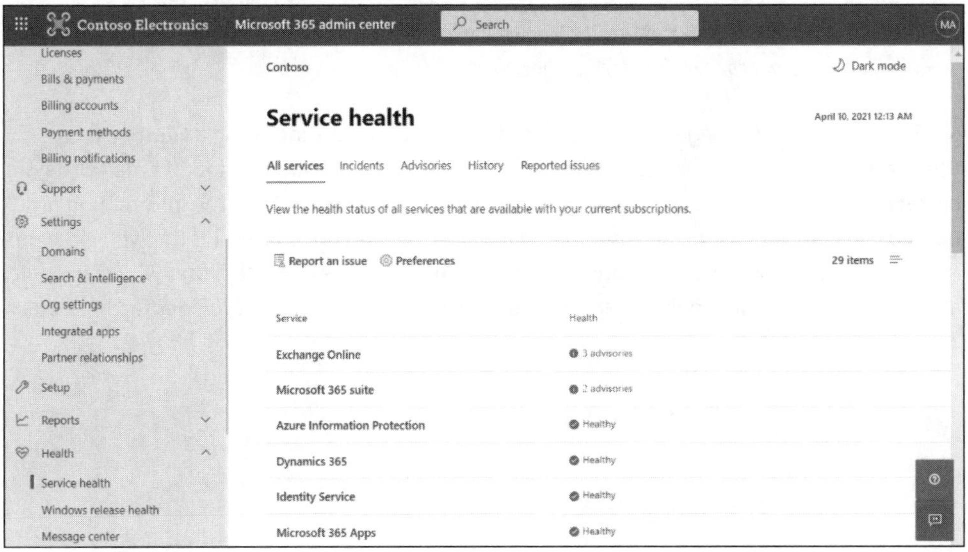

FIGURE 1-25 The Service Health dashboard

Table 1-8 defines the various statuses associated with services.

TABLE 1-8   Microsoft 365 service status definitions

Status	Definition
Investigating	Microsoft is aware of the issue and is investigating its cause and scope of impact.
Service degradation	Microsoft has confirmed that an issue is present in a specific Microsoft 365 service or feature. This status is often assigned when a service is performing in a slower-than-normal fashion or when intermittent interruptions are occurring.
Service interruption	Microsoft is aware that significant disruption is occurring with the listed system.
Restoring service	Microsoft has determined the cause of the issue and is in the process of restoring full functionality.
Extended recovery	Microsoft has restored full functionality for most users, but some users may require more time before the fix reaches them.
Investigation suspended	Microsoft has requested additional information from customers to determine the cause of the disruption.
Service restored	Microsoft has confirmed that remediation actions have resolved the problem and that the service is in a healthy state. You can view service issues to learn details of the disruption.
Post-incident report published	Microsoft has published a detailed post-incident report that includes root cause information and steps that have been taken to ensure that the issue does not arise again.

> **MORE INFO   MICROSOFT 365 SERVICE HEALTH**
>
> You can learn more about the Service Health dashboard at *https://learn.microsoft.com/microsoft-365/enterprise/view-service-health*.

The **Service Health** page includes several tabs along the top, including a **History** tab. Select this tab to display the status history of services over a specified period of time (30 days by default). Figure 1-26 shows the status history over the last seven days. The information on this tab can help you diagnose issues that may have occurred previously and that you were unaware of. For example, this information is useful if you need to explain to a user why they could not access specific functionality over the weekend. Selecting each item provides further details.

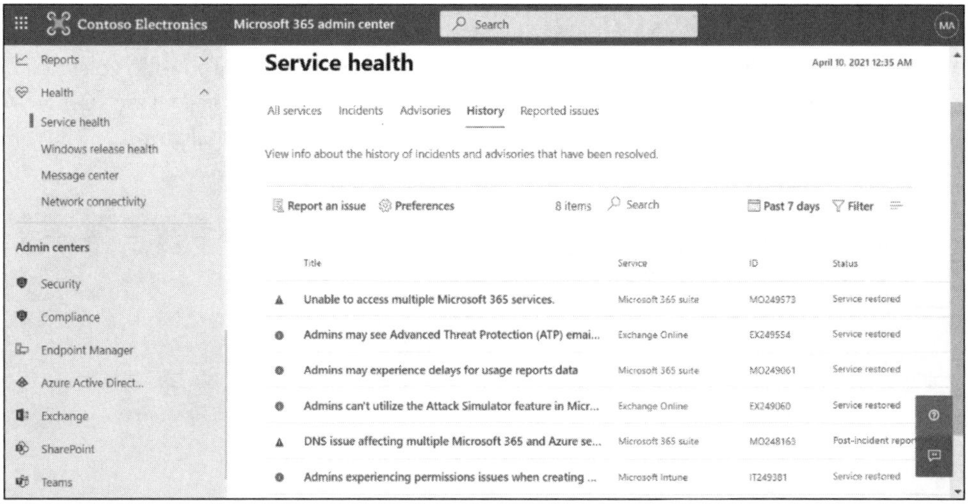

FIGURE 1-26 The History tab of the Service Health page

Create an internal service health response plan

Microsoft provides a variety of methods to notify your organization of a service disruption beyond end users ringing the service desk to complain that they "can't get the thing to work." You can monitor these service communication channels to become aware of potential issues and take steps to notify users before it affects them. Service communication channels include the following:

- **The Microsoft 365 Admin App** This app enables Microsoft 365 and Office 365 administrators to monitor service status from a mobile device. Tenant administrators can also use the app to view service health information and maintenance status updates.

- **Microsoft 365 Management Pack for System Center Operations Manager** Organizations that use System Center Operations Manager to monitor their environment can install the Microsoft 365 Management Pack to make alerts visible within the Operations Manager console. The management pack includes Subscription Health, Service Status, Active Incidents, Resolved Incidents, and the Message Center.

- **Microsoft 365 Service Communications API** This API enables you to interact with Microsoft 365 service communications in a manner that suits your organization. This API provides a method for connecting existing monitoring tools to Microsoft 365 service communications. The API lets you monitor real-time service health, Message Center communications, and planned maintenance notifications.

> **MORE INFO** **SERVICE HEALTH RESPONSE**
>
> You can learn more about service health response at *https://learn.microsoft.com/ en-us/office365/servicedescriptions/office-365-platform-service-description/ service-health-and-continuity.*

Monitor service health

Microsoft 365 informs administrators about upcoming maintenance events through planned maintenance notifications. You can view planned maintenance events in the Message Center (see Figure 1-27). To access this page, select **Health** in the left pane of the Microsoft 365 admin center and then select **Message Center**.

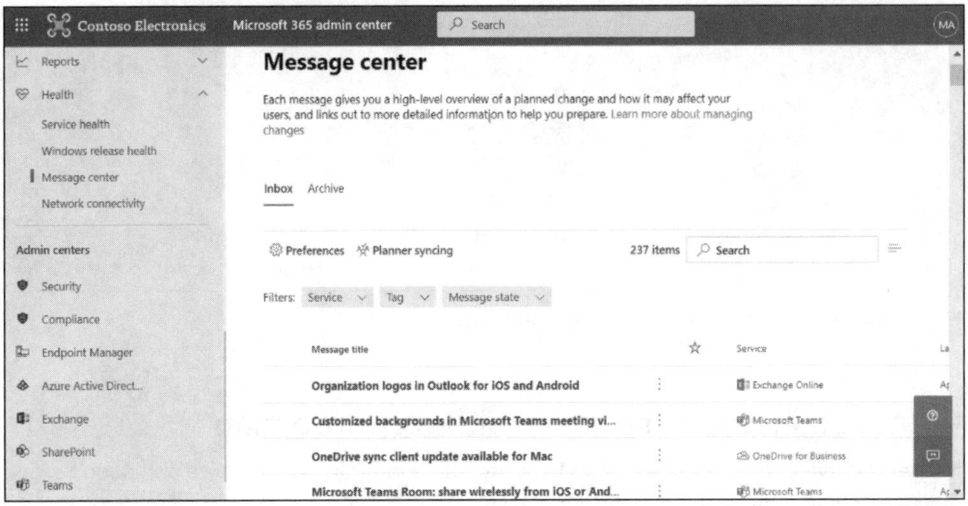

FIGURE 1-27 The Message Center

> **MORE INFO** **MESSAGE CENTER**
>
> You can learn more about the Message Center at *https://learn.microsoft.com/en-us/ microsoft-365/admin/manage/message-center*.

EXAM TIP

Remember the differences between each Microsoft 365 service status definition.

Skill 1.5: Monitor adoption and usage

By monitoring Microsoft 365 usage patterns, you can gain insights into which services and applications are used most frequently and which ones are underutilized. Monitoring adoption and usage can also help you ensure compliance with internal policies and external regulations.

Configure and review reports

You can integrate Microsoft 365 usage analytics with Power BI to visualize and analyze Microsoft 365 usage data. To enable Microsoft 365 usage analytics for Power BI, perform the following steps:

1. In the left pane of the Microsoft 365 admin center, under **Reports**, select **Usage**.
2. On the **Usage** page, in the **Microsoft 365 Usage Analytics section**, select **Get Started**.
3. On the **Reports** pane, shown in Figure 1-28, select the **Enable Power BI For Usage Analytics** checkbox. Then select Save.

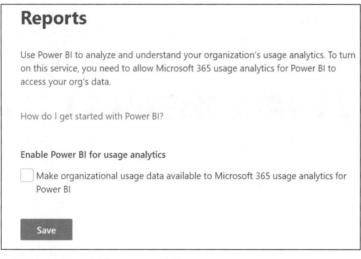

FIGURE 1-28 Power BI for usage analytics

To start the template app, follow these steps:

1. Copy the tenant ID. Alternatively, locate it in the Azure Active Directory Console.
2. Select **Go To Power BI**.
3. Sign in to Power BI, and then select **Apps**.
4. Type **Microsoft 365** and select **Search In AppSource**.
5. On the Power BI Apps page, type **Microsoft 365**, select **Microsoft 365 Usage**, and then select **Get It Now**.

Microsoft 365 usage analytics includes the following reports:

- **Executive Summary** A high-level view of Microsoft 365 business adoption, usage, mobility, communication, collaboration, and storage

- **Overview** Includes Adoption, Usage, Communication, Collaboration, Storage, and Mobility reports

- **Activation and Licensing** Information about activations and the license types in use

- **Product Usage** Information on usage of Exchange, Microsoft 365 groups, OneDrive, SharePoint, Microsoft Teams, and Yammer

- **User Activity** User activity reports for individual services

> **MORE INFO** **USAGE ANALYTICS REPORT**
>
> You can learn more about usage analytics reports at *https://learn.microsoft.com/ microsoft-365/admin/usage-analytics/usage-analytics*.

Schedule and review security and compliance reports

Certain Microsoft 365 reports reveal how security and compliance rules and technologies are used across your Microsoft 365 organization. You can view some of these reports from the Microsoft 365 admin center. Other reports are available in the Security & Compliance Center (see Figure 1-29).

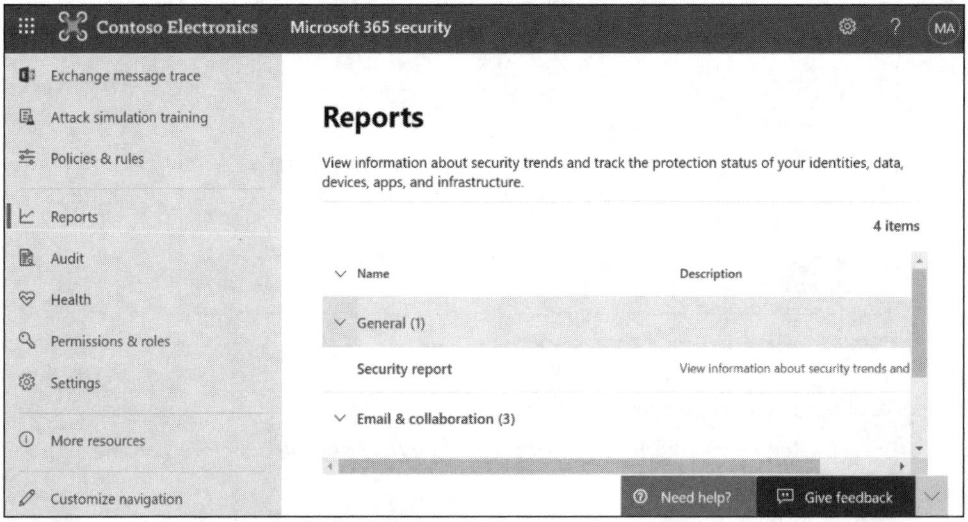

FIGURE 1-29 The Reports dashboard

Reports that relate to security and compliance are split across four categories:

- Auditing reports
- Data loss prevention (DLP) reports
- Protection reports
- Rules reports

You need one of the following roles to view reports in the Security & Compliance Center:

- **The Security Reader role in Exchange**   This role is assigned by default to the organization management and security reader role groups.

- **The DLP Compliance Management role in the Security & Compliance Center**   You must have this role to view DLP reports and policies. This role is assigned by default to the compliance administrator, organization management, and security administrator role groups.

> *MORE INFO* **SECURITY AND COMPLIANCE REPORTS**
>
> You can learn more about the Microsoft 365 security and compliance reports at *https://learn.microsoft.com/microsoft-365/admin/activity-reports/activity-reports*.

Auditing reports

The following security and compliance reports are available through the Security & Compliance Center:

- **Audit Log**   View user and administrator activity for the Microsoft 365 organization, including changes made to administrator role groups.

- **Azure AD**   View Entra ID (previously Azure AD) reports, including reports for unusual or suspicious sign-in activity. This requires a paid Azure AD subscription. This report will eventually refer to Entra ID when the user interface is updated.

- **Exchange Audit**   View and search for mailboxes accessed by people other than their owners. (Mailbox audit logging must be enabled.)

Data loss prevention reports

The following data loss prevention (DLP) reports are available through the Office 365 admin center:

- **Top DLP Policy Matches for Mail**   View the top DLP policy matches for sent and received email.

- **Top DLP Rule Matches for Mail**   View the top DLP rule matches for sent and received email.

- **DLP Policy Matches by Severity for Mail**   Track DLP policy matches by severity.

- **DLP Policy Matches, Overrides, and False Positives for Mail**   View DLP matches, overrides, and false positives for incoming and outgoing messages.

Protection reports

The following protection reports are available through the Microsoft 365 admin center:

- **Top Senders and Recipients**   View the top mail senders, mail recipients, spam recipients, and malware recipients across the Microsoft 365 subscription.
- **Top Malware for Mail**   View the amount of malware received through email for the reporting period.
- **Malware Detections**   View the amount of malware sent and received through the Microsoft 365 subscription for the reporting period.
- **Spam Detections**   View the amount of spam based on the content being filtered or the original sending host being blocked.
- **Sent and Received Mail**   View the amount of sent and received mail categorized by good mail, malware, spam, and messages dealt with by rules.

Rules reports

The following rules reports are available through the Office 365 admin center:

- **Top Rule Matches for Mail**   View the number of messages based on sent and received transport rule matches.
- **Rule Matches for Mail**   View all rule matches for received and sent email.

Schedule and review usage metrics

Usage reports (see Figure 1-30) show how users in your organization are employing Microsoft 365 services. You can review reports over periods of 7 days, 30 days, 90 days, and 180 days. Reports are not generated immediately but become available after 48 hours.

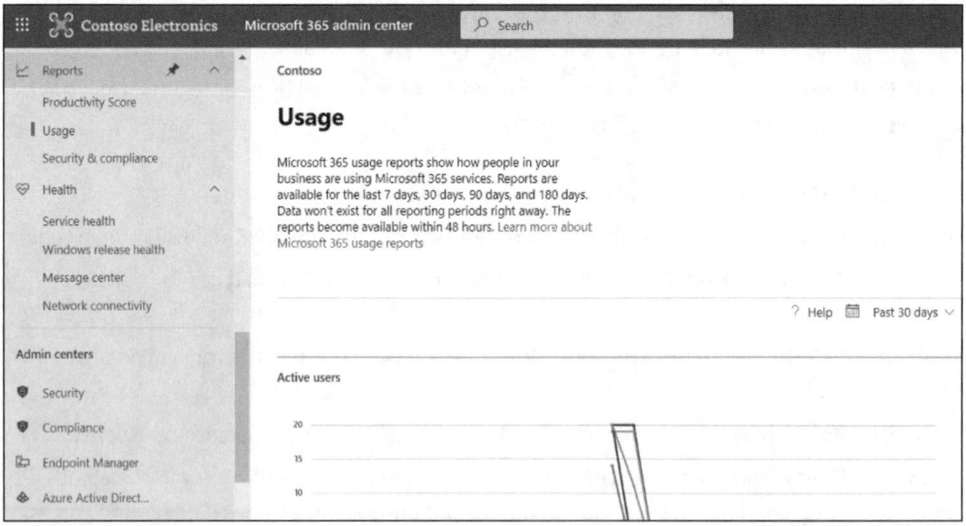

FIGURE 1-30 Usage reports

Users who hold the following roles can view these reports:

- Global Administrator
- Exchange Administrator
- SharePoint Administrator
- Report Reader
- Teams Service Administrator
- Teams Communications Administrator

The following sections detail the types of available usage reports.

Email Activity report

The Email Activity report, shown in Figure 1-31, displays the number of send, receive, and read actions across the organization, with a per-user breakdown. You can use this report to get high-level information about email traffic at your organization, including the last activity date and number of send, receive, and read actions.

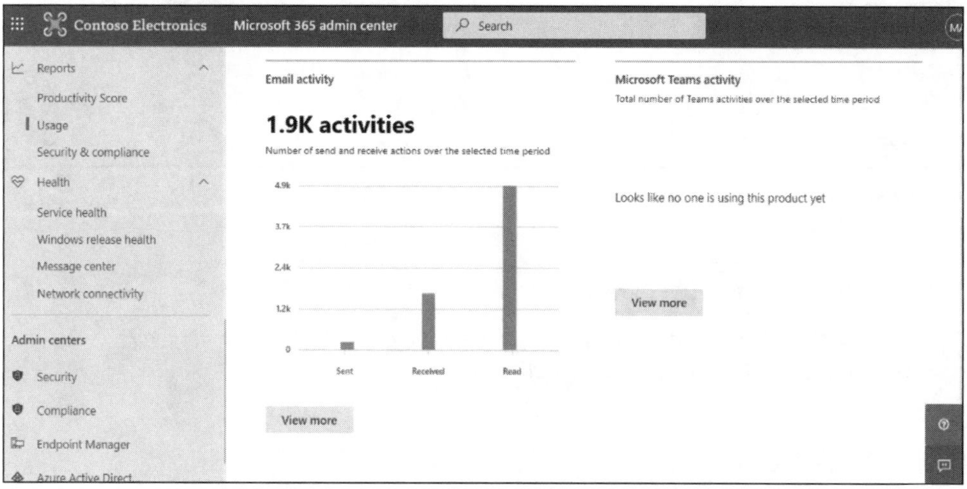

FIGURE 1-31 Email Activity report

> **MORE INFO   EMAIL ACTIVITY REPORT**
>
> You can learn more about the Email Activity report at *https://learn.microsoft.com/ microsoft-365/admin/activity-reports/email-activity-ww*.

Mailbox Usage report

The Mailbox Usage report, shown in Figure 1-32, shows the total number of mailboxes, the total number of active user mailboxes, the amount of storage used across all mailboxes, and the mailboxes by quota status (good, warning issued, send prohibited, and send/receive prohibited). You can also view the number of deleted items, the last activity date, and the number of items in each user's mailbox.

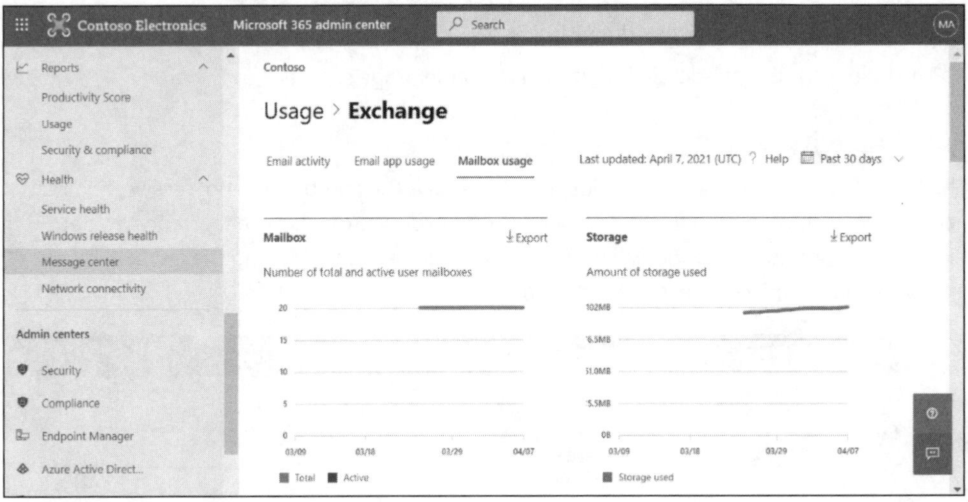

FIGURE 1-32 Mailbox Usage report

> **MORE INFO** **MAILBOX USAGE REPORT**
>
> You can learn more about the Mailbox Usage report at *https://learn.microsoft.com/microsoft-365/admin/activity-reports/mailbox-usage*.

Office Activations report

The Office Activations report provides data on users who have activated their Office 365 subscription on one or more devices. You can use it to track activations for Microsoft 365 Apps for Enterprise, Project, and Visio Pro for Office 365. You can also view activation information, including whether the product was activated on a Windows or macOS computer or on iOS or Android mobile operating system devices.

> **MORE INFO** **OFFICE ACTIVATIONS REPORT**
>
> You can learn more about the Office Activations report at *https://learn.microsoft.com/microsoft-365/admin/activity-reports/microsoft-office-activations*.

Active Users report

The Active Users report, shown in Figure 1-33, tracks the number of licenses being used across your organization. It also provides information about the products licensed by specific users. You can use this report to determine which products are not being fully used.

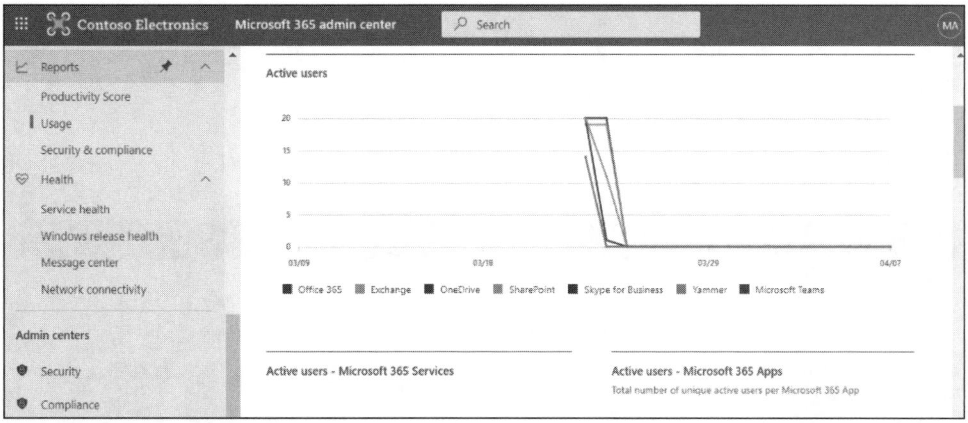

FIGURE 1-33 Active Users report

> **MORE INFO ACTIVE USERS REPORT**
>
> You can learn more about the Active Users report at *https://learn.microsoft.com/microsoft-365/admin/activity-reports/active-users*.

Email App Usage report

The Email App Usage report tracks the email app used by each user to access Exchange Online. This enables you to view each user's app usage profile. This report tracks usage through Outlook on Windows, Outlook on Mac OSX, Outlook on the web, and mobile clients.

> **MORE INFO EMAIL APP USAGE REPORT**
>
> You can learn more about the Email App Usage report at *https://learn.microsoft.com/microsoft-365/admin/activity-reports/email-apps-usage*.

OneDrive Activity report

The OneDrive Activity report, also known as the OneDrive for Business Activity Report, allows you to view the activity of all Office 365 OneDrive users. This report, shown in Figure 1-34, provides information on the following:

- Last OneDrive activity
- Files viewed or edited
- Files synced
- Files shared internally
- Files shared externally

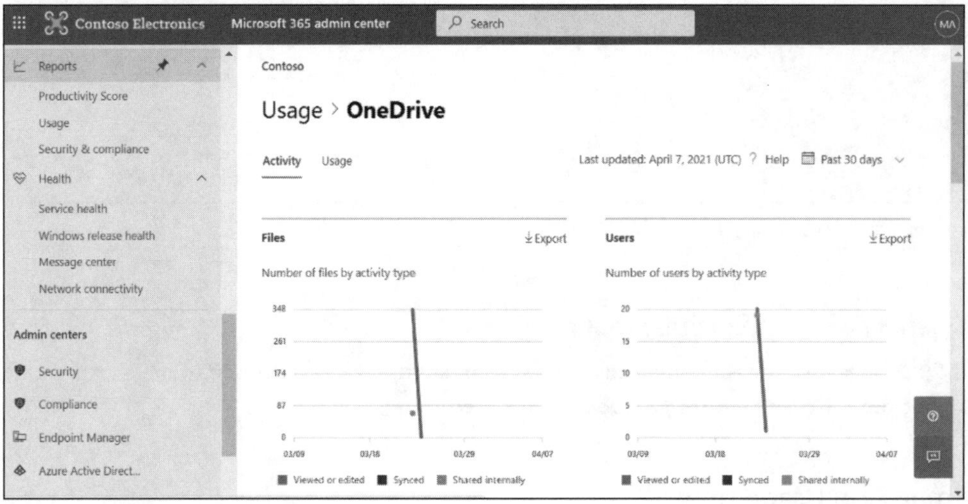

FIGURE 1-34 OneDrive Activity report

> **MORE INFO ONEDRIVE ACTIVITY REPORT**
>
> You can learn more about the OneDrive Activity report at *https://learn.microsoft.com/microsoft-365/admin/activity-reports/onedrive-for-business-activity-ww*.

OneDrive Usage report

The OneDrive Usage report, also known as the OneDrive for Business Usage report, provides a high-level overview of how files are used in your organization's OneDrive for Business subscription. The report, shown in Figure 1-35, provides details of the following:

- **URL**   The file's location within OneDrive for Business
- **Owner**   The Office 365 account associated with the file
- **Last activity date (UTC)**   The last date that the file was accessed

- **Files** The number of files associated with the user
- **Active Files** The number of the user's files actively in use
- **Storage used (MB)** Storage consumed by the user's files

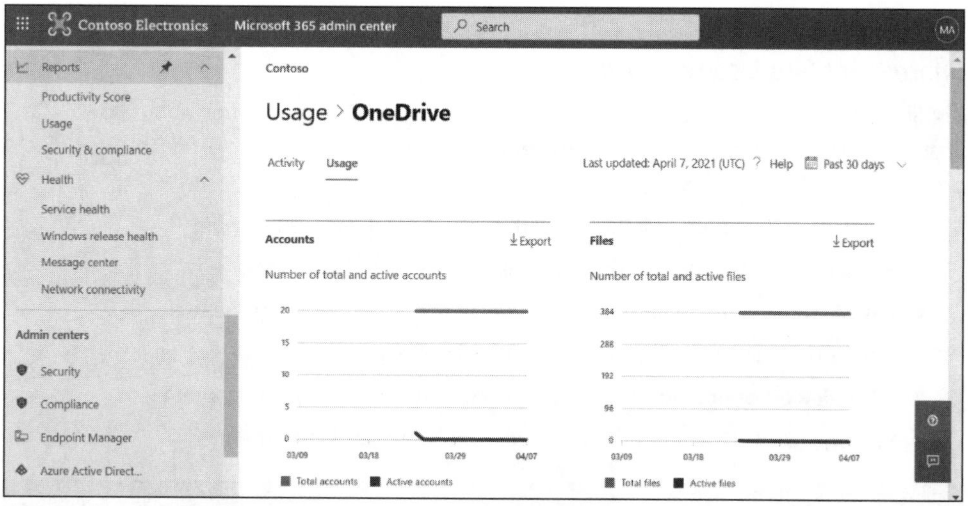

FIGURE 1-35 OneDrive Usage Report

> **MORE INFO** **ONEDRIVE USAGE REPORT**
>
> You can learn more about the OneDrive Usage report at *https://learn.microsoft.com/ microsoft-365/admin/activity-reports/onedrive-for-business-usage*.

SharePoint Activity report

The SharePoint Activity report enables you to track how Microsoft 365 users in your organization interact with SharePoint Online. This report provides the following information on a per-user basis:

- **Last activity date** The last time the user interacted with SharePoint Online
- **Files viewed or edited** The number of files with which the user has interacted that were hosted on the organization's SharePoint Online instance
- **Files synced** The number of files that have synchronized between devices used by the user and SharePoint Online
- **Files shared internally** The number of files shared with other Office 365 users through SharePoint Online
- **Files shared externally** The number of files shared through Office 365 with external users

SharePoint Site Usage report

The SharePoint Site Usage report shown in Figure 1-36 provides information about how SharePoint sites in your organization's SharePoint Online deployment are used. This report provides you with the following information:

- **Site URL**   The address of the site within your SharePoint deployment
- **Site owner**   The Microsoft 365 user assigned ownership of the site
- **Last Activity date**   The last time activity was recorded against the site
- **Files**   The number of files stored on the SharePoint online site
- **Files viewed or edited**   Files that have recently been viewed or modified
- **Storage used**   The amount of storage consumed by files on the site

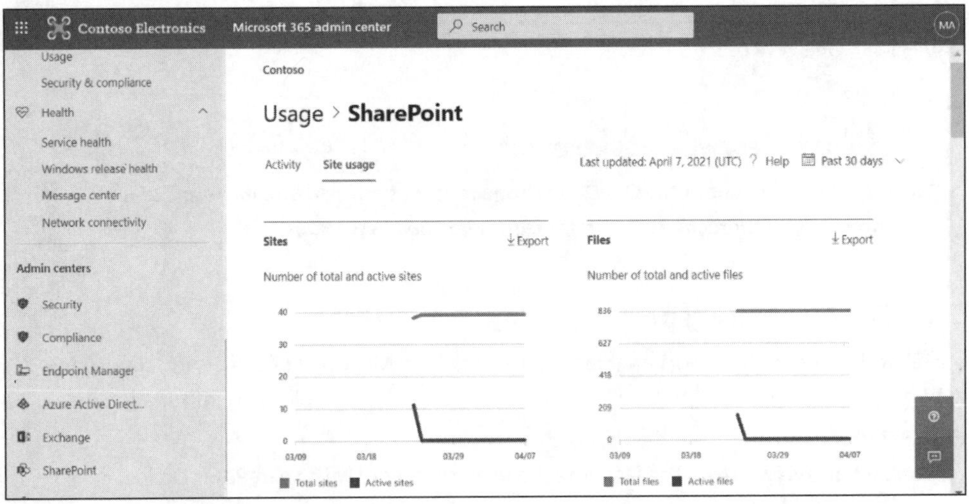

FIGURE 1-36   SharePoint Site Usage report

Yammer Activity report

The Yammer Activity report tracks how much your organization' 's users interact with Yammer. It provides information about the number of unique users posting to Yammer, how many users read a specific message, how many liked a specific message, and the general level of interaction across the organization.

> **MORE INFO** **YAMMER ACTIVITY REPORT**
>
> You can learn more about the Yammer Activity report at *https://learn.microsoft.com/ office365/admin/activity-reports/yammer-activity-report*.

Yammer Device Usage report

The Yammer Device Usage report provides data about the specific types of devices used to interact with the organization's Yammer instance. The report provides information on the following:

- Number of daily users by device type
- Number of users by device type
- Per-user device usage

> **MORE INFO** **YAMMER DEVICE USAGE REPORT**
>
> You can learn more about the Yammer Device Usage report at *https://learn.microsoft.com/ office365/admin/activity-reports/yammer-device-usage-report*.

Yammer Groups Activity report

The Yammer Groups Activity report tracks how users in your organization interact with Yammer groups. The report provides information on the number of groups created, as well as the following:

- Group name
- Group administrator
- Group type
- Connection to Office 365
- Last activity date
- Members
- Messages posted
- Messages read
- Messages liked

MORE INFO **YAMMER GROUPS ACTIVITY REPORT**

You can learn more about the Yammer Groups Activity report at *https://learn.microsoft. com/office365/admin/activity-reports/yammer-groups-activity-report.*

Microsoft Teams User Activity report

The Microsoft Teams User Activity report provides information on how users in your organization interact with the tenancy's Microsoft Teams instance. Activities tracked by this report include the following:

- Channel messages
- Chat messages
- Calls
- Meetings
- Other activities

MORE INFO **MICROSOFT TEAMS USER ACTIVITY REPORT**

You can learn more about the Microsoft Teams User Activity report at *https://learn. microsoft.com/office365/admin/activity-reports/microsoft-teams-user-activity.*

Microsoft Teams Device Usage report

The Microsoft Teams Device Usage report provides information about the specific devices that Microsoft 365 users are employing to interact with the tenancy's Microsoft Teams instance. The report tracks the following operating systems and devices:

- Windows
- macOS
- Web
- iOS
- Android phone
- Windows phone

MORE INFO **MICROSOFT TEAMS DEVICE USAGE REPORT**

You can learn more about the Microsoft Teams Device Usage report at *https://learn. microsoft.com/en-us/microsoft-365/admin/activity-reports/microsoft-teams-device- usage-preview?view=o365-worldwide.*

EXAM TIP

The best way to learn about the reports available in Microsoft 365 is to access them through your organization's subscription or to create your own trial subscription and investigate them there.

Chapter summary

- When you create a Microsoft 365 subscription, the subscription tenancy is automatically assigned a custom *onmicrosoft.com* domain.
- No two organizations can share the same tenant name.
- The tenant name chosen at setup remains with the subscription throughout the subscription's existence.
- You can assign a domain name that you own to the tenant so that you don't have to use the *onmicrosoft.com* tenant name.
- To use a domain with Microsoft 365, the DNS servers used as name servers for the domain must support CNAME, SPF/TXT, SRV, and MX records.
- You can confirm domain ownership by configuring special TXT or MX records.
- Setting the default domain configures which domain suffix will automatically be used with Microsoft 365 user accounts.
- Mail reports allow you to view how Office 365 mailboxes are used.
- Usage reports allow you to view browsers, operating systems, and license consumption information.
- SharePoint reports allow you to see how SharePoint is being used with the Office 365 subscription.
- Data loss prevention (DLP) reports allow you to view how DLP rules and policies apply to message traffic.
- The Service Health dashboard is available from the Microsoft 365 admin center, allowing you to determine the status of the various elements of Microsoft 365, including fault history and planned maintenance.
- Users assigned the Global Administrator role have access to all administrative features.
- Users assigned the billing administrator role can make purchases, manage subscriptions, manage support tickets, and monitor service health.
- Users assigned the helpdesk (password) administrator role can reset the passwords of most Office 365 user accounts (except those assigned the Global Administrator, service administrator, or billing roles).
- Users assigned the service administrator role can manage service requests and monitor service health.

Thought experiment

In this thought experiment, demonstrate your skills and knowledge of the topics covered in this chapter. You can find answers to this thought experiment in the next section.

Deploying a Microsoft 365 tenancy at Tailwind Traders

You are in the process of planning and implementing Microsoft 365 at Tailwind Traders. As a part of this deployment, you need to associate the *tailwindtraders.org* DNS zone with your Microsoft 365 tenancy. You'll also use an IT support service desk vendor to create user accounts, assign and manage Microsoft 365 licenses, and reset user passwords. You also want to determine which roles to assign to view reports across all Security & Compliance Center elements.

With this information, answer the following questions:

1. What type of DNS record will you need to configure to ensure that email addressed to users in the *@tailwindtraders.org* email domain is routed correctly to your Microsoft 365 Exchange online service?

2. Which partner type should you assign to allow your support vendor?

3. Which roles are able to view reports in the Security & Compliance Center?

Thought experiment answers

This section contains the solution to the thought experiment. Each answer explains why the answer choice is correct.

1. You will need to configure an MX record to ensure that email addressed to users in the *@tailwindtraders.org* email domain is routed correctly to the Microsoft 365 Exchange online service.

2. You assign the delegated administrator partner type to your support vendor if you want them to be able to create user accounts, assign and manage licenses, and perform password resets.

3. The roles needed to review reports in the Security & Compliance Center depend on the reports you access. For Exchange-related reports, you need the security reader role in Exchange. This role is assigned by default to the organization management and security reader role groups. For Data Loss Prevention-related reports, you need the DLP compliance management role in the Security & Compliance Center. This role is assigned by default to the compliance administrator, organization management, and security administrator role groups.

CHAPTER 2

Managing M365 users, groups, and identity synchronization

A key aspect of deploying Microsoft 365 is configuring user identity properly, so users can seamlessly access resources in the on-premises and Microsoft 365 environments. If it is not done correctly, users must juggle different accounts, depending on whether the accessible resources are hosted locally or in the cloud. In this chapter, you will learn about designing an identity strategy, managing Microsoft Entra ID identities, planning identity synchronization with Microsoft Entra Connect and Microsoft Entra Cloud Sync, and managing and trouble-shooting identity synchronization.

Skills in this chapter:

- Skill 2.1: Manage Microsoft 365 identities
- Skill 2.2: Prepare for identity synchronization
- Skill 2.3: Synchronize identities using Microsoft Entra Connect
- Skill 2.4: Synchronize identities using Microsoft Entra Cloud Sync

> **IMPORTANT**
>
> In August 2023, Microsoft announced that it was rebranding Azure Active Directory to Microsoft Entra ID. In addition, products such as Azure AD Connect, Azure AD Connect Cloud Sync, and Azure Active Directory Domain Services have also been renamed Microsoft Entra Connect, Microsoft Entra Cloud Sync, and Microsoft Entra Domain Services, respectively.

The actual functionality of these products has not been changed, and it is also likely that it will be some time before UI elements in various administrative portals and Microsoft's official documentation are also completely updated to use the new brand guidelines. Practice tests and study materials that use the original names will still provide you with relevant information on functionality. However, for the foreseeable future, multiple names will be used to label the same product or service.

Skill 2.1: Manage Microsoft 365 identities

Planning Microsoft 365 identities involves managing internal and external users who need to access Microsoft 365 resources and applications. When managing these identities, you must ensure that users are appropriately licensed for the necessary tools. External identities are users not part of your organization who might need access to internal resources and applications.

> **This section covers the following skills:**
> - Plan Microsoft 365 and Microsoft Entra ID identities
> - Manage users
> - Manage groups
> - Perform bulk user management
> - Manage external identities
> - Manage Microsoft 365 contacts

Plan Microsoft 365 and Microsoft Entra ID identities

Microsoft 365 uses Microsoft Entra ID (previously Azure Active Directory) as its identity store. In hybrid environments, you'll manage identities primarily using on-premises management tools such as Active Directory Users and Computers. In environments where Microsoft Entra ID is the primary authority source, you can use the Microsoft 365 admin center to manage user identities. You can also use the Microsoft Entra admin center to perform these tasks.

When planning the use of Azure identities, you'll need to consider the following questions:

- What UPN will be used with the identity for login to Microsoft 365 resources? You can change the UPN suffix to any domain configured and authorized for use with the directory.
- What authentication and authorization options will be required to access Microsoft 365 resources? Will users need to change their passwords regularly? Will users be required to perform multifactor authentication?
- What roles will be assigned to users? Will you need to assign Microsoft Entra ID roles to specific users? What method will you use to perform this task?
- Will Microsoft Entra ID groups be used? What strategy will you use to manage collections of users into groups? Will your organization use a group naming convention?

You'll learn more about how to perform user-management tasks later in this chapter.

Manage users

You can use the Microsoft 365 admin center or the Entra ID admin center available at *https://entra.microsoft.com* to manage Microsoft Entra ID user accounts. The Entra ID admin center gives you a larger set of options for managing the properties of user accounts than the Microsoft 365 admin center because you can edit extended user properties.

To create a new Microsoft Entra ID user, perform the following steps:

1. In the Microsoft Entra admin center, select **Users** > **All Users** > **New User**.

2. On the **New User** blade, provide the following information:

   - **Name** The user's actual name.
   - **User Name** The user's sign-in name in UPN format.
   - **Profile** The user's first name, last name, job title, and department.
   - **Properties** The user's source of authority. By default, if you are creating the user using the Entra ID admin center or the Microsoft 365 admin center, this will be Entra ID.
   - **Groups** The groups the user should be a member of.
   - **Directory Role** Whether the account has a User, Global Administrator, or a limited administrator role.
   - **Password** The automatically generated password. With the **Show Password** option, you can transmit the password to the user through a secure channel.

You can also use the Microsoft Entra admin center to perform the following user administrator tasks:

- Update profile information
- Assign directory roles
- Manage group membership
- Manage licenses
- Manage devices
- Manage access to Azure resources
- Manage authentication methods

Another option is to use the **Active Users** section of the Microsoft 365 admin center shown in Figure 2-1. From this console, you can add users using the **Add A User** item, which will require the user's first name, last name, display name, and username in UPN format and will provide the option of an automatically generated password that must be changed and the ability to assign a role and add profile details.

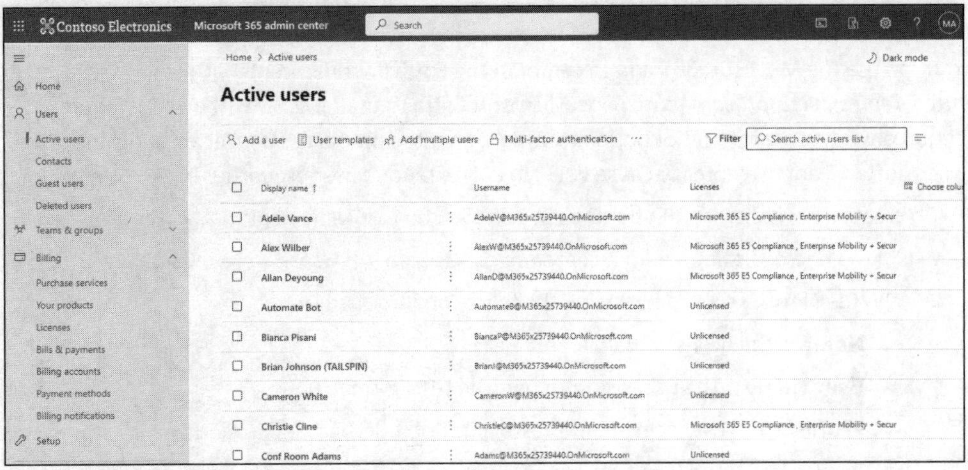

FIGURE 2-1 Active Users

User templates allow you to create users with specific configurations, including assigning a specific set of licenses, app access, roles, and profile information. Figure 2-2 shows the **Assign Licenses** page of the **Add User Template** dialog.

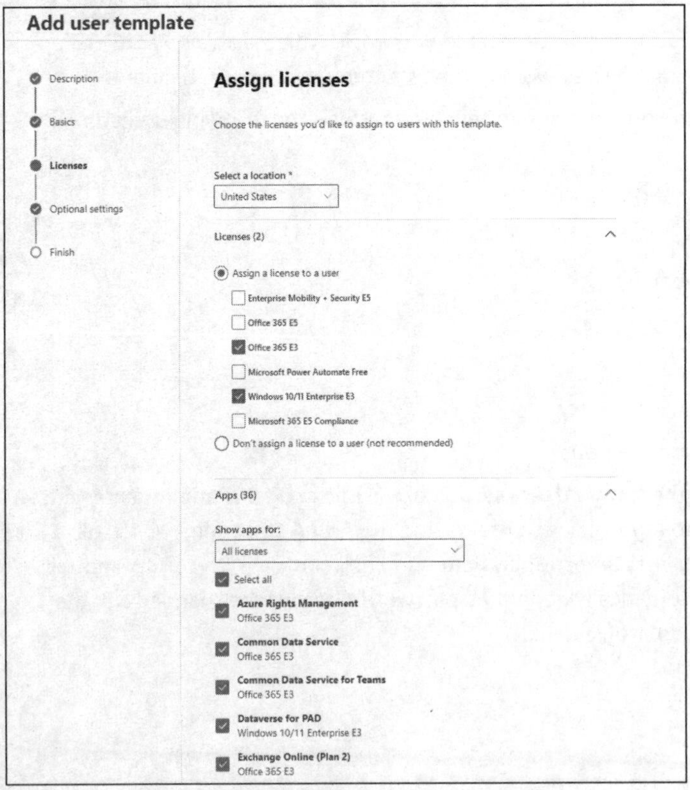

FIGURE 2-2 Creating a new user template in the Microsoft 365 admin center

MORE INFO **MANAGE MICROSOFT 365 USERS**

You can learn more about Managing Microsoft 365 users at *https://learn.microsoft.com/microsoft-365/enterprise/manage-microsoft-365-accounts*.

Manage groups

Groups enable you to collect users and assign them privileges and access to workloads or services. Rather than assign privileges and access to workloads or services directly to users, you can assign these rights to a group and then indirectly assign them to users by adding the user accounts to the appropriate group. Using groups in this way is a long-standing administrative practice because it allows you to determine a user's level of access and rights by looking at the user's group memberships rather than checking each workload and service to determine if the user account has been assigned rights to that service. You can manage groups in the **Active Teams And Groups** area of the Microsoft 365 admin center, as shown in Figure 2-3.

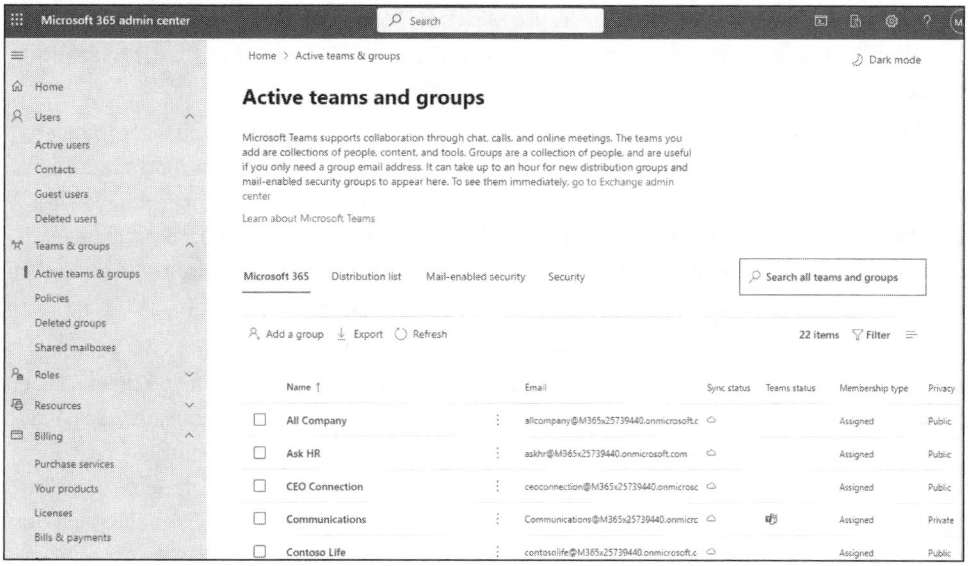

FIGURE 2-3 The Active Teams And Groups page in the Microsoft 365 admin center

Microsoft 365 supports the following group types:

- **Microsoft 365 groups** Used for collaboration between users. These users can be inside or external to the organization. Each Microsoft 365 group has an associated email address, shared workspace for conversations, shared location for files, calendar events, and a planner.
- **Security groups** Used to grant access to specific Microsoft 365 resources, such as SharePoint sites. Security groups can contain user accounts as well as device accounts. Device-related groups are most often used with services such as Intune.

- **Mail-enabled security groups**   Can be used to grant access to specific Microsoft 365 resources. Cannot be dynamically managed and cannot contain devices.
- **Distribution groups**   Used for sending notifications to groups of people.

Group membership for Microsoft 365 groups and security group types can be configured as **Assigned** or **Dynamic**. When the **Assigned** option is selected, membership is managed manually. When the **Dynamic** option is selected, group membership is determined based on the results of a query against user or device attributes. For example, suppose you have a user located in a specific department or city and managed by a specific person. That user could automatically be put in a specific group.

Source of authority is important when modifying users and groups. Modifications occurring in the on-premises Active Directory overwrite the current state of the objects within the Microsoft Entra ID instance that supports the Microsoft 365 tenancy. The only exception to this rule is the assignment of licenses, which only occurs using the Microsoft 365 admin center or PowerShell tools.

Modifications made to on-premises user and group objects will be present only in the Microsoft Entra ID instance that supports the Microsoft 365 tenancy after synchronization has occurred. By default, synchronization occurs every 30 minutes. You can force synchronization to occur by using the Synchronization Service Manager tool.

With deletion, the source of authority concept is very important. When you want to delete a user or group account created in the on-premises Active Directory instance, you should use tools such as Active Directory Users and Computers or the Active Directory admin center. When you delete a user or group using this method, the user will be deleted from the on-premises Active Directory instance and then, when synchronization occurs, from the Microsoft Entra ID instance that supports the linked Microsoft 365 tenancy.

Deleting a user from Microsoft 365 keeps their account in the Microsoft Entra ID Recycle Bin for 30 days. This means you can recover the account online if necessary. If you delete a user from your on-premises Active Directory environment but have enabled the on-premises Active Directory Recycle Bin, recovering the user from the on-premises Active Directory Recycle Bin will recover the user account in the Entra ID instance associated with Microsoft 365. You must create another account with a new GUID if your Active Directory Recycle Bin is enabled in your on-premises Active Directory instance.

> *MORE INFO*   **MICROSOFT 365 GROUPS**
>
> You can learn more about Microsoft 365 groups at *https://learn.microsoft.com/ microsoftteams/office-365-groups*.

Manage external identities by using Microsoft Entra External ID

Sometimes you want to enable people in a partner organization or external users such as temporary contractors to interact with resources hosted in Microsoft 365. For example, you might want to allow someone to collaborate with content hosted in SharePoint Online.

When planning external access to Microsoft 365 resources, you should understand that Microsoft 365 external sharing and Microsoft Entra External ID collaboration are almost the same thing. Except for OneDrive and SharePoint Online, all external sharing uses the Microsoft Entra External ID collaboration invitation APIs. Although Microsoft Entra External ID is not a direct replacement for Azure AD B2B and Azure AD B2C, the functionality of these products addresses the same use cases.

> **MORE INFO** **MICROSOFT ENTRA EXTERNAL ID**
>
> You can learn more about Microsoft Entra External ID at *https://learn.microsoft.com/azure/active-directory/external-identities/customers/faq-customers*.

You manage external sharing for SharePoint Online by using the **Sharing** page of the SharePoint admin center. To configure SharePoint so that only Microsoft Entra External ID sharing is enabled, select **Allow Sharing Only With The External Users That Already Exist In Your Organization's Directory**, as shown in Figure 2-4.

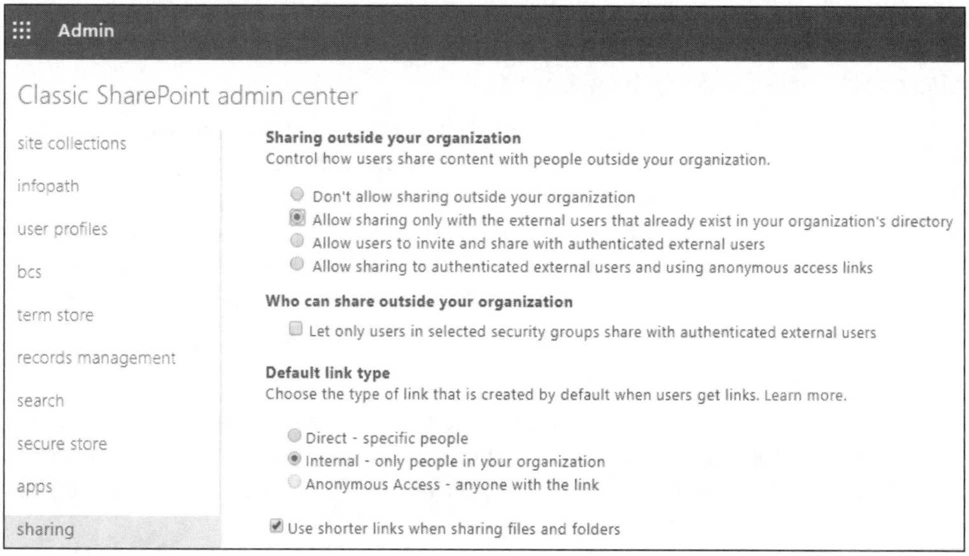

FIGURE 2-4 SharePoint Online Sharing options

You can use the **External Collaboration Settings** page, accessible from the **Entra ID External Identities** blade, to configure the following collaboration settings:

- **Guest Users Permissions Are Limited**   Enabled by default, this option enables you to configure guest users to have the same permissions as standard users.

- **Admins And Users In The Guest Inviter Role Can Invite**   Invitations can be sent from users who hold the administrator and guest inviter roles.

- **Members Can Invite**   Invitations can be sent by users who are not administrators and who have not been assigned the **Guests Can Invite** role.

- **Guests Can Invite**   Users with **Guests Can Invite** status can invite other users as B2B users or guests.

- **Enable Email One-Time Passcode For Guests**   This is a one-time passcode for guests who do not have an Azure AD or Microsoft account and for which Google Federation has not been configured. Guests who use one-time passcodes remain authenticated for 24 hours.

- **Allow Invitations To Be Sent To Any Domain**   This is the default setting, which enables guest and B2B invitations to be sent to any domain.

- **Deny Invitations To Specified Domains**   This enables you to create a block list of domains to which guest and B2B invitations cannot be sent.

- **Allow Invitations Only To The Specified Domains**   Use this option to allow guest and B2B invitations only to specific domains. Invitations to domains not on the allowed list are blocked.

Microsoft Entra External ID accounts

Microsoft Entra External ID accounts are a special type of guest user account that resides within the Microsoft Entra ID instance to which you can assign privileges. Microsoft Entra External ID accounts are generally used when you want to allow one or more users from a partner organization to access resources hosted within your organization's Microsoft 365 tenancy. For example, if users in Contoso's partner organization, Tailwind Traders, need to interact with and publish content to a Contoso SharePoint Online site, one method of providing the necessary access is to create a set of Microsoft Entra External ID accounts.

Microsoft Entra External ID accounts have the following properties:

- They are stored in a separate Microsoft Entra ID tenancy from your organization but are represented as a guest user in your organization's tenancy. The Microsoft Entra External ID user signs in using their organization's Microsoft Entra ID account to access resources in your organization's tenancy.

- They are stored in your organization's on-premises Active Directory and then synced using Microsoft Entra Connect (previously Azure AD Connect) and a guest user type. This is different from the usual type of synchronization, where user accounts are synced from an on-premises directory, but the Microsoft Entra ID accounts are traditional Microsoft Entra ID accounts and are not assigned the guest user type.

Microsoft Entra ID accounts use the user type to display information about the account's relationship to the organization's tenancy. The two following values are supported:

- **Member** If the user type is **Member**, the user is considered to belong to the host organization. This is appropriate for full-time employees, some types of contractors, or anyone else on the organizational payroll or within the organizational structure.

- **Guest** The Guest user type indicates that the user is not directly associated with the organization. The Guest user type applies to Microsoft Entra External ID and, more generally, to guest accounts. It is used when the account is based in another organization's directory or associated with another identity provider, such as a social network identity.

The account's user type does not determine how the user signs in; it merely indicates the user's relationship to the organization that controls the Microsoft Entra ID tenancy. It can also be used to implement policies that depend on the value of this attribute. It is the source attribute property that indicates how the user authenticates. This property can have the following values:

- **Invited User** A guest or Microsoft Entra External ID user who has been invited but has not accepted yet.

- **External Active Directory** An account that resides in a directory managed by a partner organization. When the user authenticates, they do so against the partner organization's Microsoft Entra ID instance. This field will eventually be updated to represent the Microsoft Entra ID branding.

- **Microsoft Account** A guest account that authenticates using a Microsoft account, such as an *Outlook.com* or *Hotmail.com* account.

- **Windows Server Active Directory** A user signed in from an on-premises instance of Active Directory managed by the same organization that controls the tenancy. This usually involves the deployment of Microsoft Entra Connect. In the case of a Microsoft Entra External ID user, though, the user type attribute is set to **Guest**.

- **Azure Active Directory** A user signed in using a Microsoft Entra ID account that your organization manages. The user type attribute is set to **Guest** for a Microsoft Entra External ID user. This field will eventually be updated to represent the Microsoft Entra ID branding.

When you create the first type of Microsoft Entra External ID account, an invitation is sent to the user to whom you want to grant Microsoft Entra External ID access. The process of creating and sending this invitation also creates an account within your organization's Microsoft Entra ID instance. This account will not have any credentials associated with it because authentication will be performed by the Microsoft Entra External ID user's identity provider.

Until the invitation is accepted, the **Source** property of an invited guest user account will be set to **Invited User**. You can also resend the invitation if the target user does not receive or respond to the first invitation. When the user accepts the invitation, the **Source** attribute will be updated to **External Entra ID**. If the user's account is synchronized from an on-premises Active Directory instance, but the **User Type** is set to **Guest**, the **Source** property will be listed as **Windows Server Active Directory**.

Guest accounts

A Guest account might be considered a type of account where the account is a Microsoft account or a social account rather than one associated with an Entra ID tenancy. For example, a Guest account might have an *@outlook.com* email address or a social media account (such as Facebook). The main difference between the two is that, in general, an Entra External ID account implies a business-to-business relationship, whereas a Guest account implies a business-to-individual relationship.

You create a Guest account in exactly the same way as an External ID account, as outlined in the preceding section. You send an invitation, an account is created, the user accepts the invitation, and then the individual uses the account to access Microsoft 365 resources to which they have been granted permissions.

Guest users are blocked from performing certain tasks, including enumerating users, groups, and other Entra ID resources. You can remove the guest user default limitations by performing the following steps:

1. On the Microsoft Entra ID blade, under **Manage**, select **User Settings**.

2. On the **User Settings** blade, select **Manage External Collaboration Settings**.

3. On the **External Collaboration Settings** page, select **No** under **Guest Users Permissions Are Limited**.

> ***MORE INFO*** **ADDING GUEST USERS**
>
> You can learn more about this skill at *https://learn.microsoft.com/en-us/azure/ active-directory/external-identities/b2b-quickstart-add-guest-users-portal*.

Manage Microsoft 365 contacts

Contacts are people not part of your organization that you want to be present within address books. For example, there might be specific partners or vendors you want people in your organization to find quickly; in that case, you can add them as contacts. When people type a contact's name into Outlook or Microsoft Teams, their details will be prepopulated as though they were typical members of your organization. You can provide a contact's email address, phone number, fax number, website, street address, city, state, zip, and country and configure a MailTip for them.

You can add contacts from the Microsoft 365 admin center by going to **Contacts** under **Users**, as shown in Figure 2-5.

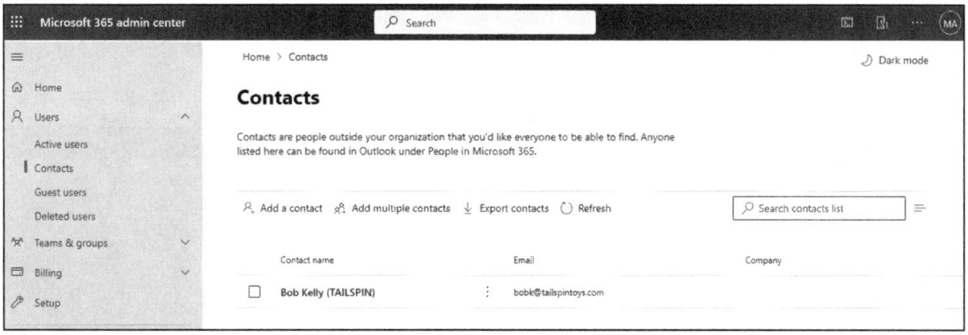

FIGURE 2-5   Contacts

You can add contacts individually or import up to 40 contacts at a time by using a specially formatted CSV file. You can also add and manage contacts using the New-MailContact, Get-MailContact, Enable-MailContact, Remove-MailContact, Disable-MailContact, and Set-MailContact Exchange PowerShell cmdlets.

> **MORE INFO   ADDING GUEST USERS**
>
> Microsoft 365 contacts function just as Exchange Online contacts do. Any contacts you create in the Exchange admin center will be visible in the Microsoft 365 admin center, and any you create in Microsoft 365 admin center will be in the Exchange admin center. You can learn more about Contacts at *https://learn.microsoft.com/en-us/exchange/recipients/mail-contacts*.

EXAM TIP

You can configure an allow list of specific domains to which invitations can be sent, and you can configure a block list where you only block invitations to specific domains.

Manage product licenses

Microsoft 365 users require licenses to use Outlook, SharePoint Online, Office 365, and other services. Users assigned the Global Administrator or User Management Administrator roles can assign licenses when creating new Microsoft 365 user accounts. They can also assign licenses to accounts created through directory synchronization or federation.

When a license is assigned to a user, the following occurs:

- An Exchange Online mailbox is created for the user.
- Edit permissions for the default SharePoint Online team site are assigned to the user.
- For Microsoft 365 Apps for enterprise, the user can download and install Microsoft Office on up to five Windows or macOS computers.

You can view the number of valid licenses and the number of those licenses that have been assigned on the Licenses page. You access this page by selecting **Billing** in the left pane of the Microsoft 365 admin center and then selecting **Licenses**, as shown in Figure 2-6.

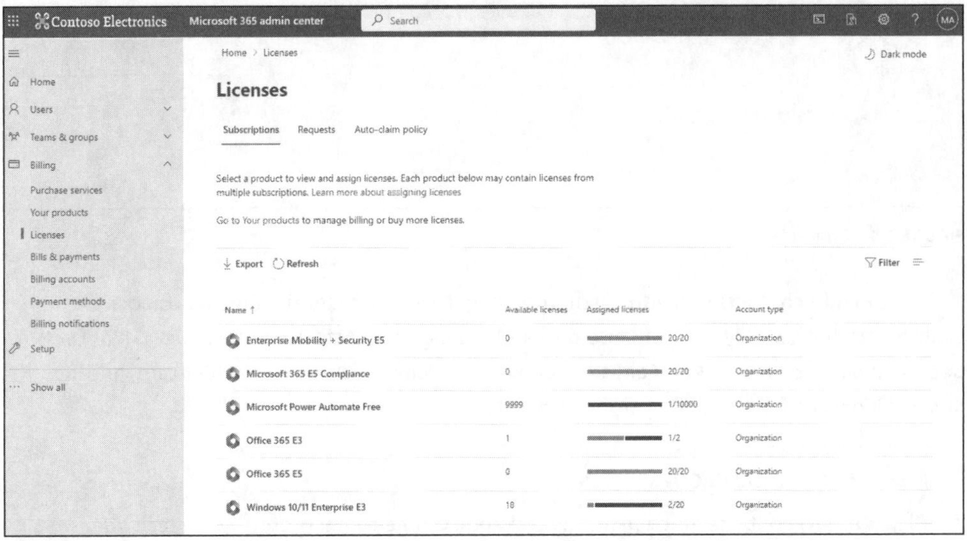

FIGURE 2-6   The Licenses page

> **MORE INFO   ASSIGN LICENSES**
>
> You can learn more about assigning licenses at *https://docs.microsoft.com/microsoft-365/admin/add-users/add-users*.

To assign a license to a user, perform the following steps:

1.   In the Microsoft 365 admin center, select the **Active Users** node under **Users**, as shown in Figure 2-7.

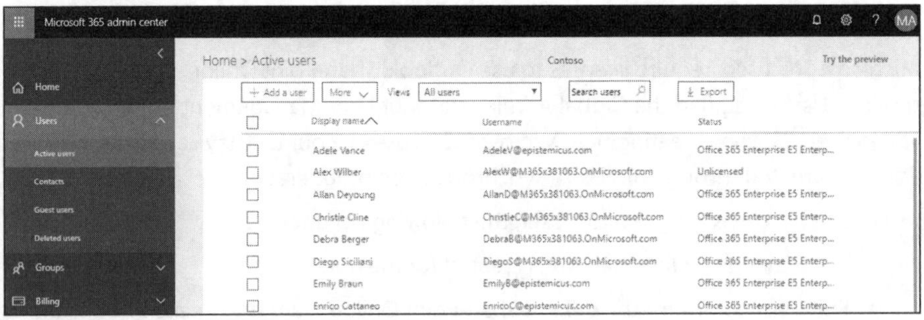

FIGURE 2-7   The Active Users node

2. Select the checkbox next to the user to whom you want to assign a license. This will open the user's properties page, as shown in Figure 2-8.

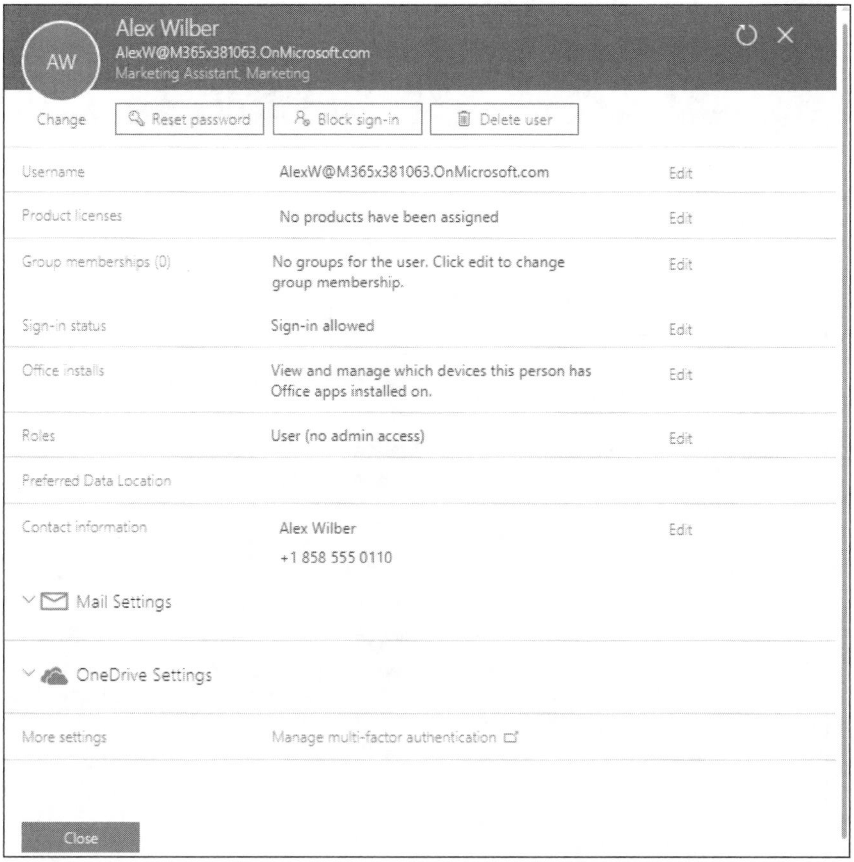

FIGURE 2-8 User properties page

3. On the user's properties page, select **Edit** next to **Product Licenses**.

4. Use the **Location** dropdown to choose your location. Then, assign licenses as needed: **Enterprise Mobility And Security**, **Office 365 Enterprise**, and **Windows 10/11 Enterprise**, as shown in Figure 2-9.

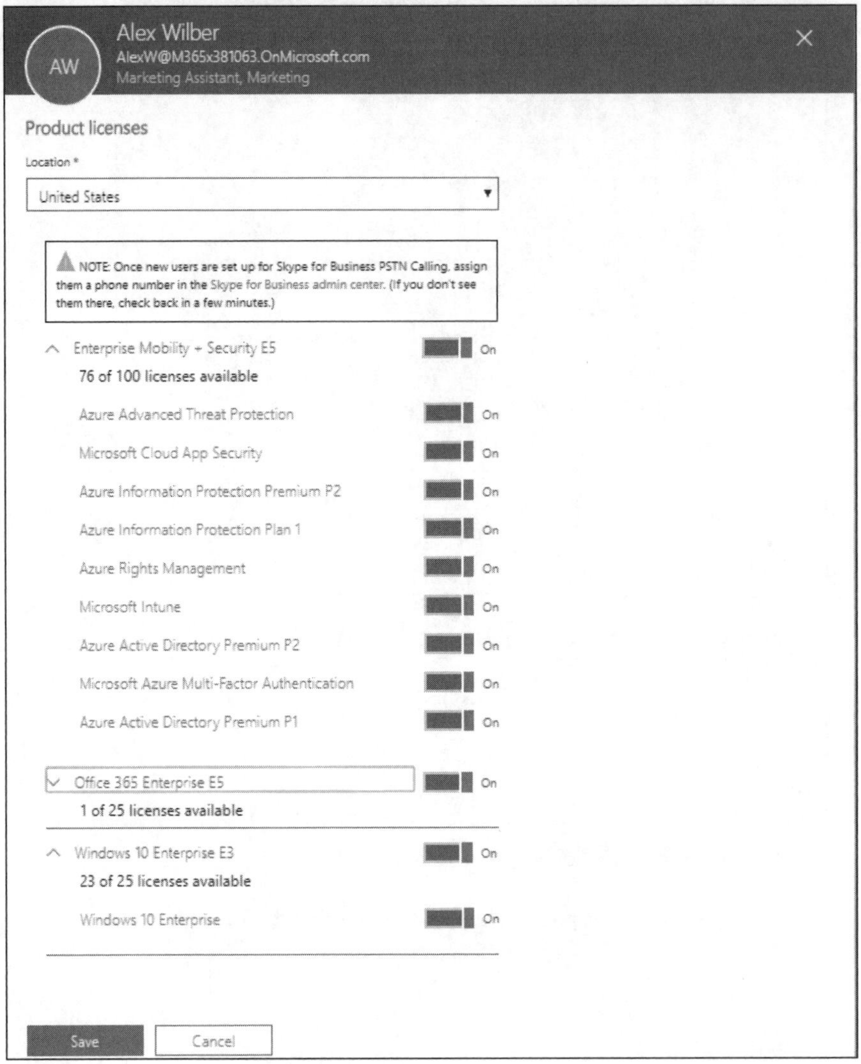

FIGURE 2-9 The Product Licenses page

5. Select **Save** to assign the licenses to the user.

User accounts created in Microsoft 365 by the synchronization process will not automatically be assigned Microsoft 365 licenses. This means that when creating new user accounts in the on-premises environment after initially configuring Microsoft Entra Connect, you'll also need to use Microsoft 365 admin center or PowerShell to provision those accounts with Microsoft 365 licenses.

MORE INFO **ASSIGN LICENSES TO USERS**

You can learn more about assigning licenses to users at *https://learn.microsoft.com/ microsoft-365/admin/add-users/add-users.*

Skill 2.2: Prepare for identity synchronization

Synchronization is the process of replicating on-premises identities, such as users and groups, to the cloud. Synchronization is necessary only when an on-premises identity provider is present. In some synchronization models, every on-premises identity is replicated to the cloud. In other models, only a subset of the on-premises identities is replicated. Most organizations that use Microsoft 365 use some form of identity synchronization as they adopted Microsoft 365 after using Active Directory Domain Services for some time, and it was simpler to use existing identities synchronized to Microsoft Entra ID than to create new ones.

> **This section covers the following topics:**
> ■ Evaluate synchronization requirements
> ■ Prepare for directory synchronization

Evaluate synchronization requirements

An important step in evaluating synchronization requirements is determining what information about a user's identity needs to be synchronized to the cloud. Depending on the model chosen, some or all of the properties of those on-premises identities can be replicated. For example, some organizations store sensitive private data about employees within Active Directory. Only replicating what is necessary is especially important given the increasing regulation of data involving personal information and where it can and cannot be stored.

Should an organization choose, it is possible to completely replicate every aspect of an Active Directory object to the cloud. For example, an organization can deploy a domain controller, SharePoint Farm, System Center, and Exchange Server in Azure infrastructure-as-a-service (IaaS) virtual machines (VMs). Those VMs can be connected via VPN or an ExpressRoute connection to an on-premises Active Directory instance. In this scenario, the Azure IaaS VMs would essentially function as an expensive branch office site running in the Azure cloud.

When evaluating requirements and a solution for synchronization, consider the following questions:

■ Which identities need to be replicated to the cloud?

■ How often do those identities need to be replicated to the cloud?

■ What properties of those identities need to be replicated to the cloud?

Which identities to replicate?

The deployment of Microsoft 365 allows organizations to assess their identity needs. If an organization has been using Active Directory for a long time, it's likely that objects don't need to be replicated to the cloud or in the on-premises Active Directory instance. Before implementing any Microsoft 365 replication scheme, it's a good idea to thoroughly audit all the objects present within the on-premises directory and clean out those that are no longer required.

Another issue is whether every on-premises identity must be present in Microsoft Entra ID. Many organizations take a phased approach to introducing Microsoft 365, migrating small groups of users to the service at a time rather than every user in the organization all at once. Users only present in the on-premises directory service won't need Microsoft 365 licenses assigned to them.

Special account types are commonly present in an on-premises Active Directory instance that does not need to be—or simply cannot be—replicated to Microsoft Entra ID. For example, there is no need to replicate service accounts or accounts used for specific administrative purposes for on-premises resources, such as managing an on-premises SQL Server database server or other workload.

Another challenge to consider is that many on-premises environments are more complicated than a single Active Directory domain. Some organizations have multidomain Active Directory forests. In addition, since it is a recommended Microsoft secure administrative practice, an increasing number of large organizations have multiforest deployments—for example, an Enhanced Security Administrative Environment (ESAE) forest to store privileged accounts for the production forest.

User accounts are not the only identity that an organization might want to replicate to the cloud. Replicating some groups to the cloud might be necessary because these groups can be useful in mediating access to Microsoft 365 workloads. For example, if your organization already has a local security group used to collect together members of the accounting team, you might want that group also present as a method of mediating access to resources and workloads within Microsoft 365.

How often to replicate?

When evaluating requirements and a solution for synchronization, you need to answer several important questions. For example, how often do the properties of an on-premises identity change, and how soon must those changes be present within Microsoft Entra ID?

You don't want a user who changes their password to have to wait 24 hours before that new password can be used against cloud identities. Similarly, suppose you deprovision a user account because a person's employment with the organization has been terminated. In that case, you'll want that action reflected in limiting access to Microsoft 365 workloads rather than the user account having continued access for some time after the user's on-premises identity has been disabled.

Although there can be bandwidth considerations around identity synchronization, most such traffic will replicate changes, also known as delta, rather than constant replications of the entire identity database. The amount of bandwidth consumed by delta identity synchronization traffic is often insignificant compared to that consumed by other Microsoft 365 workloads and services.

Which properties to replicate?

Active Directory has been present at some organizations for more than two decades. One of the original selling points of Active Directory was that it could store far more information than just user names and passwords. Because of this, many organizations use Active Directory to store a substantive amount of information about personnel, including telephone numbers, the user's position within the organization, and the branch office where the user works.

When considering a synchronization solution, determine which on-premises Active Directory attribute information needs to be replicated to Microsoft Entra ID. For example, you might have an application running in Azure that needs access to the **Job Title**, **Department**, **Company**, and **Manager** attributes, as shown in Figure 2-10.

FIGURE 2-10 Which attributes to replicate

Evaluate requirements and solutions for identity management

Evaluating the requirements and solutions for identity management first involves determining your organization's source of authority. The source of authority is the directory service that functions as the primary location for creating and managing user and group accounts. You can choose between having an on-premises Active Directory instance function as a source of authority or Microsoft Entra ID function as the source of authority.

Even though Microsoft Entra ID is present in a hybrid deployment, the source of authority will be the on-premises AD DS instance. Hybrid deployment accounts with existing on-premises resources and Microsoft 365 workloads are used for authentication and authorization purposes.

Source of authority is a very important concept when it comes to creating users and groups in an environment where Microsoft Entra Connect is configured to synchronize an on-premises Active Directory with the Microsoft Entra ID instance that supports the Microsoft 365 tenancy. When you create a user or group in the on-premises Active Directory instance, the on-premises Active Directory instance retains authority over that object. Objects created within the on-premises Active Directory instance within the filtering scope of objects synchronized via Microsoft Entra Connect will replicate to the Microsoft Entra ID instance that supports the Microsoft 365 tenancy.

Newly created on-premises user and group objects will only be present within the Microsoft Entra ID instance that supports the Microsoft 365 tenancy after synchronization. You can use the Microsoft Entra Connect Synchronization Service Manager tool to force synchronization.

Prepare for directory synchronization

Before you deploy Microsoft Entra Connect, ensuring that your on-premises Active Directory environment is healthy is prudent. You should also have an excellent understanding of the current state of the Active Directory environment, including performing an audit to determine the following:

- Do any Active Directory objects use invalid characters?
- Do any Active Directory objects have incorrect Universal Principal Names (UPNs)?
- What are the current domain and forest functional levels?
- Are any schema extensions or custom attributes in use?

Before deploying any form of identity synchronization, you should also ensure that you have performed the following tasks:

- Remove any duplicate `proxyAddress` attributes.
- Remove any duplicate `userPrincipalName` attributes.

- Ensure that blank or invalid `userPrincipalName` attribute settings have been altered so that the setting contains only a valid UPN.

- Ensure that the `cn` and `samAccountName` attributes have been assigned values for user accounts.

- Ensure that the member, alias, and `displayName` (for groups with a valid mail or `proxyAddress` attribute) are populated for group accounts.

- Ensure that the following attributes do not contain invalid characters:

```
givenName
sn
samAccountName
givenName
displayName
mail
proxyAddress
mailNickName
```

UPNs that are used with Microsoft 365 can only contain the following characters:

- Letters

- Numbers

- Periods

- Dashes

- Underscores

Rather than performing this operation manually, Microsoft provides tools that allow you to automatically remediate problems that might exist with attributes before deploying Microsoft Entra Connect.

IdFix

The IdFix tool, which you can download from Microsoft's website, allows you to scan an Active Directory instance to determine whether any user accounts, group accounts, or contacts have problems that will cause them not to synchronize between the on-premises instance of Active Directory and the Microsoft 365 instance of Microsoft Entra ID. IdFix can also perform repairs on objects that would otherwise be unable to sync. IdFix runs with the security context of the currently signed-on user. If you want to use IdFix to repair objects in the forest that have problems, the security account you use to run IdFix must have permission to modify those objects. The IdFix tool is shown in Figure 2-11, displaying an account detected with an incorrectly configured `userPrincipalName` attribute.

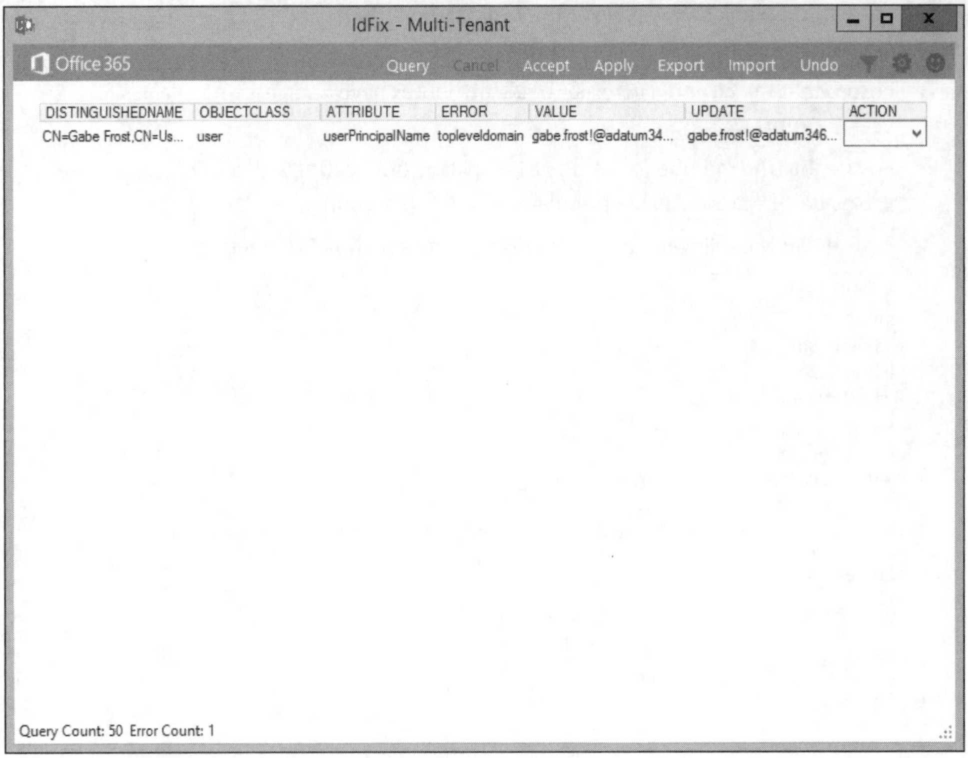

FIGURE 2-11 IdFix finds a user with a problematic UPN.

> **MORE INFO IDFIX**
>
> You can download IdFix at the following address: *https://microsoft.github.io/idfix/*.

Use UPN suffixes and nonroutable domains

Before performing synchronization between an on-premises Active Directory environment and a Microsoft Entra ID instance used to support a Microsoft 365 tenancy, you must ensure that all user account objects in the on-premises Active Directory environment are configured with a value for the UPN suffix that can function for both the on-premises environment and Microsoft 365.

This is not a problem when an organization's internal Active Directory domain suffix is a publicly routable domain. For example, a domain name—such as *contoso.com* or *adatum.com*—resolvable by public DNS servers will suffice. Things become more complicated when the organization's internal Active Directory domain suffix is not publicly routable. For example, Figure 2-12 shows the *adatum346ER.internal* nonroutable domain.

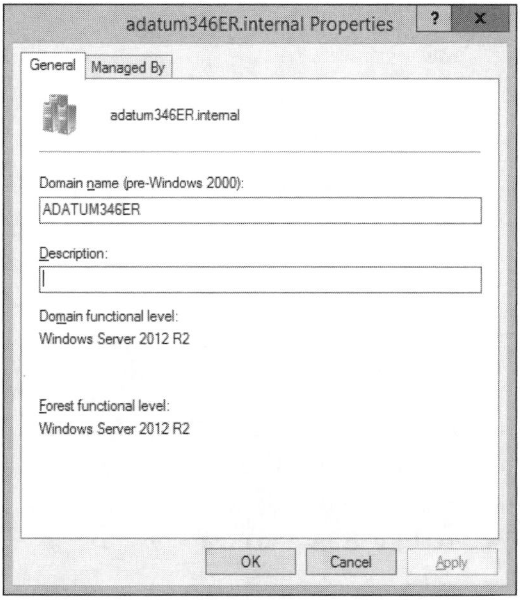

FIGURE 2-12 Nonroutable domain

If a domain is nonroutable, the default routing domain, such as *adatum346ER.onmicrosoft.com*, should be used for the Microsoft 365 UPN suffix. This requires modifying the UPN suffix of accounts stored in the on-premises Active Directory instance. Modification of UPNs after initial synchronization has occurred is not supported. So, you must ensure that on-premises Active Directory UPNs are properly configured before performing initial synchronization using Microsoft Entra Connect.

Perform the following steps to add a UPN suffix to the on-premises Active Directory if the Active Directory domain uses a nonroutable namespace:

1. Open the **Active Directory Domains And Trust** console and select **Active Directory Domains And Trusts**.

2. On the **Action** menu, select **Properties**.

3. On the **UPN Suffixes** tab, enter the UPN suffix to be used with Microsoft 365. Figure 2-13 shows the UPN suffix of *epistemicus.com*.

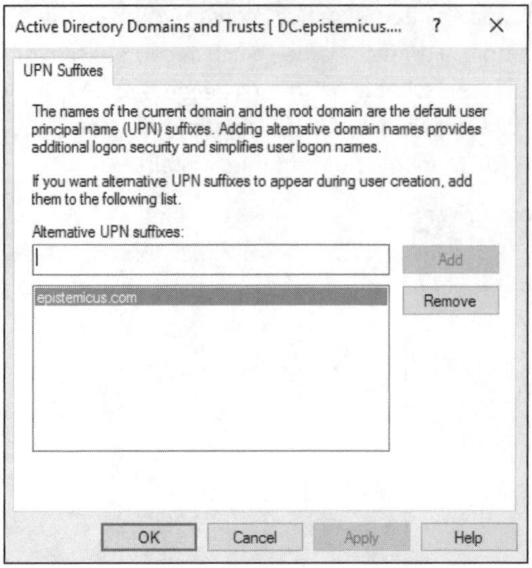

FIGURE 2-13   Routable domain

Once the UPN suffix has been added in **Active Directory Domains And Trusts**, you assign the UPN suffix to user accounts. You can do this in one of three ways:

- **Manually**   As shown in Figure 2-14, this can be done manually using the **Account** tab of the user's **Properties** dialog in **Active Directory Users And Computers**.

FIGURE 2-14   Configuring the UPN

- **Using Microsoft PowerShell scripts to reset the UPNs of multiple user accounts**
  For example, the following script resets the UPN suffixes of all user accounts in the
  epistemicus.internal domain to *epistemicus.onmicrosoft.com*:

```
Get-ADUser -Filter {UserPrincipalName -like "*@epistemicus.internal"} -SearchBase
"DC=epistemicus,DC=internal" |
ForEach-Object {
$UPN =
$_.UserPrincipalName.Replace("epistemicus.internal","epistemicus.onmicrosoft.com")
Set-ADUser $_ -UserPrincipalName $UPN
}
```

Skill 2.3: Manage identity synchronization by using Microsoft Entra Connect

This skill section deals with managing identity synchronization with Microsoft Entra Connect once deployed. To master this skill, you must understand how to monitor Microsoft Entra Connect Health, manage Microsoft Entra Connect synchronization, configure object filters, and configure password synchronization.

This section covers the following skills:

- Configure directory synchronization by using Microsoft Entra Connect
- Monitor Microsoft Entra Connect Health
- Manage Microsoft Entra Connect synchronization
- Configure object filters
- Configure password synchronization
- Implement multiforest AD Connect scenarios

Microsoft Entra Connect

Microsoft Entra Connect is designed to streamline configuring connections between the on-premises deployment and a Microsoft Entra ID instance. The Microsoft Entra Connect tool is designed to make configuring synchronization between an on-premises Active Directory deployment and Microsoft Entra ID as frictionless as possible.

Microsoft Entra Connect can automatically configure and install simple password synchronization or Federation/single sign-on, depending on your organizational needs. When you choose the Federation with AD FS option, Active Directory Federation Services is installed and configured, as well as a web application proxy server to facilitate communication between the on-premises AD FS deployment and Microsoft Entra ID.

The Microsoft Entra Connect tool supports the following optional features:

- **Exchange Hybrid Deployment** This option is suitable for organizations with an Office 365 deployment in which mailboxes are hosted on-premises and in the cloud.

- **Exchange Mail Public Folders** This feature allows organizations to synchronize mail-enabled public folder objects from an on-premises Active Directory environment to Microsoft 365.

- **Azure AD App And Attribute Filtering** Selecting this option allows you to be more selective about which attributes are synchronized between the on-premises environment and Azure AD.

- **Password Synchronization** This synchronizes a hash of the user's on-premises password with Azure AD. When the user authenticates to Azure AD, the submitted password is hashed using the same process, and if the hashes match, the user is authenticated. Each time the user updates their password on-premises, the updated password hash synchronizes to Azure AD.

- **Password Writeback** Password writeback allows users to change their passwords in the cloud and have the changed password written back to the on-premises Active Directory instance.

- **Group Writeback** With this option, changes made to groups in Azure AD are written back to the on-premises AD instance.

- **Device Writeback** Here, information about devices registered by the user in Azure AD is written back to the on-premises AD instance.

- **Directory Extension Attribute Sync** This option allows you to extend the Azure AD schema based on extensions made to your organization's on-premises Active Directory instance.

> *MORE INFO* **MICROSOFT ENTRA CONNECT**
>
> You can learn more about Microsoft Entra Connect at *https://learn.microsoft.com/azure/active-directory/hybrid/whatis-azure-ad-connect*.

Microsoft Entra Connect user sign-in options

Microsoft Entra Connect supports a variety of user sign-in options related to the method you use to synchronize directory information from Active Directory Domain Services to Azure AD. You configure which sign-in option you will use when setting up Microsoft Entra Connect. The default method, password sync, is appropriate for the majority of organizations that will use Microsoft Entra Connect to synchronize identities to the cloud.

Password synchronization

Hashes of on-premises Active Directory user passwords synchronize to Microsoft Entra ID, and changed passwords immediately synchronize to Microsoft Entra ID. Actual passwords are never sent to Microsoft Entra ID and are not stored in Microsoft Entra ID. This allows for single sign-on for users of computers that are joined to an Active Directory domain that synchronizes to Microsoft Entra ID. Password synchronization also allows you to enable password writeback for self-service password reset functionality through Microsoft Entra ID.

Pass-through authentication

The user's password is validated against an on-premises Active Directory domain controller when authenticating to Microsoft Entra ID. Passwords and password hashes are not present in Microsoft Entra ID. Pass-through authentication allows for on-premises password policies to apply. Pass-through authentication requires Microsoft Entra Connect to have an agent on a computer joined to the domain that hosts the Active Directory instance containing the relevant user accounts. Pass-through authentication also allows single sign-on for users of domain-joined machines.

Pass-through authentication validates the user's password against the on-premises Active Directory controller. The password doesn't need to be present in Microsoft Entra ID in any form. This allows for on-premises policies, such as sign-in hour restrictions, to be evaluated during authentication to cloud services.

Pass-through authentication uses a simple agent on a Windows Server 2012 R2, Windows Server 2016, Windows Server 2019, or Windows Server 2022 domain–joined machine in the on-premises environment. This agent listens for password-validation requests. It doesn't require any inbound ports to be open to the internet.

You can also enable single sign-on for users on domain-joined machines that are on the corporate network. With single sign-on, enabled users only need to enter a user name to help them securely access cloud resources.

Active Directory Federation

Active Directory Federation allows users to authenticate to Microsoft Entra ID resources using on-premises credentials. It also requires the deployment of an Active Directory Federation Services infrastructure. This is the most complicated identity synchronization configuration for Microsoft 365 and is only likely to be implemented in environments with complicated identity configurations.

> *MORE INFO* **MICROSOFT ENTRA CONNECT SIGN-IN OPTIONS**
>
> To learn more about sign-in options, consult the following article: *https://learn.microsoft.com/azure/active-directory/hybrid/plan-connect-user-signin*.

EXAM TIP

Remember the difference between password sync and pass-through authentication.

Installing Microsoft Entra Connect

To configure Microsoft Entra Connect synchronization, install the Microsoft Entra Connect software and then run the Microsoft Entra Connect Installation Wizard. The process of installing Microsoft Entra Connect is simply a matter of installing the appropriate MSI file on a Windows Server computer in an environment that meets the necessary prerequisites. After installing the software, you use the Microsoft Entra Connect Setup Wizard to perform the initial configuration. Run the Setup Wizard again if you want to change any Microsoft Entra Connect synchronization settings. You can also use PowerShell or the Synchronization Service Manager to configure synchronization settings, which you'll learn about later in this section.

Meeting the Microsoft Entra Connect installation requirements

Before installing Microsoft Entra Connect, you should ensure that your environment, Microsoft Entra Connect computer, and account used to configure Microsoft Entra Connect meet the software, hardware, and privilege requirements. So, you need to ensure that your Active Directory environment is configured at the appropriate level, that the computer on which you will run Microsoft Entra Connect has the appropriate software and hardware configuration, and that the account used to install Microsoft Entra Connect has been added to the appropriate security groups.

> **MORE INFO** **MICROSOFT ENTRA CONNECT PREREQUISITES**
>
> You can learn more about Microsoft Entra Connect prerequisites at *https://learn.microsoft.com/azure/active-directory/hybrid/how-to-connect-install-prerequisites*.

Microsoft Entra ID and Microsoft 365 requirements

Before installing and configuring Microsoft Entra Connect, you must ensure that you have configured an additional DNS domain for Microsoft 365. By default, a Microsoft Entra ID tenant will allow 50,000 objects; however, when you add and verify an additional domain, this limit increases to 300,000. You can open a support ticket with Microsoft if you require more than 300,000 objects in your Microsoft Entra ID instance. If you require more than 500,000 objects in your Microsoft Entra ID instance, you must acquire a Microsoft Entra P1 or P2 license or Enterprise Mobility and Security license. Having the DNS domain configured before you set up identity synchronization will allow you to ensure that user UPNs aren't using the default onmicrosoft.com DNS domain.

On-premises Active Directory environment requirements

Microsoft Entra Connect requires configuring the on-premises Active Directory environment at the Windows Server 2003 forest functional level or higher. The forest functional level depends on the minimum domain functional level of any domain in a forest. For example, if you have five domains in a forest—four of them running at the Windows Server 2012 R2 domain functional level and one running at the Windows Server 2003 domain functional level—Windows Server 2003 will be the maximum forest functional level.

Because Microsoft no longer supports Windows Server 2008 without a custom support agreement, your organization should have domain controllers running at least Windows Server 2012 (Windows Server 2012 and Windows Server 2012 R2 will only be supported through custom support agreements from 2024 onward). The Microsoft security best practice is to have domain controllers deployed with Microsoft's most recent version of the server operating system, so in theory, you should have domain controllers running Windows Server 2022 or later.

To support Microsoft Entra Connect password writeback functionality, you'll need domain controllers running either Windows Server 2008 R2 or Windows Server 2008 with all service packs applied and hotfix KB2386717 or domain controllers running later operating systems. Domain and forest functional levels are not automatically upgraded when you install domain controllers. Some organizations have deployed domain controllers but still have older functional levels.

You can check the forest functional level using the **Active Directory Domains And Trusts** console. To do this, perform the following steps:

1. Open the **Active Directory Domains And Trusts** console.

2. Select the **Active Directory Domains And Trusts** node.

3. On the **Actions** menu, select **Raise Forest Functional Level**.

The **Raise Forest Functional Level** dialog displays the current functional level and, if possible, allows you to upgrade the forest functional level. Figure 2-15 shows the forest functional level configured at Windows Server 2012 R2, the highest possible forest functional level for an organization where all domain controllers run the Windows Server 2012 R2 operating system. If all the domain controllers are running the Windows Server 2016 operating system, it is possible to raise the domain and forest functional level to Windows Server 2016. Note that domains with exclusively Windows Server 2019 and Windows Server 2022 domain controllers can only be raised to the Windows Server 2016 domain and forest functional level.

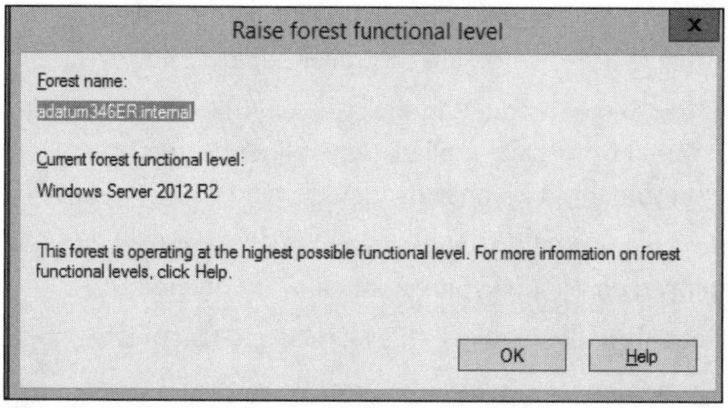

FIGURE 2-15   Forest functional level

You can also check the forest functional level by using the following Microsoft PowerShell command:

```
(Get-ADForest).ForestMode
```

Microsoft Entra Connect Server requirements

Microsoft Entra Connect is software installed on a computer that manages synchronizing objects between the on-premises Active Directory and the Microsoft Entra ID instance that supports the Microsoft 365 tenancy. You can install Microsoft Entra Connect on computers running the following operating systems:

- Windows Server 2008 (x86 and x64)
- Windows Server 2008 R2 (x64)
- Windows Server 2012 (x64)
- Windows Server 2012 R2 (x64)
- Windows Server 2016 (x64)
- Windows Server 2019 (x64)
- Windows Server 2022 (x64)

Microsoft Entra Connect cannot be installed on Windows Server 2003. Given that Microsoft no longer supports Windows Server 2003—and you are a diligent administrator—you will not have Windows Server 2003 in your environment. Although the requirements below are the minimum because it synchronizes important identities with Microsoft Entra ID, the best practice when this book was published was to only deploy on a computer running Windows Server 2022.

Microsoft Entra Connect has the following requirements:

- It must be installed on a Windows Server instance with the GUI version of the operating system. You cannot install Microsoft Entra Connect on a Server Core operating system computer.
- You can deploy Microsoft Entra Connect on a domain controller, member server, or stand-alone server computer if you use the custom options. As it is best practice not to allow AD DS domain controllers to be able to contact hosts on the internet directly and to have AD DS domain controllers run the Server Core version of the Windows Server operating system, you should generally avoid domain controller deployment.
- If installing on versions of Windows Server before Windows Server 2012, ensure that all service packs, updates, and relevant hotfixes are applied. (As a diligent administrator, you have already done this, so presumably it is unnecessary to remind you.)
- If you want to use the password synchronization functionality, you must ensure that Microsoft Entra Connect is deployed on Windows Server 2008 R2 SP1 or later.
- The server hosting Microsoft Entra Connect requires .NET Framework 4.5.1 or later.
- The server hosting Microsoft Entra Connect requires Microsoft PowerShell 3.0 or later.
- Microsoft Entra Connect's server hosting must not have PowerShell Transcription enabled through Group Policy.
- If you are deploying Microsoft Entra Connect with Active Directory Federation Services, you must use Windows Server 2012 R2 or later for the web application proxy, and Windows remote management must be enabled on the servers that will host AD FS roles.

If Global Administrators enable multifactor authentication (MFA), then the *https://secure. aadcdn.microsoftonline-p.com* URL must be configured as a trusted site.

Connectivity requirements

The computer with Microsoft Entra Connect installed must be a member of a domain in the forest that you want to synchronize, and it must have connectivity to a writable domain controller in each domain of the forest you want to synchronize on the following ports:

- **DNS** TCP/UDP port 53
- **Kerberos** TCP/UDP port 88
- **RPC** TCP port 135
- **LDAP** TCP/UDP port 389
- **SSL** TCP port 443
- **SMB** TCP port 445

The computer with Microsoft Entra Connect installed must be able to establish communication with the Microsoft Azure servers on the internet over TCP port 443. This computer can be located on an internal network if it can initiate communication on TCP port 443. It does not need a publicly routable IP address. The computer hosting Microsoft Entra Connect always initiates synchronization communication to Microsoft Azure. Microsoft Entra ID does not initiate synchronization communication to the computer hosting Microsoft Entra Connect on the on-premises network.

Although you can install Microsoft Entra Connect on a domain controller, Microsoft recommends deploying Microsoft Entra Connect on a computer that does not have the domain controller role. If you will be replicating more than 50,000 objects, Microsoft recommends deploying SQL Server on a computer separate from the one hosting Microsoft Entra Connect. If you plan to host the SQL Server instance on a separate computer, ensure that communication is possible between the computer hosting Microsoft Entra Connect and the computer hosting the SQL instance on TCP port 1433.

If you will use a separate SQL Server instance, ensure that the account used to install and configure Microsoft Entra Connect has systems administrator rights on the SQL instance and that the service account used for Microsoft Entra Connect has public permissions on the Microsoft Entra Connect database.

Hardware requirements

The hardware requirements of the computer that hosts Microsoft Entra Connect depend on the number of objects in the Active Directory environment that you need to sync. These requirements would also apply to a virtual machine configured to host Microsoft Entra Connect. The greater the number of objects you need to sync, the steeper the hardware requirements. Table 2-1 provides a guide to the requirements, with all configurations requiring at least a 1.6 GHz processor.

TABLE 2-1 Microsoft Entra Connect computer hardware requirements

Number of objects in Active Directory	Memory	Storage
Fewer than 10,000	4 GB	70 GB
10,000–50,000	4 GB	70 GB
50,000–100,000	16 GB	100 GB
100,000–300,000	32 GB	300 GB
300,000–600,000	32 GB	450 GB
More than 600,000	32 GB	500 GB

During the planning phase, a new Microsoft 365 tenancy has a limit of 50,000 objects. However, once the first DNS domain is verified, this limit is increased to 300,000 objects. Organizations that need to store more than 300,000 objects in a Microsoft Entra ID instance that supports a Microsoft 365 tenancy should contact Microsoft Support.

SQL Server requirements

When you deploy Microsoft Entra Connect, you can have Microsoft Entra Connect install a SQL Server Express instance, or you can choose to have Microsoft Entra Connect leverage a full instance of SQL Server. SQL Server Express is limited to a maximum database size of 10 GB. This means that Microsoft Entra Connect can only manage 100,000 objects. This is likely to be adequate for all but the largest environments.

For environments that require Microsoft Entra Connect to manage more than 100;000 objects, you'll need to have Microsoft Entra Connect leverage a full instance of SQL Server. Microsoft Entra Connect can use all versions of Microsoft SQL Server, from Microsoft SQL Server 2008 with the most recent service pack to SQL Server 2022. However, SQL Azure is not supported as a database for Microsoft Entra Connect. If deploying a full instance of SQL Server to support Microsoft Entra Connect, ensure that the following prerequisites are met:

- **Use a case-insensitive SQL collation**   Case-insensitive collations include the _CI_ identifier in their names. Case-sensitive collations (those that use the _CS_ designation) are not supported for use with Microsoft Entra Connect.

- **Use only one sync engine per SQL instance**   If you have an additional Microsoft Entra Connect sync engine or are using Microsoft Identity Manager in your environment, each sync engine requires its own separate SQL instance.

Installation account requirements

The accounts that you use to install and configure Microsoft Entra Connect have the following requirements:

- The account used to configure Microsoft Entra Connect must have the Global Administrator permission in the Microsoft 365 tenant. If you create a service account in Microsoft 365 to use in place of the account with tenant administrator permissions, be sure to configure the account with a password that does not expire.

- If you use express installation settings, the account used to install and configure Microsoft Entra Connect must have enterprise administrator permissions within the on-premises Active Directory forest. This account is required only during installation and configuration. Once Microsoft Entra Connect is installed and configured, this account no longer needs enterprise administrator permissions. Best practices are creating a separate account for Microsoft Entra Connect installation and configuration and temporarily adding this account to the enterprise administrators group during the installation and configuration process. After installing and configuring Microsoft Entra Connect, this account can be removed from the enterprise administrators group. You should not attempt to change the account used after Microsoft Entra Connect is set up and configured because Microsoft Entra Connect always attempts to run using the original account.

- The account used to install and configure Microsoft Entra Connect must be a member of the Local Administrators group on the computer on which Microsoft Entra Connect is installed.

- Microsoft Entra Connect installation can create a new account specifically for synchronization. To do this, you will have to provide Enterprise Administrator credentials.

Installing Microsoft Entra Connect

Installing Microsoft Entra Connect with express settings is appropriate if your organization has a single Active Directory forest and you want to use password sync for authentication. The Microsoft Entra Connect express settings are appropriate for most organizations.

To install Microsoft Entra Connect with Express settings, perform the following steps:

1. Double-click the installation file downloaded from the Microsoft Download Center or the Microsoft Entra portal to the computer hosting the synchronization service. You will be presented with a security warning, and the installation will complete, prompting you to perform configuration. Before performing the configuration, you will be asked to agree to the license terms and privacy notice.

2. You must use custom settings if your organization has an internal nonroutable domain. To use custom settings, select **Customize**.

3. On the **Install Required Components** page, choose from the following options:

- **Specify A Custom Installation Location**   Choose this option to install Microsoft Entra Connect in a separate location, such as on another volume.

- **Specify An Existing SQL Server**   Choose this option to specify an alternate SQL server instance. By default, Microsoft Entra Connect will install a SQL Server Express instance.

- **Use An Existing Service Account**   You can configure Microsoft Entra Connect to use an existing service account. By default, Microsoft Entra Connect will create a service account. If you install Microsoft Entra Connect on a computer running Windows Server 2012 or later, you can configure Microsoft Entra Connect to use a group-managed service account. You'll need to use an existing service account if you are using Microsoft Entra Connect with a remote SQL Server instance or if communication with Azure will occur through a proxy server that requires authentication.

- **Specify Custom Sync Groups**   When you deploy Microsoft Entra Connect, it creates four local groups on the server that hosts the Microsoft Entra Connect instance: the Administrators group, operators group, password reset group, and browse groups. If you want to use your own set of groups, you can specify them here. These groups must be local to the host server and not a domain member.

4. You don't have to select any custom options, but because you have a nonroutable domain on-premises, you must perform a custom installation; select **Install**.

5. On the **User Sign-In** page, specify what type of sign-in you want to allow. You can choose between the following options, the details of which were covered earlier in this chapter (except for PingFederate, which is a third-party tool and is not addressed by the MS-102 exam). Most organizations choose **Password Synchronization** because it is the most straightforward.

- **Password Synchronization**
- **Pass-Through Authentication**
- **Federation With AD FS**
- **Federation With PingFederate**
- **Do No Configure**
- **Enable Single Sign-On**

6. On the **Connect To Microsoft Entra ID** page, provide the credentials of a Global Administrator account. Microsoft recommends using an account in the default *onmicrosoft.com* domain associated with the Microsoft Entra ID instance you will connect to. If you choose the **Federation With AD FS** option, ensure that you do not sign in using an account in a domain you will enable for Federation.

7. After Microsoft Entra Connect has connected to Microsoft Entra ID, you can specify the directory type to synchronize and the forest. Select **Add Directory** to add a specific forest. When you add a forest by selecting **Add Directory**, you must specify the

credentials of an account that will perform periodic synchronization. Unless you are certain that you have applied the minimum necessary privileges to an account, you should provide enterprise administrator credentials and allow Microsoft Entra Connect to create the account (choose **Create New AD Account**). Doing so will ensure that the account is assigned only the privileges necessary to perform synchronization tasks.

8. After verifying the credentials, select **Next** and review the UPN suffix on the **Microsoft Entra ID Sign-In Configuration** page. Inspect the on-premises attribute to use as the Microsoft Entra ID user name. When doing this, you must ensure that accounts use a routable Microsoft Entra ID user name.

9. On the **Domain And OU Filtering** page, select whether you want to sync all objects (**Sync All Domains And OUs**) or just objects in specific domains and OUs (**Sync Selected Domains and OUs**).

10. On the **Uniquely Identifying Your Users** page, specify how users will be identified. By default, users should have only one representation across all directories (**Users Are Represented Only Once Across All Directories**). If users exist in multiple directories, you can have matches identified by a specific Active Directory attribute (**User Identities Exist Across Multiple Directories. Match Using <*AD Attribute*>**), with the default being the **Mail Attribute**.

11. On the **Filter Users And Devices** page, specify whether you want to synchronize all users and devices or only members of a specific group.

12. On the **Optional Features** page, select any optional features that you want to configure. These features include the following:
    - **Exchange Hybrid Deployment**
    - **Exchange Mail Public Folders**
    - **Microsoft Entra ID App And Attribute Filtering**
    - **Password Hash Synchronization**
    - **Password Writeback**
    - **Group Writeback**
    - **Device Writeback**
    - **Directory Extension Attribute Sync**

13. On the **Ready To Configure** page, you can choose to start synchronization (**Start The Synchronization Process When Configuration Completes**) or enable staging mode (**Enable Staging Mode: When Selected, Synchronization Will Not Export Any Data to AD or Microsoft Entra ID**), where synchronization will prepare to be run but will not synchronize any data with Microsoft Entra ID.

> **MORE INFO**   **MICROSOFT ENTRA CONNECT CUSTOM INSTALLATION**
>
> To install Microsoft Entra Connect with the custom settings, consult the following article: *https://learn.microsoft.com/azure/active-directory/hybrid/how-to-connect-install-custom.*

Identifying synchronized attributes

Microsoft Entra Connect synchronizes some, but not all, attributes from the on-premises Active Directory instance to the Microsoft Entra ID instance that supports a Microsoft 365 tenancy. Depending on whether the object is a user account, group account, or mail-enabled contact object, 143 separate attributes synchronize. These attributes are listed in Table 2-2.

TABLE 2-2 List of attributes synchronized by Microsoft Entra Connect

accountEnabled	MsExchArchiveGUID	msExchTeamMailboxOwners
Assistant	MsExchArchiveName	msExchTeamMailboxSharePointLinkedBy
altRecipient	msExchArchiveStatus	msExchTeamMailboxSharePointUrl
Authoring	msExchAssistantName	msExchUCVoiceMailSettings
C	msExchAuditAdmin	msExchUsageLocation
Cn	msExchAuditDelegate	msExchUserHoldPolicies
Co	msExchAuditDelegateAdmin	msOrg-IsOrganizational
Company	msExchAuditOwner	msRTCSIP-ApplicationOptions
countryCode	MsExchBlockedSendersHash	msRTCSIP-DeploymentLocator
Department	msExchBypassAudit	msRTCSIP-Line
Description	MsExchBypassModerationFrom DLMembersLink	msRTCSIP-OwnerUrn
displayName	MsExchBypassModerationLink	msRTCSIP-PrimaryUserAddress
dLMemRejectPerms	msExchCoManagedByLink	msRTCSIP-UserEnabled
dLMemSubmitPerms	msExchDelegateListLink	msRTCSIP-OptionFlags
ExtensionAttribute1	msExchELCExpirySuspensionEnd	objectGUID
ExtensionAttribute10	msExchELCExpirySuspensionStart	oOFReplyToOriginator
ExtensionAttribute11	msExchELCMailboxFlags	otherFacsimileTelephone
ExtensionAttribute12	MsExchEnableModeration	otherHomePhone
ExtensionAttribute13	msExchExtensionCustomAttribute1	otherIpPhone
ExtensionAttribute14	msExchExtensionCustomAttribute2	otherMobile
ExtensionAttribute15	msExchExtensionCustomAttribute3	otherPager
ExtensionAttribute2	msExchExtensionCustomAttribute4	otherTelephone
ExtensionAttribute3	msExchExtensionCustomAttribute5	pager

ExtensionAttribute4	MsExchGroupDepartRestriction	photo
ExtensionAttribute5	MsExchGroupJoinRestriction	physicalDeliveryOfficeName
ExtensionAttribute6	msExchHideFromAddressLists	postalCode
ExtensionAttribute7	MsExchImmutableID	postOfficeBox
ExtensionAttribute8	msExchLitigationHoldDate	PreferredLanguage
ExtensionAttribute9	msExchLitigationHoldOwner	proxyAddresses
Facsimiletelephonenumber	MsExchMailboxGuid	PublicDelegates
givenName	msExchMailboxAuditEnable	pwdLastSet
GroupType	msExchMailboxAuditLogAgeLimit	reportToOriginator
hideDLMembership	MsExchModeratedByLink	ReportToOwner
Homephone	MsExchModerationFlags	samAccountName
Info	MsExchRecipientDisplayType	Sn
Initials	msExchRecipientTypeDetails	St
ipPhone	MsExchRemoteRecipientType	streetAddress
L	msExchRequireAuthToSendTo	targetAddress
legacyExchangeDN	MsExchResourceCapacity	TelephoneAssistant
Mail	MsExchResourceDisplay	telephoneNumber
Mailnickname	MsExchResourceMetaData	thumbnailphoto
managedBy	MsExchResourceSearchProperties	title
Manager	msExchRetentionComment	unauthOrig
Member	msExchRetentionURL	url
middleName	MsExchSafeRecipientsHash	userAccountControl
Mobile	MsExchSafeSendersHash	userCertificate
msDS-HABSeniorityIndex	MsExchSenderHintTranslations	UserPrincipalName
msDS-PhoneticDisplayName	msExchTeamMailboxExpiration	userSMIMECertificate

> **MORE INFO** **ATTRIBUTES SYNCHRONIZED BY MICROSOFT ENTRA CONNECT**
>
> You can learn more about which attributes are synchronized by Microsoft Entra Connect at *https://learn.microsoft.com/azure/active-directory/hybrid/reference-connect-sync-attributes-synchronized.*

Monitor Microsoft Entra Connect Health

Microsoft Entra Connect Health is a tool available in the Microsoft Entra admin center that allows you to monitor the health of synchronization between your organization's on-premises directory and Microsoft Entra ID.

You can use Microsoft Entra Connect Health to view the following information:

- **Synchronization Errors** These include duplicate attributes, data mismatches, data validation failure, large attributes, Federated domain change, and existing admin role conflicts.

- **Synchronization Services** This handles information about which services synchronize with Microsoft Entra ID.

- **AD FS Services** This is information about AD FS when Microsoft Entra Connect is configured for Federation, including information about errors and issues.

- **AD DS Services** This is information about domains and forests connected to Microsoft Entra ID.

> **MORE INFO** **MICROSOFT ENTRA CONNECT HEALTH**
>
> You can learn more about Microsoft Entra Connect Health at *https://learn.microsoft.com/ azure/active-directory/hybrid/whatis-azure-ad-connect*.

Manage Microsoft Entra Connect synchronization

By default, synchronization occurs between the on-premises instance of Active Directory and Microsoft Entra ID every 30 minutes. However, in some cases, you'll change a user account or create a collection of user accounts and want to get those changes or new accounts into the Microsoft Entra ID instance that supports the Microsoft 365 tenancy as fast as possible. You can force synchronization by running the Microsoft Entra Connect Wizard again or by using the Synchronization Service Manager.

To perform a full synchronization using the Synchronization Service Manager, follow these steps:

1. Open the Synchronization Service Manager by selecting **Synchronization Service** in the **Start** menu or by running the miisclient.exe file in the C:\Program Files\Microsoft Microsoft Entra ID Sync\UIShell folder.

2. Select the **Connectors** tab.

3. On the **Connectors** tab, select the name of your Active Directory domain service, as shown in Figure 2-16.

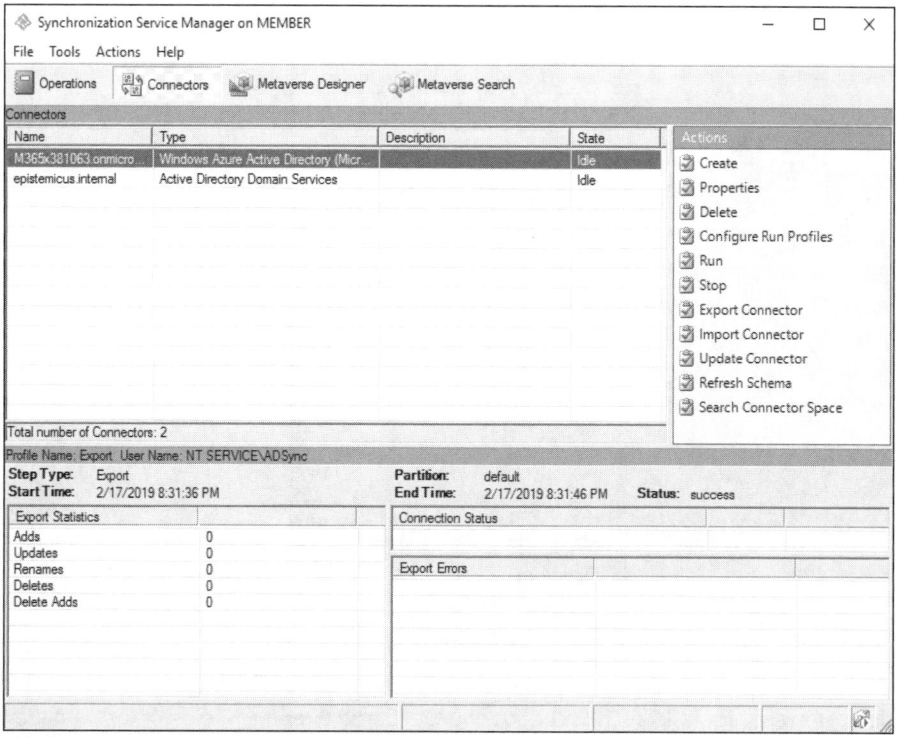

FIGURE 2-16 Synchronization Service Manager

4. In the **Actions** pane, select **Run**.

5. The **Run Connector** dialog contains a list of synchronization options (see Figure 2-17):

   ■ **Full Synchronization**   Performs a full synchronization

   ■ **Delta Import**   Imports changed schema and objects

   ■ **Delta Synchronization**   Synchronizes only objects that have changed since the last sync

   ■ **Export**   Writes data from the Azure instance to the on-premises instance

   ■ **Full Import**   Suitable for initiating the first full synchronization or the first full synchronization after you have changed the filtering parameters

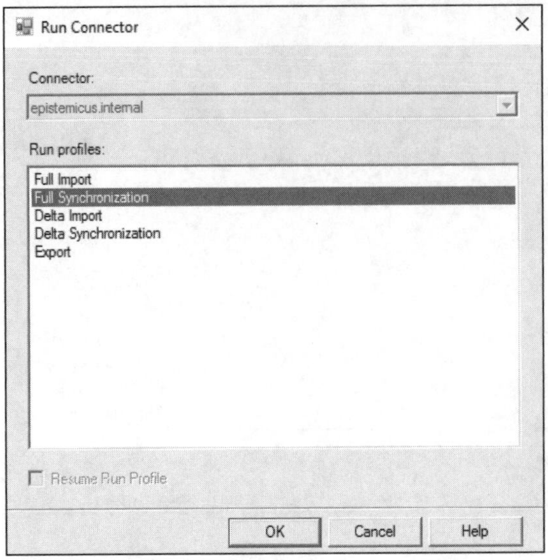

FIGURE 2-17 Full Synchronization

6. Select **Full Synchronization** and select **OK**.

You can also use the Synchronization Service Manager to configure extensive filtering options. However, for tasks such as configuring OU-based filtering, Microsoft recommends first attempting to configure filtering using the Microsoft Entra Connect Setup Wizard and relying on a tool such as the Synchronization Service Manager only if problems arise.

> *MORE INFO* **SYNCHRONIZATION SERVICE MANAGER**
>
> You can learn more about the Synchronization Service Manager at *https://learn.microsoft.com/en-us/azure/active-directory/hybrid/connect/how-to-connect-sync-service-manager-ui*.

Configure object filters

When you use Microsoft Entra Connect to synchronize on-premises Active Directory to a Microsoft Entra ID instance, the default setting is to have all user accounts, group accounts, and mail-enabled contact objects synchronized to the cloud. For some organizations, synchronizing everything is exactly what they want. Other organizations want to be more selective about which objects are synchronized from the on-premises Active Directory environment to the Microsoft Entra ID instance that supports the Office 365 tenancy.

With Microsoft Entra Connect, you can choose to filter based on the following options:

- **Domain based** In a forest with multiple domains, you can configure filtering so that only objects from some domains, and not others, are filtered.

- **Organizational unit (OU) based** With this filtering type, you choose which objects are filtered based on their location within specific organizational units.

You can also configure filtering based on group membership. Using Microsoft Entra Connect, you can configure separate group-based filters for each synchronized forest or domain.

> **MORE INFO   CONFIGURE FILTERING**
>
> You can learn more about Microsoft Entra ID sync filtering at *https://learn.microsoft.com/azure/active-directory/hybrid/how-to-connect-sync-configure-filtering*.

Although Microsoft Entra Connect will address most organizations' synchronization requirements, the most comprehensive tool you can use to filter synchronization is the Synchronization Rules Editor, shown in Figure 2-18. You can use this tool to modify and create new synchronization rules. Rather than configuring synchronization on a per-domain or per-OU basis, you can tailor rules for individual objects and specific Active Directory attributes.

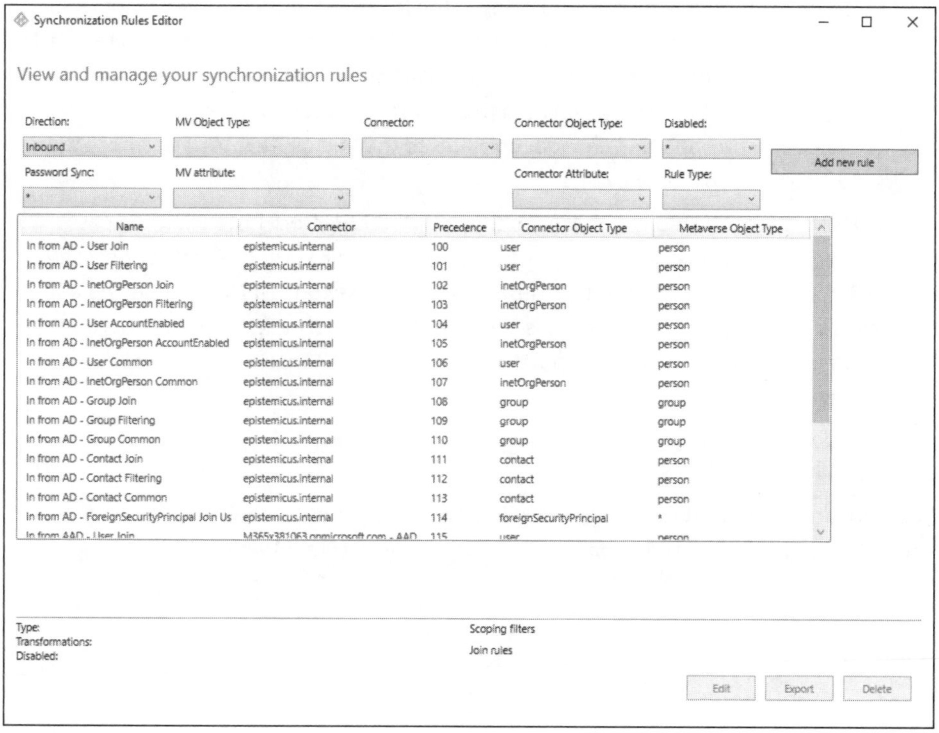

FIGURE 2-18   Synchronization Rules Editor

Configure password synchronization

Password sync allows the synchronization of user account passwords from an on-premises Active Directory to the Microsoft Entra ID instance that supports the Office 365 tenancy. The advantage of this is that users can sign in to Microsoft 365 using the same password that they use to sign in to computers on the on-premises environment. Password sync does not provide single sign-on or federation.

When you enable password sync, the on-premises password complexity policies override password complexity policies configured for the Microsoft Entra ID instance that supports the Microsoft 365 tenancy. This means any password valid for an on-premises user will be valid within Microsoft 365, even if it would not be normally.

Password expiration works as follows: The password of the account of the cloud user object is set to never expire. Each time the user account password is changed in the on-premises Active Directory instance, this change replicates to the Microsoft Entra ID instance that supports the Microsoft 365 tenancy. This means that a user account's password can expire on the on-premises Active Directory instance, but that user can still use the same password to sign in to Microsoft 365. The next time they sign in to the on-premises environment, they are forced to change their password, and that change replicates to the Microsoft Entra ID instance that supports the Microsoft 365 tenancy.

If you disable a user's account in the on-premises Active Directory instance when password sync is enabled, the user's account in the Microsoft Entra ID instance that supports the Microsoft 365 tenancy is disabled within a few minutes. If password sync is not enabled and you disable a user account in the on-premises Active Directory instance, the user's account in the Microsoft Entra ID instance that supports the Microsoft 365 tenancy is not disabled until the next full synchronization.

Implement multiforest AD DS scenarios

The Microsoft Entra Connect tool supports synchronization from multiple on-premises Active Directory forests to a single Microsoft Entra ID instance. Multiple-forest synchronization to a single Microsoft Entra ID instance is supported only when a single Microsoft Entra Connect server is in use. Microsoft does not support multiple Microsoft Entra Connect servers synchronizing with a single Microsoft Entra ID instance, whether one or multiple forests are being synchronized.

By default, Microsoft Entra Connect assumes that

- A user has a single enabled account. Also, the forest where this account is located must host the directory that is used to authenticate the user. This assumption is used in both password sync and Federation scenarios. Based on this assumption, the UserPrincipalName and sourceAnchor/immutableID attributes are drawn from this forest.

- Each user has a single mailbox, and the forest that hosts that mailbox is the best source of attributes visible in the Exchange global address list (GAL). If a user doesn't have an associated mailbox, any configured forest can function as the source for the attribute values.

If a user account has a linked mailbox, an account in an alternate forest will be used for the sign-in process.

The key to synchronizing user accounts from multiple forests is that only one user account from all synchronized forests should represent the user, meaning the synchronization engine should have a way to determine when accounts in separate forests represent the same user. You can configure how the Microsoft Entra Connect sync engine identifies users on the **Uniquely Identifying Your Users** page using one of the following options:

- Matching users using the **Mail Attribute**
- Matching users using ObjectSID and msExchangeMasterAccountSID/msRTCIP-OriginatorSID attributes
- Matching users using the SAMAccountName and MailNickName attributes
- Specifying a custom attribute on which to match names

> **MORE INFO**   **MULTIFOREST SYNCHRONIZATION**
>
> You can learn more about multiforest synchronization and supported topologies for Microsoft Entra Connect at *https://learn.microsoft.com/azure/active-directory/hybrid/plan-connect-topologies*.

EXAM TIP

Remember what tools you can use to trigger synchronization.

Skill 2.4: Manage identity synchronization by using Microsoft Entra Cloud Sync

This skill deals with Microsoft Entra Cloud Sync. This rather confusingly named utility performs some, but not all, of the same functions as Microsoft Entra Connect. Microsoft might intend to replicate all the existing tools' functionality and function as an eventual replacement. Currently, the tool provides a lightweight option for organizations that do not require all of Microsoft Entra Connect's functionality.

> **This section covers the following skills:**
> - Microsoft Entra Cloud Sync
> - Installing Microsoft Entra Cloud Sync
> - Comparing Cloud Sync with AD Connect
> - Troubleshooting Microsoft Entra Cloud Sync

Microsoft Entra Cloud Sync

Microsoft Entra Cloud Sync is a separate product from Microsoft Entra Connect. The product is very much in development and far from feature parity with the more established Microsoft Entra Connect. Like Microsoft Entra Connect, Microsoft Entra Cloud Sync synchronizes users, groups, and contacts from an on-premises AD DS instance to Microsoft Entra ID. The primary architectural difference between the two products is that the synchronization engine is hosted on an on-premises server with Microsoft Entra Connect. With Microsoft Entra Cloud Sync, the synchronization engine runs in Azure. Microsoft Entra Cloud Sync can be deployed alongside Microsoft Entra Connect.

> **MORE INFO   MICROSOFT ENTRA CLOUD SYNC**
>
> You can learn more about Microsoft Entra Cloud Sync at *https://learn.microsoft.com/azure/active-directory/cloud-sync/what-is-cloud-sync*.

Installing Microsoft Entra Cloud Sync

To install the Microsoft Entra Cloud Sync agent, perform the following steps:

1. In the Microsoft Entra admin center (*entra.microsoft.com*), select **Microsoft Entra Connect** > **Manage Microsoft Entra Cloud Sync**.

2. On the **Microsoft Entra Cloud Sync** page, click **Download Agent** and then click **Accept Terms & Download**. The installation file will be downloaded to your computer.

3. Open this file on the computer that you want to have as your Microsoft Entra Cloud Sync server. You can have multiple computers in this role. While you can install the Microsoft Entra Cloud Sync agent on a domain controller, the best practice is to avoid allowing AD DS domain controllers to communicate directly with any host on the internet. It is also a best practice to have AD DS domain controllers run the Server Core version of Windows Server to minimize the operating system's attack surface.

4. On the **Microsoft Entra Connect Provisioning Agent Package** page, agree to the license terms and conditions and click **Install**. In the **User Account Control** dialog, click **Yes**.

5. On the **Microsoft Entra Connect Provisioning Agent Configuration** page, click **Next**.

6. On the **Select Extension** page , select **HR-Driven Provisioning (Workday And Success Factors) / Microsoft Entra Cloud Sync** and click **Next**.

7. You'll then be prompted to sign in to your Microsoft 365 tenancy with an account with Global Administrator permissions. Authenticate with your Microsoft 365 or Microsoft Entra ID credentials.

8. On the **Configure Service Account** page, provide domain administrator credentials for the on-premises AD DS domain you want to synchronize with Microsoft Entra ID.

9. On the **Connect Active Directory** page, select the domain you want to synchronize and click **Add Directory**. Add each directory in the forest you want to synchronize and then click **Next**.

10. On the **Confirm** page, review the configuration and then click **Confirm**.

You can verify that the agent is running by opening the Services console and verifying that the following services are present and running:

- Microsoft Entra Connect Agent Updater
- Microsoft Entra Connect Provisioning Agent

> **MORE INFO**   **INSTALL MICROSOFT ENTRA CLOUD SYNC**
>
> You can learn more about installing Microsoft Entra Cloud Sync at *https://learn.microsoft. com/azure/active-directory/cloud-sync/how-to-install*.

Comparing Microsoft Entra Cloud Sync with Microsoft Entra Connect

The primary benefit of Microsoft Entra Cloud Sync is that it has a minimal on-premises foot-print. The drawback is that it doesn't support all the same features as Microsoft Entra Connect. Most organizations that need the full feature set will continue to use Microsoft Entra Connect. For example, if you need support for Pass-Through Authentication, you'll need Microsoft Entra Connect. Organizations with new synchronization requirements or that are reducing their on-premises footprints and only need Microsoft Entra Cloud Sync's features should deploy Microsoft Entra Cloud Sync.

Table 2-3 compares Microsoft Entra Connect and Microsoft Entra Cloud Sync features.

TABLE 2-3   Feature comparison of Microsoft Entra Connect and Microsoft Entra Cloud Sync

Feature	Microsoft Entra Connect	Microsoft Entra Cloud Sync
Connect to single on-premises AD forest	Yes	Yes
Connect to multiple on-premises AD forests	Yes	Yes
Connect to multiple disconnected on-premises AD forests	No	Yes
Lightweight agent installation model	No	Yes
Multiple active agents for high availability	No	Yes
Connect to LDAP directories	Yes	No
Support for user objects	Yes	Yes
Support for group objects	Yes	Yes
Support for contact objects	Yes	Yes
Support for device objects	Yes	No
Allows basic customization for attribute flows	Yes	Yes
Synchronize Exchange online attributes	Yes	Yes
Synchronize extension attributes (1-15)	Yes	Yes
Synchronize customer-defined AD attributes (directory extensions)	Yes	Yes
Support for Password Hash Sync	Yes	Yes
Support for Pass-Through Authentication	Yes	No
Support for federation	Yes	Yes
Seamless Single Sign-on	Yes	Yes
Supports installation on a domain controller	Yes	Yes
Filter on domains/OUs/groups	Yes	Yes
Filter on objects' attribute values	Yes	No

Allows minimal set of attributes to be synchronized (MinSync)	Yes	Yes
Allows removing attributes from flowing from AD to Microsoft Entra ID	Yes	Yes
Allows advanced customization for attribute flows	Yes	No
Support for password writeback	Yes	Yes
Support for device writeback	Yes	No
Support for group writeback	Yes	No
Support for merging user attributes from multiple domains	Yes	No
Microsoft Entra Domain Services support	Yes	No
Exchange hybrid writeback	Yes	No
Unlimited number of objects per AD domain	Yes	No
Support for up to 150,000 objects per AD domain	Yes	Yes
Groups with up to 50,000 members	Yes	Yes
Large groups with up to 250,000 members	Yes	No
Cross-domain references	Yes	Yes
On-demand provisioning	No	Yes

Troubleshooting Microsoft Entra Cloud Sync

When troubleshooting the Microsoft Entra Cloud Sync, first verify that the agent is installed and running on the server on which you deployed it by checking the Microsoft Entra Connect Agent Updater and Microsoft Entra Connect Provisioning Agent services.

The next step is to determine whether the agent is present in the Microsoft Entra admin center. Open the Microsoft Entra admin center (*entra.microsoft.com*), select **Microsoft Entra Connect**, and then click **Manage Microsoft Entra Cloud Sync**. Click **Review All Agents** to view deployed agents and their status.

The agent cannot communicate with Azure if it cannot open a TCP port 80 or 443 connection to Azure services on the internet or resolve the DNS addresses of Azure services on the internet.

The agent stores log files in the C:\ProgramData\Microsoft\Microsoft Entra Connect Provisioning Agent\Trace folder. You can use the Export-AADCloudSyncToolsLogs cmdlet to interrogate these logs. This cmdlet is located in the AADCloudSyncTools PowerShell module you learned about earlier in this chapter.

If you need to repair the cloud sync service account, you can use the `Repair-AADCloudsyncToolsAccount` cmdlet. This cmdlet is also found in the `AADCloudSyncTools` PowerShell module.

The **Provisioning Logs** page, available from the Microsoft Entra Cloud Sync page of the Microsoft Entra ID portal, shows details of object synchronization between on-premises AD DS and Azure AD. If there are synchronization problems for specific objects, you can review these logs to determine more information.

> **MORE INFO   TROUBLESHOOT AZURE AD CLOUD SYNC**
>
> You can learn more about troubleshooting Microsoft Entra Cloud Sync at
> *https://learn.microsoft.com/azure/active-directory/cloud-sync/how-to-troubleshoot.*

Chapter summary

- When determining an appropriate identity strategy, determine which identities need to be replicated to the cloud, how often that replication should occur, and which aspects must be replicated.

- Microsoft Entra Connect can be installed on a local member server, allowing the synchronization of identities and password hashes to Azure AD.

- Before deploying Microsoft Entra Connect, the on-premises directory should be cleaned up to remove any current settings that can block successful synchronization. Tools such as IdFix and ADModify.NET can be used to perform this task.

- If your on-premises directory uses a nonroutable domain, you must update on-premises accounts with a routable UPN suffix configured to work with Microsoft 365. This will usually be a registered domain name associated with the tenancy.

- The health of Microsoft Entra Connect can be monitored through the Microsoft Entra admin center.

- Synchronization can be forced using the Synchronization Service Manager or through PowerShell.

- Azure AD identities can be managed through the Microsoft Entra admin center, the Microsoft 365 admin center, or Azure PowerShell.

- Users must be assigned licenses to use Microsoft 365 resources. This task can be performed through the Microsoft 365 admin center or Microsoft Entra admin center.

Thought experiment

In this thought experiment, demonstrate your skills and knowledge of the skills covered in this chapter. You can find answers to this thought experiment in the next section.

You are implementing and managing identity synchronization at Tailwind Traders. You have a five-domain AD DS forest running at the Windows Server 2016 forest functional level with Active Directory Recycle Bin enabled. You currently have Microsoft Entra Connect deployed but want to know if you can migrate to Microsoft Entra Cloud Sync. One of your identity synchronization requirements is support for Azure AD Domain Services. Tailwind Traders only uses password hash synchronization and does not need pass-through authentication.

Yesterday a new person responsible for network security was hired. They've been auditing the existing configuration and asked you if firewall rules might have been set up on the external firewall to support identity synchronization.

While you are researching these questions, your assistant has been experimenting with generative AI and is using it to create PowerShell scripts. One such experiment deletes five user accounts from your on-premises AD DS forest. This deletion replicates to Azure AD through synchronization, and the objects are no longer present in Azure AD or on-premises AD DS.

With this information, answer the following questions:

1. What tool can you use to recover the deleted users, both on-premises and in Microsoft 365?

2. Are you able to use Microsoft Entra Cloud Sync for synchronization?

3. Which firewall ports do you need to open for the synchronization server on the external firewall?

Thought experiment answers

This section contains the solution to the thought experiment. Each answer explains why the answer choice is correct.

1. Active Directory Recycle Bin can recover the five accounts from on-premises and Azure. Deleting a user from Microsoft 365 keeps their account in the Microsoft Entra ID Recycle Bin for 30 days. This means you can recover the account online should you need to do so. If you delete a user from your on-premises Active Directory environment but have enabled the on-premises Active Directory Recycle Bin, recovering the user from the on-premises Active Directory Recycle Bin will recover the user account in Microsoft 365. If you don't have the Active Directory Recycle Bin enabled, you must create another account with a new GUID.

2. You cannot use Microsoft Entra Cloud Sync for synchronization because Microsoft Entra Cloud Sync does not support Microsoft Entra Domain Services.

3. You will not need to open ports on the external firewall for the synchronization server. Microsoft Entra Connect synchronization servers establish contact with services in Azure, so services in Azure don't need to initiate contact with Microsoft Entra Connect synchronization servers.

CHAPTER 3

Managing Microsoft 365 Roles

A role is a set of privileges that a Microsoft 365 user assigned the role can perform. Rather than assigning permissions to individual users on a per-permission basis, you assign the role to a user instead. You can also create custom roles if a role does not meet your organization's exact requirements. In this chapter, you will learn about managing roles in Microsoft 365 and other important topics related to assigning administrative permissions in Microsoft 365 and Microsoft Entra ID.

Skills in this chapter:

- Skill 3.1: Manage role membership
- Skill 3.2: Microsoft 365 administrative roles
- Skill 3.3: Microsoft Defender roles and role groups
- Skill 3.4: Microsoft Purview roles
- Skill 3.5: Microsoft Entra ID role-based access control

Important note: In August 2023, Microsoft announced that it was rebranding Azure Active Directory to Microsoft Entra ID. Also, products such as Microsoft Entra ID Connect, Microsoft Entra ID Connect Cloud Sync, and Azure Active Directory Domain Services have been renamed to Microsoft Entra Connect, Microsoft Entra Cloud Sync, and Microsoft Entra Domain Services, respectively.

The actual functionality of these products has not been changed, and it is also likely that it will be some time before UI elements in various administrative portals and Microsoft's official documentation are also completely updated to use the new brand guidelines. Practice tests and study materials that use the original names will still provide you with relevant information on functionality. However, for the foreseeable future, multiple names will be used to label the same product or service.

Skill 3.1: Manage role membership

> **This section covers the following skills:**
> - Manage admin roles
> - Manage role allocations by using Microsoft Entra ID

Rather than assign the Global Administrator role to all users who need to perform administrative tasks, an organization's approach to planning and assigning user roles should follow the principle of least privilege. This principle dictates that you should assign the minimum necessary privileges to an account required for the user associated with that account to perform tasks.

When planning user roles, determine precisely what tasks the user needs to perform and then assign the role that allows them to perform only those tasks. For example, if a support desk technician needs to be able to reset passwords, assign that technician the password administrator role rather than a more privileged role such as Security Administrator or Global Administrator.

You can view a list of users assigned a particular role by opening the **Roles** page in the Microsoft 365 admin center and selecting the role whose membership you want to view. Figure 3-1 shows the members of the Helpdesk Admin role.

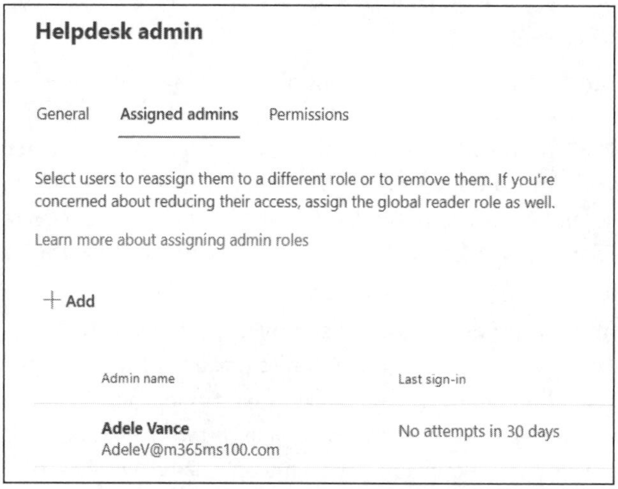

FIGURE 3-1   List of Helpdesk Admins

To assign an administrative role to a Microsoft 365 user, open the **Manage Admin Roles** page of the user's properties, as shown in Figure 3-2. Simply specify the administrative role you want to assign and an alternate email address. You assign the alternate email address so that it is possible to perform password recovery if necessary. You can only add Microsoft 365 users to a role.

Manage admin roles

> **Manage admin roles**
>
> ○ User (no admin center access)
>
> ⦿ Admin center access
>
> Global readers have read-only access to admin centers, while Global admins have unlimited access to edit all settings. Users assigned other roles are more limited in what they can see and do.
>
> ☐ Exchange Administrator ⓘ
>
> ☐ Global Administrator ⓘ
>
> ☐ Global reader ⓘ
>
> ☑ Helpdesk admin ⓘ
>
> ☐ Service support admin ⓘ
>
> ☐ SharePoint Administrator ⓘ
>
> ☐ Teams Administrator ⓘ
>
> ☐ User Administrator ⓘ
>
> [Save changes]

FIGURE 3-2   Assigning the Helpdesk Administrator role

You can also use this page of a user's account to remove an assigned role. To do this, deselect the role you want to remove and select **Save**.

Manage admin roles

Microsoft Entra ID includes many roles that provide various permissions to different aspects of Microsoft Entra ID and Microsoft 365 workloads. Microsoft Entra ID roles address permissions and functionality beyond that available in Microsoft 365, but because Microsoft 365 uses Microsoft Entra ID to store security principal information, it is important to understand how Microsoft Entra ID roles work for the MS-102 exam.

Several Microsoft Entra ID roles, such as Exchange Administrator, Intune Administrator, and SharePoint Administrator, are specific to certain Microsoft 365 workloads. These roles often provide complete administrative rights for those workloads but no administrative permissions beyond those workloads. In organizations where staff are responsible for one or more Microsoft 365 workloads but not responsible for tasks such as user management or other workloads, ensure that you follow the principle of least privilege and assign roles only at the workload level.

Microsoft Entra ID roles, and the permissions that they grant, are listed in Table 3-1. This table briefly outlines all Microsoft Entra ID privileged roles you can assign to Microsoft 365 security principles. Later in this chapter, you will learn more about commonly used Microsoft

365 administrative roles. While the general approach as products have been integrated into Microsoft 365 is to move toward using a Microsoft Entra ID role scoped to a specific product, many Microsoft 365 products still have their own idiosyncratic roles and role groups.

TABLE 3-1 Microsoft Entra ID roles

Role	Description
Application Administrator	Can administer enterprise applications, application registrations, and application proxy settings.
Application Developer	Can create application registrations.
Attack Payload Author	Can create attack payloads for security testing.
Attack Simulation Administrator	Can create and manage all elements of attack simulation campaigns.
Attribute Assignment Administrator	Can configure custom security attribute keys and values for supported Microsoft Entra ID objects.
Attribute Assignment Reader	Can view custom security attribute keys and values for supported Microsoft Entra ID objects.
Attribute Definition Administrator	Can define and manage custom security attribute definitions.
Attribute Definition Reader	Can view custom security attribute definitions.
Authentication Administrator	Can view current authentication method settings. Can set or reset non-password credentials. Can force MFA on the next sign-in. Limited to performing actions on non-administrative users.
Authentication Policy Administrator	Can author and apply authentication methods policy, configure tenant-wide multi-factor authentication settings, and configure password protection policy and verifiable credentials.
Microsoft Entra ID (Azure AD) Joined Device Local Administrator	Any users assigned to this role will be added to the Local Administrators group on computers joined to Microsoft Entra ID.
Azure DevOps Administrator	Can configure Azure DevOps settings and policies.
Azure Information Protection Administrator	Can manage all elements of Azure Information Protection.
B2C IEF Keyset Administrator	Can configure secrets for encryption and Federation for the Identity Experience Framework (IEF).
B2C IEF Policy Administrator	Can create and configure trust framework policies in the Identity Experience Framework (IEF).
Billing Administrator	Can purchase and manage subscriptions. Can manage support tickets and monitor service health.
Cloud App Security Administrator	Can configure and manage Defender for Cloud Apps.
Cloud Application Administrator	Can manage all aspects of enterprise applications and registrations but cannot manage application proxy.
Cloud Device Administrator	Can enable, disable, and remove devices in Microsoft Entra ID. Can view Windows 10 BitLocker drive encryption keys through the Azure portal.

Compliance Administrator	Can manage features in the Microsoft 365 compliance center, Microsoft 365 admin center, Azure, and Microsoft 365 Security & Compliance Center.
Compliance Data Administrator	Can create and manage compliance content.
Conditional Access Administrator	Has administrative rights over Microsoft Entra ID conditional access configuration.
Customer Lockbox Access Approver	Manages customer lockbox requests. Can also enable and disable the Customer Lockbox feature.
Desktop Analytics Administrator	Can access and manage desktop management tools and services.
Directory Readers	Can view basic directory information. Often used to provide Microsoft Entra ID read access to applications and guests.
Directory Synchronization Accounts	Assigned to the Microsoft Entra ID Connect service and not used for user accounts.
Directory Writers	Can read and write basic Microsoft Entra ID information. Should be assigned only to applications, not user accounts.
Domain Name Administrator	Can manage domain names in cloud and on-premises environments.
Dynamics 365 Administrator	Provides administrative access to Dynamics 365 Online.
Edge Administrator	Manage and configure Microsoft Edge.
Exchange Administrator	Provides administrative access to Exchange Online.
Exchange Recipient Administrator	Can create and edit Exchange Online recipients.
External ID User Flow Administrator	Can create and configure user flows.
External Id User Flow Attributed Administrator	Can create and configure attribute schema available to user flows.
External Identity Provider Administrator	Can manage identity providers used in direct Federation.
Global Administrator	Provides administrative access to all Microsoft Entra ID features. The account used to sign up for the tenancy becomes the Global Administrator. Global Administrators can reset the passwords of any user, including other Global Administrators.
Global Reader	Can view the same cloud deployment elements as a Global Administrator but cannot make configuration changes.
Groups Administrator	Can create and manage groups. Can manage naming and expiration policies.
Guest Inviter	Can manage Microsoft Entra ID B2B guest user invitations.
Helpdesk Administrator	Can reset passwords for accounts not assigned to administrative roles and other users assigned the Helpdesk Admin role.
Hybrid Identity Administrator	Configure and edit AD DS to Microsoft Entra ID cloud provisioning, Microsoft Entra ID Connect, pass-through authentication (PTA), Password hash synchronization (PHS), seamless single sign-on (seamless SSO), and Federation settings.
Identity Governance Administrator	Manage access through Microsoft Entra ID for identity governance scenarios.
Insights Administrator	Administrative permissions to configure and manage Viva Insights.

Insights Analyst	Run custom queries against Microsoft Viva Insights.
Insights Business Leader	Can share dashboards and insights through Microsoft Insights.
Intune Administrator	Has full administrative rights to Microsoft Intune.
Kaizala Administrator	Can manage and configure Microsoft Kaizala
Knowledge Administrator	Can configure settings related to knowledge and learning content.
Knowledge Manager	Can organize and manage topics related to knowledge content.
License Administrator	Can manage license assignments on users and groups. Cannot purchase or manage subscriptions.
Lifecycle Workflows Administrator	Create and manage all aspects of workflows in Microsoft Entra ID.
Message Center Privacy Reader	Can read security messages in Office 365 Message Center.
Message Center Reader	Can monitor notifications and Microsoft advisories in the Microsoft 365 message center.
Microsoft Hardware Warranty Administrator	Create and manage warranty claims for Microsoft hardware.
Microsoft Hardware Warranty Specialist	Create warranty claims for Microsoft hardware.
Modern Commerce User	Can manage commercial purchases.
Network Administrator	Can configure network locations and review enterprise network insights for Microsoft 365 Software as a Service (SaaS) applications.
Office Apps Administrator	Can configure Office apps cloud services, including policy and settings management.
Organizational Messages Writer	Write, publish, manage, and review organizational messages.
Password Administrator	Can reset passwords for non-administrators and users that hold the Password Administrator role.
Permissions Management Administrator	Manage Entra Permissions Management.
Power BI Administrator	Has administrator permissions over Power BI.
Power Platform Administrator	Can create and manage all aspects of Microsoft Dynamics 365, Power Apps, and Power Automate.
Printer Administrator	Able to manage all aspects of printers and printer connectors and can configure status messages, including PC Load Letter.
Printer Technician	Can register and unregister printers. Also able to update printer status.
Privileged Authentication Administrator	Can configure the authentication method, including resetting, for any user, including administrators.
Privileged Role Administrator	Can manage all aspects of Microsoft Entra ID Privileged Identity Management (PIM). Can manage role assignments in Microsoft Entra ID.
Reports Reader	Can view reporting data in the Microsoft 365 Reports dashboard.
Search Administrator	Can configure Microsoft Search settings.
Search Editor	Can create, manage, and delete content for Microsoft Search.

Security Administrator	Has administrator-level access to manage security features in the Microsoft 365 Security & Compliance Center, Microsoft Entra ID Identity Protection, and Azure Information Protection.
Security Operator	Can configure and manage security events.
Security Reader	Has read-only access to Microsoft 365–related security features.
Service Support Administrator	Can open and view support requests for Microsoft 365–related services.
Sharepoint Administrator	Has Global Administrator permissions for SharePoint Online workloads.
Skype For Business Administrator	Has Global Administrator permissions for Skype for Business workloads. Still in existence for tenants using older systems.
Teams Administrator	Can administer all elements of Microsoft Teams.
Teams Communications Administrator	Can manage Microsoft Teams workloads related to voice and telephony, including telephone number assignment and voice and meeting policies.
Teams Communications Support Engineer	Can troubleshoot communication issues within Microsoft Teams and Skype for Business. Can view details of call records for all participants in a conversation.
Teams Communications Support Specialist	Can troubleshoot communication issues within Microsoft Teams and Skype for Business. Can only view user details in the call for a specific user.
Teams Devices Administrator	Can manage and configure Microsoft Teams–certified devices.
Tenant Creator	Can create new Microsoft Entra ID or Microsoft Entra ID B2C tenants.
Usage Summary Reports Reader	Can view tenant-level information in Microsoft 365 Usage Analytics and Productivity Score.
User Administrator	Can create and manage user accounts. Can create and manage groups. Can manage user views and support tickets and monitor service health.
Virtual Visits Administrator	Manage and share Virtual Visits information and metrics.
Viva Goals Administrator	Can configure and manage Viva Goals.
Windows 365 Administrator	Can provision and manage Cloud PCs.
Windows Update Deployment Administrator	Can configure and manage all elements of Windows Update deployments through Windows Update for Business.
Yammer Administrator	Can manage all Yammer elements.

> **MORE INFO   MICROSOFT ENTRA ID ADMINISTRATOR ROLES**
>
> You can learn more about Microsoft Entra ID administrator roles at *https://learn.microsoft. com/azure/active-directory/roles/permissions-reference*.

EXAM TIP

Remember that in role-based access control, you can take a set of permissions that comprise a role and apply them at a specific scope, which may be a specific product. A user-assigned Security Administrator role on the scope of one product does not necessarily have any rights on another product.

Manage role allocations by using Microsoft Entra ID

To assign a user to a specific role within Microsoft Entra ID at the tenancy level, perform the following steps:

1. In the Microsoft Entra ID admin center, select **Roles And Administrators**.

2. Select the role to which you want to add a user. This will open the role's properties page.

3. On the role's properties page, select **Add Member**.

> **MORE INFO**   **VIEW AND ASSIGN MICROSOFT ENTRA ID ADMINISTRATOR ROLES**
>
> You can learn more about viewing and assigning administrator roles at
> *https://learn.microsoft.com/azure/active-directory/roles/manage-roles-portal.*

Skill 3.2: Microsoft 365 administrative roles

This section covers the following skills:

- Global Administrator
- Global Reader
- Service Support Administrator
- Exchange Administrator (Exchange Online Administrator)
- Helpdesk Administrator
- SharePoint Administrator
- Teams Administrator
- User Administrator
- Delegated Administrator

In this section, you will learn about the most commonly used Microsoft 365 administrative roles and how they can be used to manage specific workload settings. By default, the roles visible in the Microsoft 365 admin center are a subset of all the Microsoft Entra ID roles listed earlier in Table 3-1. In most environments, this small set of roles will likely meet your needs. A list of common role assignments is shown in Figure 3-3. You can click **Show All Roles** to switch from the list of suggested roles to the list of all available roles if you prefer to assign these roles from the Microsoft 365 admin center instead of the **Microsoft Entra ID** blade in the Azure portal.

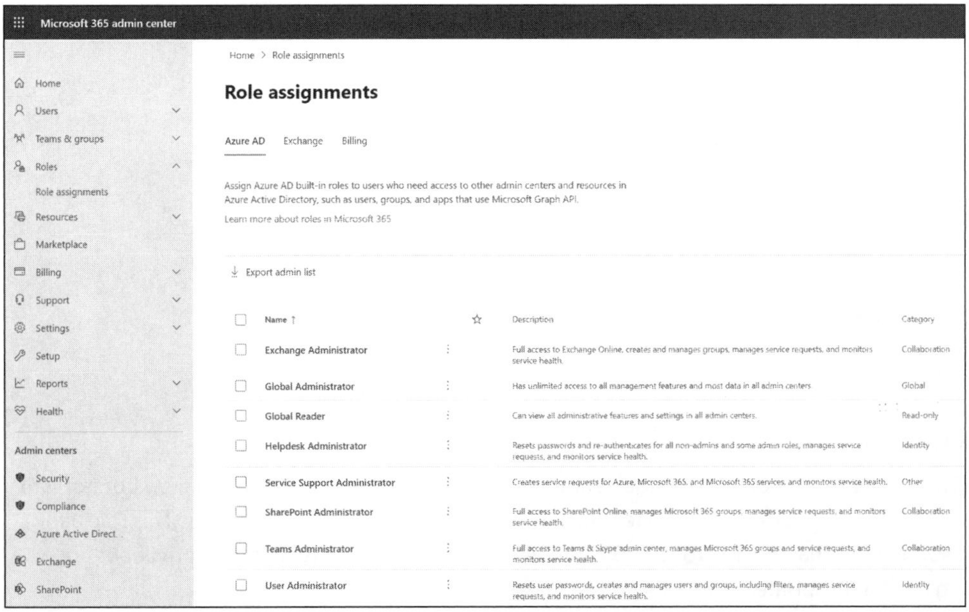

FIGURE 3-3 Microsoft 365 Role Assignments

When considering which role to assign, always assign the role that has the minimum permissions required to accomplish the task. The more powerful an administrative role, the less likely it is to be appropriate for a specific set of tasks. Also, remember that multiple roles can be assigned to a user account. Rather than assigning a role such as Global Administrator to someone responsible for managing SharePoint, Exchange, and Microsoft Teams, you can instead assign the relevant SharePoint, Exchange, and Microsoft Teams roles to the user's account.

General guidelines for assigning roles include:

- **Limit the number of Global Administrators as much as possible**   If a Global Administrator accidentally locks their account and requires a password reset, another user with the Global Administrator or Privileged Authentication Administrator roles can reset that password.

- **Require multifactor authentication for administrators**   While it is best practice to have all users configured so that they must perform multifactor authentication to sign in, you should require multifactor authentication for any user assigned a privileged role.

Global Administrator

Global Administrators have the most permissions over a Microsoft 365 tenancy. A Global Administrator has the following permissions:

- View organization and user information
- Manage support tickets
- Reset user passwords

- Perform billing and purchasing operations
- Create and manage user views
- Create, edit, and delete users
- Create, edit, and delete groups
- Manage user licenses
- Manage domains
- Manage organization information
- Delegate administrative roles to others
- User directory synchronization

Global Reader

Often assigned to auditors or legal team members, members of this role can view but not alter settings in all the administrative features related to the Microsoft 365 tenancy. This role allows people other than the Microsoft 365 administration team to verify that their privileges are being used appropriately.

Service Support Administrator

Service Support Administrators manage support tickets and monitor the health of Microsoft 365 services. They can create and manage support requests with Microsoft for Azure and Microsoft 365 services and view the service dashboard and message center.

Exchange Administrator (Exchange Online Administrator)

The Exchange Administrator role is also known as the Exchange Online Administrator role. Users with this role can manage mailboxes and anti-spam policies for their tenancy:

- Recover deleted items from mailboxes
- Configure how long deleted items will be retained before permanent deletion
- Configure mailbox-sharing policies
- Configure **Send As** and **Send On Behalf Of** delegates for a mailbox
- Configure anti-spam and malware filters
- Create shared mailboxes

> *MORE INFO*   **EXCHANGE ONLINE ADMINISTRATOR**
>
> You can learn more about the Exchange Administrator role at *https://learn.microsoft.com/ en-us/microsoft-365/admin/add-users/about-exchange-online-admin-role.*

Helpdesk Administrator

Members of the Helpdesk Administrator role are responsible for resetting passwords for non-privileged users and other members of the Password Administrator role. Members can manage service requests and monitor service health and have the following permissions:

- View organization and user information.
- Manage support tickets.
- Reset nonprivileged user passwords as well as passwords of other password administrators. Members of this role cannot reset the passwords of Global Administrators, user management administrators, or billing administrators.
- Manage the Exchange Online Help Desk Administrator role.
- Manage the Skype For Business Online Administrator role.

SharePoint Administrator

Also known as the SharePoint Online Administrator, this role enables users to use the SharePoint Online admin center and perform the following tasks:

- Create and manage site collections
- Manage site collections and global settings
- Designate site collection administrators
- Manage site collection storage limits
- Manage SharePoint online user profiles

> **MORE INFO** **SHAREPOINT ADMINISTRATOR**
>
> You can learn more about the SharePoint Administrator role at *https://learn.microsoft.com/en-us/sharepoint/sharepoint-admin-role*.

Teams Administrator

Also known as the Teams Service Administrator, users who hold this role can administer all aspects of Microsoft Teams except the assignment of licenses:

- Manage calling policies
- Manage messaging policies
- Manage meeting policies
- Use call analytics tools
- Manage users and their telephone settings
- Manage Microsoft 365 groups

User Administrator

Also known as the User Management Administrator, members can reset some user passwords, monitor service health, manage some user accounts and groups, and handle service requests. Members have the following permissions:

- View organization and user information
- Manage support tickets
- Reset the passwords of all user accounts except those assigned the Global Administrator, billing administrator, and service administrator roles
- Create and manage user views
- Create, edit, and delete users and groups except for users who are assigned Global Administrator privileges
- Manage user licenses

Delegated Administrator

Delegated Administrators are people outside the organization who perform administrative duties within the Office 365 tenancy. Administrators within the tenancy control who receives delegated administrator permissions. You can only assign delegated administrator permissions to users who have Office 365 accounts in their own tenancy.

When you configure delegated administration, you can choose one of the following permission levels:

- **Full administration**   The delegated administrator has the same privileges as a member of the Global Administrator role.
- **Limited administration**   The delegated administrator has the same privileges as a Helpdesk (Password) Administrator role member.

> ***MORE INFO***   **DELEGATED ADMINISTRATORS**
>
> You can learn more about delegated administrators at *https://support.office.microsoft.com/ article/Partners-Offer-delegated-administration-26530dc0-ebba-415b-86b1-b55bc06b073e.*

Skill 3.3: Microsoft Defender roles and role groups

> **This section covers the following skills:**
> - Microsoft 365 Defender and AAD global roles
> - Microsoft Defender for Endpoint roles
> - Microsoft Defender for Office 365 roles
> - Defender for Office 365 administrative role groups
> - Defender for Cloud Apps roles
> - Microsoft Defender for Identity administrative roles
> - Microsoft Defender for Business administrative roles
> - Creating custom roles in Microsoft 365 Defender

Microsoft 365 Defender is a portfolio of security-related products that provide threat detection, prevention, attack investigation, and response functionality across client computers, Microsoft 365 services, and Azure services used by Microsoft 365, including Microsoft Entra ID. The Defender products available to your Microsoft 365 tenancy depend on your plan and subscription details. The functionality of Microsoft Defender products is covered in more detail in Chapter 5, "Manage Microsoft 365 security." In this chapter, you'll learn about the different administrative roles and role groups you can assign to users and the permissions they grant related to Microsoft Defender functionality.

A role is a collection of permissions associated with a specific discrete task or related set of tasks. A role group is a collection of roles. You can assign roles and role groups to individual users. While you can also assign the individual permissions that constitute a role to a user, the best practice is to add the individual permissions to a custom role and then assign the custom role to the user. Collecting permissions into roles and role groups makes it simpler to ascertain which permissions have been delegated to which users, though sometimes that is more challenging if you assign permissions directly without using roles or role groups.

Microsoft 365 Defender and AAD global roles

Microsoft 365 Defender products sometimes use a dual methodology for role-based access control. The unified role-based access control approach relies on assigning one of the existing Microsoft Entra ID roles, such as Global Administrator, Security Administrator, or Security Operator, to a user account to grant permissions to accomplish specific tasks in each Microsoft Defender product. You can assign these Microsoft Entra ID roles at the tenancy level; in this case, the permissions apply to all products, or you can apply these roles scoped only at the individual product level. In general, accounts that you assign the following Microsoft Entra ID roles will be able to access Microsoft 365 Defender tools and telemetry:

- Global Administrator
- Security Administrator
- Security Operator
- Global Reader
- Security Reader

The Administrator level roles can manage all elements, and the Reader roles can view configuration settings and telemetry data but cannot alter any of these settings. In most cases, it will not be necessary for any account to hold the Global Administrator scoped to any specific Microsoft Defender product, so a role like Security Operator will be more appropriate. Using these common roles scoped for each Microsoft 365 Defender product is occasionally termed the Unified RBAC approach; one aim of this approach is to minimize the confusion of each Microsoft Defender product having its own idiosyncratic set of role groups.

Because many of these products existed separately before their inclusion in the Microsoft 365 Defender portfolio, some products, such as Defender for Identity, also support their own specific role groups. These product-specific role groups allow you to assign product-specific permissions that differ from the more generalized permissions of the Microsoft Entra ID role groups. Some of these products, including Defender for Endpoint, Defender for Office 365, and Defender for Cloud Apps, allow you to create custom roles. A custom role allows you to assign a set of tailored permissions and rights that may be more appropriate for a given scenario than those offered by one of the existing role groups.

> **MORE INFO** **MICROSOFT DEFENDER ROLES AND PERMISSIONS**
>
> You can learn more about Microsoft Defender roles at *https://learn.microsoft.com/en-us/ microsoft-365/security/defender/m365d-permissions*.

Microsoft Defender for Endpoint roles

Defender for Endpoint is designed to protect endpoint devices, including computers, phones, wireless access points, firewalls, and routers. Defender for Endpoint has the following roles that you can assign to users as a way of allocating permissions:

- **View Data**   Includes the following read-only permissions:
  - **Security Operations**   Read-only access to security operations data.
  - **Threat And Vulnerability Management**   Read-only access to vulnerability management data.

- **Active remediation Actions** Includes the following permissions that allow actions to be taken:
  - **Security Operations.** Perform response actions, manage allow and block lists for automation and indication, and approve or dismiss remediation actions.
  - **Threat And Vulnerability Management – Exception Handling** Create and manage exceptions.
  - **Threat And Vulnerability Management – Remediation Handling** Create and manage remediations.
  - **Threat And Vulnerability Management – Application Handling** Apply mitigation actions by blocking vulnerable applications.
- **Security Baselines** Includes permissions around configuring security baselines.
  - **Threat And Vulnerability Management – Manage Security Baselines Assessment Profiles** Configure profiles that allow assessment of devices against security baselines.
- **Alerts Investigation** Permissions to manage alerts, initiate automated investigations, perform scans, build investigation packages, configure device tags, and download portable execution files.
- **Manage Portal System Settings** Permissions that allow you to configure storage, SIEM, and threat intel API settings. Also allows for the configuration of roles and device groups.
- **Manage Security Settings In Security Center** Permissions allowing role holder to manage alert suppression settings, configure folder exclusions for automation, edit email notifications, and manage and configure allowed/blocked lists for indicators.
- **Live Response Capabilities** Permissions that allow the role holder to perform live-response sessions, download files from the remote device through live response, upload a file to a remote device, view scripts in the files library, and run scripts on remotely managed devices from the files library.

> *MORE INFO* **MICROSOFT DEFENDER FOR ENDPOINT ROLES**
>
> You can learn more about Microsoft Defender for Endpoint roles at *https://learn.microsoft. com/en-us/microsoft-365/security/defender-endpoint/user-roles.*

Microsoft Defender for Office 365 roles

You assign permissions in Defender for Office 365 by assigning a user account to a *role group*, which are collections of roles. The Defender for Office 365 role groups are covered later in this chapter. In this section, you'll learn about the Defender for Office 365 roles.

Defender for Office 365 compliance-related roles

The compliance-related roles allow the assignment of permissions around eDiscovery and compliance tasks:

- **Case Management**   Can manage and control access to eDiscovery cases.
- **Communication**   Manage all communications with eDiscovery custodians.
- **Communication Compliance Admin**   Manage Communication Compliance policies.
- **Communication Compliance Analysis**   Role used to perform investigations and remediate message violations. Cannot view message contents, only message metadata.
- **Communication Compliance Case Management**   View and manage Communication Compliance Cases.
- **Communication Compliance Investigation**   Used to investigate Communication Compliance violations. Can view message contents and message metadata.
- **Communication Compliance Viewer**   View communication compliance reports.
- **Compliance Administrator**   Configure compliance settings and reports.
- **Compliance Manager Administration**   Configure the creation and modification of templates.
- **Compliance Manager Assessment**   Configure assessments and improvement actions.
- **Compliance Manager Contribution**   Configure assessments and manage improvement actions.
- **Compliance Manager Reader**   View all Compliance Manager settings other than those related to Administrator functions.
- **Compliance Search**   Run compliance searches against mailboxes.
- **Custodian**   Manage eDiscovery case custodians, associating data sources (mailboxes, SharePoint sites, and Microsoft Teams) with case custodians.

Defender for Office 365 data classification–related roles

The data classification roles allow the assignment of permissions around data classification:

- **Data Classification Content Viewer**   View rendered files in Content Explorer
- **Data Classification Feedback Provider**   Provide feedback related to Content Explorer classifiers
- **Data Classification Feedback Reviewer**   Review classifier feedback
- **Data Classification List Viewer**   List all files in Content Explorer

Defender for Office 365 information protection–related roles

These information protection roles allow the assignment of permissions around Microsoft Defender's information protection functionality:

- **IB (Information Barrier) Compliance Management**   Configure Information Barrier policies.

- **Information Protection Admin**   Manage data loss prevention (DLP) policies, sensitivity labels, and classifiers.

- **Information Protection Analyst**   Manage DLP alerts and view DLP policies, sensitivity labels, and classifier types.

- **Information Protection Investigator**   View and manage DLP alerts, Activity Explorer, and Content Explorer. Also has read access to DLP policies, sensitivity labels, and all classifier types.

- **Information Protection Reader**   Read-only access to DLP policy reports and sensitivity labels.

Defender for Office 365 insider risk management–related roles

The insider risk management roles allow for the assignment of permissions related to Microsoft 365 functionality that governs insider risk management:

- **Insider Risk Management Admin**   Manage access to Insider Risk Management (IRM).

- **Insider Risk Management Analysis**   View all IRM alerts, notices templates, and cases.

- **Insider Risk Management Approval**   Permission to investigate, remediate, and review violations. Can view message contents and metadata.

- **Insider Risk Management Audit**   View IRM audit trails.

- **Insider Risk Management Investigation**   Provides access to all IRM alerts, cases, notices templates, and Content Explorer for every case.

- **Insider Risk Management Permanent contribution**   This role is used by background services in Microsoft Defender 365.

- **Insider Risk Management Sessions**   Provides access to message metadata but not contents when investigating and remediating violations.

- **Insider Risk Management Temporary contribution**   This role is used by background services in Microsoft Defender 365.

Defender for Office 365 privacy management–related roles

The following roles are often collected into role groups to assign permissions related to privacy management:

- **Privacy Management Admin**   Manage Privacy Management policies and use all elements of Privacy Management in Microsoft Defender 365
- **Privacy Management Analysis**   Perform investigation and remediation of Privacy Management message violations
- **Privacy Management Investigation**   Investigate, remediate, and view Privacy Management message violations
- **Privacy Management Permanent contribution**   Permanent contributor access to Privacy Management
- **Privacy Management Temporary contribution**   Temporary contributor access to Privacy Management
- **Privacy Management Viewer**   View Privacy Management dashboards and widgets

Defender for Office 365 view-only roles

The following roles provide read-only permissions over Microsoft 365 elements, including audit logs, cases, alerts, and recipients:

- **View-Only Audit Logs**   View and export audit reports
- **View-Only Case**   Read access to cases
- **View-Only Device Management**   Read access to device management configuration and settings
- **View-Only DLP Compliance Management**   Read access to DLP Compliance Management reports and settings
- **View-Only IB Compliance Management**   Read-only access to Information Barriers configuration and reports
- **View-Only Manage Alerts**   Read-only access to reports and configuration for Manage Alerts
- **View-Only Recipients**   View information about groups and users
- **View-Only Record Management**   View records management configuration settings
- **View-Only Retention Management role**   View retention policy configuration, retention labels, and retention label policies

Other Defender for Office 365 roles

Other roles that collect important permissions and are used by many Defender for Office 365 role groups include the following:

- **Audit Logs** Permissions that allow a holder to configure auditing for the organization, view audit reports, and export audit reports
- **Data Connector Admin** Make connectors for importing and archiving non-Microsoft data into Microsoft 365
- **Data Investigation Management** Manage access to data investigation
- **Device Management** Configure device management settings and features
- **Disposition Management** Manage Manual Disposition permissions
- **DLP Compliance Management** Manage DLP policy settings and reports
- **Export** Export Microsoft 365 content returned form searches
- **Hold** Place Microsoft 365 content on hold in a secure location
- **Knowledge Admin** Manage knowledge, learning, and assigned training
- **Manage Alerts** Configure alerts, reports, and settings
- **Manage Review Set Tags** Decrypt Rights Management–protected content when exporting the results of a search
- **Organization Configuration** Manage audit reports and compliance policies for Data Loss Prevention
- **Preview** View all items returned from content searches
- **Quarantine** View and release messages held in quarantine
- **Record Management** Manage records management
- **Retention Management** Manage retention policies, retention labels, and retention label policies
- **Review** Provides access to review sets of case data in eDiscovery
- **RMS Decrypt** Decrypt Rights Management Services–protected content when performing an export of search results
- **Role Management** Manage the membership of role groups. Also can create custom role groups
- **Scope Manager** Configure scopes for investigation
- **Search and Purge** Perform bulk removal of data matching a content search

- **Security Administrator**   Manage configuration of security features for Microsoft 365
- **Security Reader**   View the configuration of security features for Microsoft 365
- **Sensitivity Label Administrator**   Manage sensitivity labels
- **Sensitivity Label Reader**   View sensitivity labels
- **Service Assurance View**   Access documents from Service Assurance
- **Subject Rights Request Admin**   Manage supervisory review policies
- **Subject Rights Request Approver**   Manage access to custodian
- **Supervisory Review Administrator**   Manage supervisory review policies
- **Tag Manager**   Manage user tags
- **Tag Reader**   View access to user tags
- **Tenant AllowBlockList Manager**   Manage allow and block lists for tenants

> *MORE INFO*   **MICROSOFT DEFENDER FOR OFFICE 365 ROLES**
>
> You can learn more about Microsoft Defender for Office 365 roles at *https://learn.microsoft. com/microsoft-365/security/office-365-security/scc-permissions*.

Defender for Office 365 administrative role groups

The previous section listed the roles related to Defender for Office 365. These roles are associated with role groups. You assign a role group to a user as a method of assigning multiple task-related roles.

Compliance administration role groups

Depending on the specific role groups, Compliance administrators can manage settings for communication methods, device management, data loss prevention, reports, and data preservation and retention. Compliance administration–related role groups are described in the following list with their associated roles:

- **Communication Compliance role group**   Includes the Case Management, Communication Compliance Admin, Communication Compliance Analysis, Communication Compliance Case Management, Communication Compliance Investigation, Communication Compliance Viewer, Data Classification Feedback Provider, Data Connector Admin, Scope Manager, and View-Only Case roles
- **Communication Compliance Administrators role group**   Includes the Communication Compliance Admin, Communication Compliance Case Management, Data Connector Admin, and Scope Manager roles

- **Communication Compliance Analysts role group**   Includes the Communication Compliance Analysis and Communication Compliance Case Management roles

- **Communication Compliance Investigators role group**   Includes Case Management, Communication Compliance Analysis, Communication Compliance Case Management, Communication Compliance Investigation, Data Classification Feedback Provider, and View-Only Case roles

- **Communication Compliance Viewers role group**   Includes the Communication Compliance Case Management and Communication Compliance Viewer roles

- **Compliance Administrator role group**   Includes the Compliance Administrator, Compliance Manager Administrator, Compliance Search, Device Management, Disposition Management, DLP Compliance Management, IB Compliance Management, Information Protection Admin, Information Protection Analyst, Information Protection Reader, Manage Alerts, Organization Configuration, Record Management, Retention Management, Scope Manager, Sensitivity Label Administrator, View-Only Audit Logs, View-Only Device Management, View-Only DLP Compliance Management, View-Only IB Compliance Management, View-Only Manage Alerts, View-Only Recipients, View-Only Record Management, and View-Only Retention Management roles

- **Compliance Data Administrator role group**   Includes the Compliance Administrator, Compliance Manager Administrator, Compliance Search, Device Management, Disposition Management, DLP Compliance Management, IB Compliance Management, Information Protection Admin, Information Protection Analyst, Information Protection Reader, Manage Alerts, Organization Configuration, RecordManagement, Retention Management, Scope Manager, Sensitivity Label Administrator, View-Only Audit Logs, View-Only Device Management, View-Only DLP Compliance Management, View-Only IB Compliance Management, View-Only Manage Alerts, View-Only Recipients, and View-Only Record Management roles

- **Compliance Manager Administrators role group**   Includes the Compliance Manager Administration, Compliance Manager Assessment, Compliance Manager Contribution, Compliance Manager Reader, and Data Connector Admin roles

- **Compliance Manager Assessors role group**   Includes the Compliance Manager Assessment, Compliance Manager Contribution, Compliance Manager Reader, and Data Connector Admin roles

- **Compliance Manager Contributors role group**   Includes the Compliance Manager Contribution, Compliance Manager Reader, and Data Connector Admin roles

- **Compliance Manager Readers role group**   Includes only the Compliance Manager Reader role

Information protection role groups

Information protection role groups include the management of sensitive labels, policies, Data Loss Prevention (DLP), classifier types, activity, content explorers, and reports related to these elements:

- **Information Protection role group**   Includes the Data Classification Content Viewer, Data Classification List Viewer, Information Protection Admin, Information Protection Analyst, Information Protection Investigator, and Information Protection Reader roles
- **Information Protection Admins role group**   Includes only the Information Protection Admin role
- **Information Protection Analysts role group**   Includes the Data Classification List Viewer and Information Protection Analyst roles
- **Information Protection Investigators role group**   Includes the Data Classification Content Viewer, Data Classification List Viewer, Information Protection Analyst, and Information Protection Investigator roles
- **Information Protection Readers role group**   Includes the Information Protection Reader role

Insider risk management role groups

Insider risk management involves minimizing internal risks through the detection, investigation, and remediation of malicious and accidental activities within an organization:

- **Insider Risk Management role group**   Includes the Case Management, Data Connector Admin, Insider Risk Management Admin, Insider Risk Management Analysis, Insider Risk Management Approval, Insider Risk Management Audit, Insider Risk Management Investigation, Insider Risk Management Sessions, Review, and View-Only Case roles.
- **Insider Risk Management Admins role group**   Includes the Case Management, Custodian, Data Connector Admin, Insider Risk Management Admin, and View-Only Case roles.
- **Insider Risk Management Analysts role group**   Includes the Case Management, Insider Risk Management Analysis, and View-Only Case roles.
- **Insider Risk Management Approvers role group**   Includes the Insider Risk Management Approval role.
- **Insider Risk Management Auditors role group**   Includes the Insider Risk Management Audit role.
- **Insider Risk Management Investigators role group**   Includes the Case Management, Custodian, Insider Risk Management Investigation, Review, and View-Only Case roles.

- **Insider Risk Management Session Approvers role group** Includes the Insider Risk Management Sessions role.

- **IRM (Insider Risk Management) Contributors role group** Visible as a role group but not assigned to users and used for background services. Includes the Insider Risk Management Permanent contribution and Insider Risk Management Temporary contribution roles.

Privacy management role groups

Members of privacy management role groups can perform administrative functions related to Priva in the Microsoft Purview compliance portal:

- **Privacy Management role group** Includes the Case Management, Data Classification Content Viewer, Data Classification List Viewer, Privacy Management Admin, Privacy Management Analysis, Privacy Management Investigation, Privacy Management Permanent contribution, Privacy Management Temporary contribution, Privacy Management Viewer, Subject Rights Request Admin, and View-Only Case roles

- **Privacy Management Administrators role group** Includes the Case Management, Privacy Management Admin, and View-Only Case roles

- **Privacy Management Analysts role group** Includes the Case Management, Data Classification List Viewer, Privacy Management Analysis, and View-Only Case roles

- **Privacy Management Contributors role group** Includes the Privacy Management Permanent contribution and Privacy Management Temporary contribution roles

- **Privacy Management Investigators role group** Includes the Case Management, Data Classification Content Viewer, Data Classification List Viewer, Privacy Management Investigation, and View-Only Case roles

- **Privacy Management Viewers role group** Includes the Data Classification List Viewer and Privacy Management Viewer roles

Security role groups

Members of the Security named role groups are able to configure and access security features in the Identity Protection Center, Privileged Identity Management, Defender, Compliance, and service health monitoring portals:

- **Security Administrator role group** Includes the Audit Logs, Compliance Manager Administration, Device Management, DLP Compliance Management, IB Compliance Management, Manage Alerts, Quarantine, Security Administrator, Sensitivity Label Administrator, Tag Manager, Tag Reader, View-Only Audit Logs, View-Only Device Management, View-Only DLP Compliance Management, View-Only IB Compliance Management, and View-Only Manage Alerts roles

- **Security Operator role group**   Includes the Compliance Search, Manage Alerts, Security Reader, Tag Reader, Tenant AllowBlockList Manager, View-Only Audit Logs, View-Only Device Management, View-Only DLP Compliance Management, View-Only IB Compliance Management, and View-Only Manage Alerts roles

- **Security Reader role group**   Includes the Compliance Manager Reader, Security Reader, Sensitivity Label Reader, Tag Reader, View-Only Device Management, View-Only DLP Compliance Management, View-Only IB Compliance Management, and View-Only Manage Alerts roles

Other Defender for Office 365 role groups

Other Defender for Office 365 role groups that don't fit neatly into any category include the following:

- **Content Explorer Content Viewer role group**   Can view content files in Content Explorer.

- **Content Explorer List Viewer role group**   View items in Content explorer only in list format. Includes the Data Classification List Viewer role.

- **Data Investigator role group**   Can perform searches of mailboxes, SharePoint Online sites, and OneDrive for Business. Includes the Communication, Compliance Search, Custodian, Data Investigation Management, Export, Preview, Review, RMS Decrypt, and Search And Purge roles.

- **eDiscovery Manager role group.** Can perform searches and place holds on Microsoft 365 content locations including mailboxes, SharePoint Online Sites, and OneDrive for Business. Can create and manage eDiscovery cases. Differs from eDiscovery Administrator in that the manager can only access cases they create or cases to which they have been assigned. Includes the Case Management, Communication, Compliance Search, Custodian, Export, Hold, Manage Review Set Tags, Preview, Review, RMS Decrypt, and Scope Manager roles.

- **Global Reader role group**   Has read-only access to reports, alerts and can view configuration and settings. Includes the Compliance Manager Reader, Security Reader, Sensitivity Label Reader, Service Assurance View, View-Only Audit Logs, View-Only Device Management, View-Only DLP Compliance Management, View-Only IB Compliance Management, View-Only Manage Alerts, View-Only Recipients, View-Only Record Management, and View-Only Retention Management roles.

- **Knowledge Administrators role group**   Allows the role group holder to configure knowledge, learning, and training. Includes the Knowledge Admin role.

- **MailFlow Administrator role group**   Users assigned this role group can monitor and view mail flow insights. Includes the View-Only Recipients role.

- **Organization Management role group**   Includes the Audit Logs, Case Management, Communication Compliance Admin, Communication Compliance Case Management, Compliance Administrator, Compliance Manager Administration, Compliance Search, Data Connector Admin, Device Management, DLP Compliance Management, Hold, IB Compliance Management, Insider Risk Management Admin, Manage Alerts, Organization Configuration, Quarantine, RecordManagement, Retention Management, Role Management, Scope Manager, Search And Purge, Security Administrator, Security Reader, Sensitivity Label Administrator, Sensitivity Label Reader, Service Assurance View, Tag Manager, Tag Reader, View-Only Audit Logs, View-Only Case, View-Only Device Management, View-Only DLP Compliance Management, View-Only IB Compliance Management, View-Only Manage Alerts, View-Only Recipients, View-Only Record Management, and View-Only Retention Management roles.

- **Quarantine Administrator role group**   Users assigned this role group are able to access all Quarantine functionality. Includes the Quarantine role group.

- **Records Management role group**   Users assigned this role group are able to configure and manage all elements of records management. Includes the Disposition Management, RecordManagement, Retention Management, and Scope Manager roles.

- **Reviewer role group**   Members of this role group are able to access review sets in eDiscovery cases. Includes the Review role.

- **Subject Rights Request Administrators role group**   Users assigned this role can create subject rights requests. Includes the Case Management, Subject Rights Request Admin, and View-Only Case roles.

- **Subject Rights Request Approvers role group**   Members of this role group can approve subject rights requests. Includes the Subject Rights Request Approver role.

- **Supervisory Review role group**   Members of this role group can configure policies determining which communications are subject to review. Includes the Supervisory Review Administrator role.

Defender for Cloud Apps roles

Microsoft Defender for Cloud Apps is a Cloud Access Security Broker that provides guardrails for an organization using cloud services. It allows you to monitor how users interact with cloud resources, reducing the chance of leaking sensitive data, protecting against nefarious actors, and evaluating the compliance of cloud services. You can use the following roles scoped to the Defender for Cloud Apps product to assign the rights and permissions outlined in Table 3-2.

TABLE 3-2 Defender for Cloud Apps roles

Role scoped to Defender for Cloud Apps	Permissions
Global Administrator	Full permissions to all elements of Defender for Cloud Apps.
Compliance Administrator	Functions similar to the Microsoft Entra ID Compliance Administrator role, which can manage features in the Microsoft 365 compliance center, Microsoft 365 admin center, Azure, and Microsoft 365 Security & Compliance Center. It is only scoped to Defender for Cloud Apps.
Security Reader	Has read access to security settings and telemetry related to Defender for Cloud Apps.
Security Operator	Can configure and manage security settings and telemetry related to Defender for Cloud Apps.
App/Instance Admin	Configured for a specific cloud application or application instance. Provides application-specific permissions on the following: ■ Activities ■ Alerts ■ Policies (including the ability to add and edit policies) ■ Accounts ■ App permissions ■ Files ■ Permissions for the API token ■ Governance actions
User Group Admin	Provides permissions to all the data managed through Defender for Cloud Apps associated with members of the designated group. User group admin includes the following permissions: ■ View activities on group users ■ View alerts related to group users ■ View and edit policies related to group users ■ View accounts for specific users of the group ■ Configure permissions for API tokens for group users ■ Configure governance for group users
Cloud Discovery Global Admin	Assigned permissions to edit and view all Cloud Discovery settings and data: ■ Alerts related to Cloud Discovery reports ■ Create and edit Cloud Discovery policies ■ Create and delete their own API tokens
Cloud Discovery Report Admin	Can view the following: ■ Cloud Discovery activity ■ Alerts ■ Policies (can create Cloud Discovery policies without application governance) ■ Can view Cloud Discovery reports. ■ Can create and delete their own API keys

MORE INFO **MICROSOFT DEFENDER FOR CLOUD APPS ROLES**

You can learn more about Microsoft Defender for Cloud Apps roles at
https://learn.microsoft.com/en-us/defender-cloud-apps/manage-admins.

Microsoft Defender for Identity administrative roles

Microsoft Defender for Identity is a solution that runs in Azure and allows you to monitor Active Directory Domain Services telemetry to detect and investigate advanced threats, compromised identities, and malicious insider actions.

Members of the Global Administrator and Security Administrator Microsoft Entra ID roles can perform the following tasks:

- Create Defender for Identity Workspace
- Configure Defender for Identity Settings
- Configure Defender for Identity security alerts and activities
- Configure Defender for Identity security assessments (Microsoft Secure Score)

The RBAC permissions required for each of these tasks that can be assigned to a custom role are listed in Table 3-3.

TABLE 3-3   Microsoft Defender for Identity custom RBAC permissions

Microsoft Defender for Identity Action	RBAC Permissions
Configure Defender for Identity Settings	■ Authorization And Settings/Security Settings/Read ■ Authorization And Settings/Security Settings/All Permissions ■ Authorization And Settings/System Settings/Read ■ Authorization And Settings/System Settings/All Permissions
Configure Defender for Identity security alerts and activities	■ Security Operations/Security Data/Alerts (Manage) ■ Security Operations/Security Data /Security Data Basics (Read)
Configure Defender for Identity security assessments (Microsoft Secure Score)	■ Security Operations/Security Data /Security Data Basics (Read)

Defender for Identity also includes three security group types, each with a specific name format that includes the name of the workspace for which they provide permissions:

- Azure ATP (Workspace Name) Administrators
- Azure ATP (Workspace Name) Users
- Azure ATP (Workspace Name) Viewers

Table 3-4 lists the permissions each workspace-specific role group provides.

Security Group	Permissions
Azure ATP (Workspace Name) Administrators	■ Alter Health Alert Status ■ Alter Security Alert Status ■ Delete Workspace ■ Download Report ■ Export Security Alerts ■ Update Configuration ■ Update Entity Tags ■ Update Exclusions ■ Update Notifications ■ Schedule Reports ■ View Entity Profiles And Security Alerts
Azure ATP (Workspace name) Users	■ Alter Security Alert Status ■ Download Report ■ Export Security Alerts ■ Update Entity Tags ■ Update Exclusions ■ Update Notifications ■ Schedule Reports ■ View Entity Profiles And Security Alerts
Azure ATP (Workspace name) Viewers	■ Download Report ■ Export Security Alerts ■ View Entity Profiles And Security Alerts

> *MORE INFO* **MICROSOFT DEFENDER FOR IDENTITY ROLES**
>
> You can learn more about Microsoft Defender for Identity administrative roles at *https://learn.microsoft.com/en-us/defender-for-identity/role-groups*.

Microsoft Defender for Business administrative roles

Microsoft Defender for Business is an endpoint security product for small- and medium-sized software that protects against ransomware, malware, and phishing, reduces the attack surface, and provides other security features. Defender for Business is designed specifically for organizations with up to 300 employees and is included in Microsoft 365 Business Premium or as a standalone subscription.

Microsoft Defender for Business uses the following Microsoft Entra ID administrative roles:

- **Global Administrators** Users assigned this role can configure all Microsoft Defender for Business settings.
- **Security Administrators** Users assigned this role can
  - View and manage Defender for Business security policies
  - View and manage endpoint security and threats
  - View and manage security telemetry and reports

- **Security Reader** Users assigned this role can
  - View security policies
  - View security threats and alerts
  - View security telemetry and reports

> **MORE INFO** **MICROSOFT DEFENDER ROLES**
>
> You can learn more about Microsoft Defender for Business roles at *https://learn.microsoft.com/microsoft-365/security/defender-business/mdb-roles-permissions*.

Creating custom roles in Microsoft 365 Defender

In some circumstances, you might require a more detailed level of control over specific product data than is available through the Microsoft Entra ID global roles that you can use with Microsoft 365 Defender products. You can create custom roles through each product's security portal. For example, if you wanted to configure a custom role that allowed access only to Microsoft Defender for Office 365 functionality and not Microsoft Defender for Endpoint functionality, you would create a custom role in the Microsoft Defender for Office 365 portal rather than assigning the Security Operator or Security Reader Microsoft Entra ID roles. When creating a custom role, you specify which permissions you want to assign to the role while considering the principle of least privilege.

Table 3-5 lists the permissions you need to assign in each product to a custom role if you want to allow the role holder to view investigation data, including alerts, incidents, and the action center:

TABLE 3-5 Custom investigation data viewer role

Defender Workload	One of the following Role Permissions IS required to view investigation data
Defender for Endpoint	■ View Data-Security Operations
Defender for Office 365	■ View-Only Manage Alerts ■ Organization Configuration ■ Audit Logs ■ View-Only Audit Logs ■ Security Reader ■ View-Only Recipients
Defender for Cloud Apps	■ Security Operator ■ Security Reader ■ Global Reader

Table 3-6 lists the permissions you would need to assign in each product to a custom role if you want to allow the role holder to have the equivalent permissions to an existing role.

TABLE 3-6   Custom threat hunting data viewer role

Defender Workload	One of the following Role Permissions IS required to view custom threat-hunting data
Defender for Endpoint	■ View Data – Security Operations
Defender for Office 365	■ Security Reader ■ View-Only Recipients
Defender for Cloud Apps	■ Security Reader ■ Global Reader

Table 3-7 lists the permissions you would need to assign in each product to a custom role if you want to allow the role holder to have the equivalent permissions to an existing role.

TABLE 3-7   Custom managing alerts and incidents role

Defender Workload	One of the following Role Permissions IS required to manage alerts and incidents
Defender for Endpoint	■ Alerts Investigation
Defender for Office 365	■ Manage Alerts ■ Security Admin
Defender for Cloud Apps	■ Security Admin ■ Compliance Admin ■ Security Operator ■ Security Reader

Table 3-8 lists the permissions you would need to assign in each product to a custom role if you want to allow the custom role holder to have the equivalent permissions to an existing role.

TABLE 3-8   Custom action center remediation role

Defender Workload	Role Permissions required to
Defender for Endpoint	■ Active Remediation Actions – Security Operations
Defender for Office 365	■ Manage Alerts ■ Security Admin
Defender for Cloud Apps	■ Not applicable

Table 3-9 lists the permissions you would need to assign in each product to a custom role if you want to allow the custom role holder to have the equivalent permissions to an existing role.

TABLE 3-9 Custom Threat analytics role

Defender Workload	Role Permissions required to
Defender for Endpoint (Alerts and incidents data)	■ View Data – Security Operations (Alerts And Incidents Data)
Defender for Endpoint (Defender Vulnerability Management Mitigations)	■ View Data – Threat And Vulnerability Management
Defender for Office 365 (Alerts and incidents data)	■ View-Only Manage Alerts ■ Manage Alerts ■ Organization Configuration ■ Audit Logs ■ View-Only Audit Logs ■ Security Reader ■ Security Admin ■ View-Only Recipients
Defender for Office 365 (Prevented email attempts)	■ Security Reader ■ Security Admin ■ View-Only Recipients
Defender for Cloud Apps	■ Not available

> **MORE INFO   MICROSOFT DEFENDER CUSTOM ROLES**
>
> You can learn more about Microsoft Defender custom roles at *https://learn.microsoft.com/en-us/microsoft-365/security/defender/custom-roles*.

Skill 3.4: Microsoft Purview roles

Microsoft Purview is a data governance solution that allows you to manage your organization's on-premises, multi-cloud, and software-as-a-service (SaaS) data. While you will learn more about Microsoft Purview in Chapter 6, "Manage Microsoft Purview," the following are the Microsoft Purview–related administrative roles.

> **This section covers the following skills:**
> - Collection Administrators
> - Data Curators
> - Data Readers
> - Data Source Administrator
> - Insights Reader
> - Policy Author
> - Workflow Administrator
> - Assigning Purview roles

Collection Administrators

Collection administrators manage collections and assign roles to other users. If you assign the collection administrator role to a user on the root collection, that user will also have permission to access the Microsoft Purview governance portal.

Data Curators

Data Curators can access the data catalog, manage assets, create custom classifications, and configure glossary terms; also, this role provides read access to data estate insights.

Data Readers

Provides users assigned the role the ability to view data assets, classifications, classification rules, collections, and glossary terms.

Data Source Administrator

Users assigned this role can configure data sources and scans. Grant the Data Source Administrator role on a specific data source to allow them to run new scans using a preexisting scan rule. For the ability to create new scan rules, the user also requires the Data Reader or Data Curator roles.

Insights Reader

Users assigned this role have read-only access to Insights reports for Purview collections when the user with the Insights Reader role has also been assigned the Data Reader role or one with the same permissions.

Policy Author

A user assigned the Policy Author role can view, update, and delete Microsoft Purview policies using the policy management app.

Workflow Administrator

A user assigned the Workflow Administrator role can use the workflow authoring page in the Purview Governance portal to publish workflows against collections to which they have access. To publish a workflow against a collection, the user also needs a minimum role of Data Reader.

Assigning Purview roles

You manage role assignments in Azure Purview by adding users to collections. A user must have the Collection Administrator role to grant permissions to other users. To add a role assignment to another user, navigate to data map in the **Microsoft Purview Governance** portal, select the **Collections** tab, and then select the collection on which you want to add the role. On the **Role Assignments** tab, add users to the appropriate role for the collection.

> *MORE INFO* **MICROSOFT PURVIEW PERMISSIONS AND ACCESS**
>
> You can learn more about Microsoft Purview permissions and access at
> *https://learn.microsoft.com/en-us/azure/purview/catalog-permissions*.

Manage administrative units

Microsoft Entra ID administrative units are containers for Microsoft Entra ID user and group accounts that you can use to limit administrative permissions. For example, if you want to limit administrative rights to a specific set of users and groups, you could place those users and groups in an administrative unit and assign permissions using the administrative unit as the permission scope. All the user and group objects in that administrative unit will be subject to the permissions assigned at the administrative unit level.

The administrative unit structure will be dependent on the needs of each organization. Some organizations might create an administrative unit structure based on geographical boundaries; other organizations might create an administrative unit structure based on their company divisions. Administrative units in Microsoft Entra ID are analogous to Organizational Units in Active Directory Domain Services. Users with the Global Administrator or Privileged Role Administrators can

- Create administrative units
- Add users and groups to administrative units
- Delegate administrative roles to administrative units

To add an administrative unit through the Azure portal, perform the following steps:

1. In the Microsoft Entra ID admin center or Azure portal, select the **Microsoft Entra ID** node and then select **Administrative Units**.

2. In the **Administrative Units** blade, select **Add**. You will be asked to provide a name for the administrative unit in the **Name** box, and you will have the option of providing a **Description** for the administrative unit.

3. Click **Add** to complete the process of adding the administrative unit.

Once you have created the administrative unit, you can add users, groups and assign roles and administrators. To add a user using the Azure portal, open the **Administrative Unit**, select **Users**, and then click **Add Member**.

To add a group using the Azure portal, open the **Administrative Unit**, select **Groups**, and click **Add**. You will need a Microsoft Entra ID P1 or P2 license to add roles and administrators for the Administrative Unit. By default, the following Administrative roles are assigned permissions to the Administrative Unit.

- Authentication Administrator
- Groups Administrator
- Helpdesk Administrator
- License Administrator
- Password Administrator
- User Administrator

Perform the following steps to add a user or group to one of the existing roles scoped only with permissions to objects within the Administrative Unit:

1. Open the **Administrative Unit** in the Azure portal and select **Roles And Administrators**.
2. Select the role you want to assign over the objects within the administrative unit and then select **Add Assignments**.
3. On the **Add Assignments** pane, select the users or groups you want to assign to the role.

The best practice when using role-based access control technologies is to assign roles to specially created groups and then add users to that group. Removing a user's privileges is a matter of removing their account from specific groups. This process is simpler than removing privileges for a specific user on a resource-by-resource basis.

> **MORE INFO**   **MICROSOFT ENTRA ID ADMINISTRATIVE UNITS**
>
> You can learn more about Microsoft Entra ID administrative units at *https://learn.microsoft.com/azure/active-directory/roles/administrative-units*.

EXAM TIP

Remember that you can assign rights to an application by associating the application's service principal with specific Microsoft Entra ID roles.

Configure Microsoft Entra ID Privileged Identity Management (PIM)

Microsoft Entra ID Privileged Identity Management (PIM) allows you to make role assignments temporary and contingent on approval rather than making them permanent, as is the case when you manually add a member to the role. PIM requires Microsoft Entra ID P2, which must be enabled before it can be configured. To configure an Microsoft Entra ID administrative role for use with PIM, perform the following steps:

1. In the Microsoft Entra ID admin center, select **Roles And Administrators**.
2. Select the role to which you want to add a user. This will open the role's properties page.
3. On the **Role Properties** page, click **Manage In PIM**. The role will open, and any members assigned permanently to it will be listed with the **Permanent** status.
4. Select the user you want to convert from **Permanent** to **Eligible**. An eligible user can request access to the role but will not have its associated rights and privileges until that access is granted. On the user's properties page, click **Make Eligible**.

You can edit the conditions under which an eligible user can be granted by performing the following steps:

1. On the **Privileged Identity Management** blade, click **Microsoft Entra ID Roles**.
2. Under **Manage**, click **Settings**.
3. Click **Roles** and then select the role that you want to configure.

Users can activate roles they're eligible for from the **Privileged Identity Management** area of the Microsoft Entra ID Administrative console. Administrators with the appropriate permissions can also use the **Privileged Identity Management** area of the Microsoft Entra ID Administrative console to approve requests that require approval and review role activations.

> **MORE INFO**   **PRIVILEGED IDENTITY MANAGEMENT**
>
> You can learn more about PIM at *https://learn.microsoft.com/azure/active-directory/privileged-identity-management/pim-configure*.

PIM requires you to configure Microsoft Entra ID users with appropriate licenses. PIM requires one of the following license categories to be assigned to users who will perform PIM-related tasks:

- Microsoft Entra ID P2
- Enterprise Mobility + Security (EMS) E5
- Microsoft 365 M5

The PIM-related tasks that require a license are as follows:

- Any user who is eligible for a Microsoft Entra ID role that is managed using PIM
- Any user who can approve or reject PIM activation requests
- Users assigned to Azure resource roles with just-in-time or time-based assignments
- Any user who can perform an access review
- Any user who is assigned to an access review

MORE INFO   PIM LICENSE REQUIREMENTS

You can learn more about PIM license requirements at *https://learn.microsoft.com/azure/active-directory/privileged-identity-management/subscription-requirements*.

You cannot use PIM to manage the following classic subscription administrator roles:

- Account Administrator
- Service Administrator
- Co-Administrator

The first person to activate PIM will be assigned the tenancy's Security Administrator and Privileged Administrator roles.

MORE INFO   ACTIVATING PRIVILEGED IDENTITY MANAGEMENT

You can learn more about activating PIM at *https://learn.microsoft.com/en-us/azure/active-directory/privileged-identity-management/pim-security-wizard*.

Skill 3.5: Microsoft Entra ID role-based access control

This section covers the following skills:

- Delegate admin rights
- Configure administrative accounts
- Plan security and compliance roles for Microsoft 365

Role-based access control (RBAC) allows you to configure fine-grained access control to Azure resources, such as virtual machines and storage accounts. When you configure RBAC, you assign a role and a scope, with the scope being the resource you want to have managed.

Azure RBAC includes more than 70 roles, though a full listing of the details is beyond the scope of this text. However, those responsible for managing Microsoft 365 should be aware of four fundamental roles that can be assigned to specific Azure subscriptions, resource groups, or resources:

- **Owner**   Users who hold this role have full access to all resources within the scope of the assignment and can delegate access to others.
- **Contributor**   Users who hold this role can create and manage resources within the scope of the assignment but cannot grant access to others.

- **Reader**   Users who hold this role can view resources within the scope of the assignment but can't perform other tasks and cannot grant access to others.
- **User Access Administrator**   Users who hold this role can manage user access to Azure resources within the scope of the assignment.

> **MORE INFO   AZURE RBAC**
>
> You can learn more about Azure RBAC at *https://learn.microsoft.com/azure/role-based-access-control/rbac-and-directory-admin-roles*.

Delegate admin rights

To view which users are assigned a specific role, perform the following steps:

1. In the Entra ID, select **Roles And Administrators** under **Manage**,
2. Select the role whose membership you want to see. The interface will display users who have been assigned role membership.

> **MORE INFO   DELEGATING ADMINISTRATOR RIGHTS**
>
> You can learn more about delegating administrator rights at *https://learn.microsoft.com/azure/active-directory/roles/security-planning*.

Configure administrative accounts

Microsoft Entra ID Privileged Identity Management (PIM) allows you to make role assignments temporary and contingent on approval, rather than permanent, as is the case when you manually add a member to the role. PIM requires Microsoft Entra ID P2 and must be enabled before you can configure it. To configure a Microsoft Entra ID administrative role for use with PIM, perform the following steps:

1. In the Microsoft Entra ID admin center, select **Roles And Administrators** under **Manage**.
2. Select the role to which you want to add a user. This will open the role's properties page.
3. On the role's properties page, select **Manage In PIM**. The role's page will open, and any members assigned permanently to the role will be listed with a **Permanent** status.
4. Select the user you want to convert from **Permanent** to **Eligible**. An eligible user can request access to the role but will not have its associated rights and privileges until that access is granted. On the user's properties page, select **Make Eligible**.

You can edit the conditions under which an eligible user can be granted the rights and privileges associated with a role by performing the following steps:

1. On the **Privileged Identity Management** blade, select **Microsoft Entra ID Roles**. Under **Manage**, select **Settings**.

2. Select **Roles** and select the role you want to configure. On this page, you can configure the following:

   - Maximum activation duration in hours
   - Whether a notification email is sent when a role is activated
   - Whether an incident request ticked ID is required when activating the role
   - Whether multi-factor authentication must occur for the role to be activated
   - Whether another user must provide approval for activation to occur

Users can activate roles for which they are eligible from the **Privileged Identity Management** area of the Microsoft Entra ID admin center. Administrators with the appropriate permissions can also use the **Privileged Identity Management** area of the Microsoft Entra ID admin center to approve requests requiring approval and review role activations.

> **MORE INFO** **PRIVILEGED IDENTITY MANAGEMENT**
>
> You can learn more about PIM at *https://learn.microsoft.com/azure/active-directory/privileged-identity-management/pim-configure*.

Plan security and compliance roles for Microsoft 365

The Microsoft 365 Security & Compliance Center includes default role groups appropriate for the most commonly performed security and compliance tasks. To assign users permission to perform these tasks, add them to the appropriate role group in the Microsoft 365 Security & Compliance Center. Table 3-10 lists Microsoft 365 security and compliance role groups.

TABLE 3-10 Security and compliance role groups

Role Group	Description
Compliance Administrator	Can manage device-management settings, data loss–prevention settings, and data-preservation reports.
eDiscovery Manager	Can perform searches and place holds on SharePoint Online sites, OneDrive for Business locations, and Exchange Online mailboxes. Can create and manage eDiscovery cases.
Organization Management	Can control permissions for accessing the Security & Compliance Center. It can also manage data loss prevention, device management, reports, and preservation settings.
Records Management	Can manage and dispose of record content.

Reviewer	Can view the list of eDiscovery cases in the Security & Compliance Center. Cannot create or manage eDiscovery cases.
Security Administrator	Has all the permissions of the security reader role, plus administrative permissions for Azure Information Protection, Identity Protection Center, and Privileged Identity Management, and the ability to monitor Office 365 Service Health and the Microsoft 365 Security & Compliance Center.
Security Reader	Provides read-only access to security features of the Identity Protection Center, Privileged Identity Management, Microsoft 365 Service Health, and the Microsoft 365 Security & Compliance Center.
Service Assurance User	Provides reports and documentation that explain Microsoft's security practices for customer data stored in Microsoft 365.
Supervisory Review	Can create and manage policies that mediate which communications are subject to review.

> **MORE INFO** **SECURITY AND COMPLIANCE ROLES**
>
> You can learn more about security and compliance roles at *https://learn.microsoft.com/ en-us/microsoft-365/security/office-365-security/scc-permissions*.

EXAM TIP

Remember the functionality of the various security and compliance roles that can be assigned to users.

Chapter summary

- Microsoft Entra ID includes several role groups that can be used to assign privileges to different Microsoft 365 products. Privileges scoped for one product are only assigned to that product and are unavailable in others.

- Microsoft 365 can use any Microsoft Entra ID–privileged role but tends to use a specific subset. Some Microsoft 365 products have their own privileged roles and role groups.

- A role is a collection of privileges. A role group is a collection of roles. Depending on the Microsoft 365 product, assigning a user account to a role and/or a role group is possible as a method of assigning privileges.

- Microsoft Entra ID administrative units are containers for Microsoft Entra ID user and group accounts that you can use to limit administrative permissions.

- Azure role-based access control (RBAC) allows you to configure fine-grained access control to Azure resources, such as virtual machines and storage accounts. When you configure RBAC, you assign a role and a scope, with the scope being the resource you want to have managed.

Thought experiment

In this thought experiment, demonstrate your skills and knowledge of the topics covered in this chapter. You can find answers to this thought experiment in the next section.

Managing compliance at Contoso

Contoso has decided to use Defender for Office 365 to ensure they meet compliance and security requirements for their data. They have important and confidential data stored across mailboxes in Exchange, SharePoint sites, and OneDrive for Business.

Contoso has been asked to provide specific emails as part of a legal case. They must allow a designated company representative to search specific mailboxes to find these emails. It is also necessary to perform a company-wide assessment of their compliance with data protection regulations. This will involve configuring assessments and managing improvement actions. Contoso has been asked to provide a report on their communication compliance, including any violations and the actions taken in response.

With this information, answer the following questions:

1. Which role should be assigned to carry out the task related to email and the legal case?

2. Which role is most suitable for configuring assessments and managing improvement actions?

3. Which role should be tasked with preparing the communications compliance report while ensuring the principle of least privilege is adhered to?

Thought experiment answers

This section contains the solution to the thought experiment. Each answer explains why the answer choice is correct.

1. The Compliance Search role should be assigned to search for specific emails in certain mailboxes as part of a legal case,. This role is specifically designed to run compliance searches against mailboxes.

2. The Compliance Manager Assessment role is most suitable for a company-wide compliance assessment with data protection regulations, including configuring assessments and managing improvement actions. This role has the necessary permissions to configure assessments and manage improvement actions.

3. The Communication Compliance Viewer role should be assigned to prepare a report on communication compliance, including any violations and the actions taken in response. This role is designed for viewing communication compliance reports, including information about violations and responses.

CHAPTER 4

Manage secure access and authentication

Authentication allows the identity of a user, device, or application to be verified. Authentication usually occurs through credentials such as usernames and passwords or specially created digital certificates. During the authentication process, credentials are verified against a secure database. If the credentials match those stored in the database, access is granted to the entity that provided the credentials.

Skills in this chapter:

- Skill 4.1: Implement and manage authentication
- Skill 4.2: Managing passwords
- Skill 4.3: Microsoft Entra ID Password Protection
- Skill 4.4: Multifactor authentication
- Skill 4.5: Self-service password reset
- Skill 4.6: Microsoft Entra ID Identity Protection
- Skill 4.7: Conditional access policies
- Skill 4.8: Resolving authentication issues

Skill 4.1: Implement and manage authentication

Implementing and managing authentication in Microsoft Entra ID and Microsoft 365 involves determining what authentication methods you will support.

> **This section covers the following topics:**
> - Basic and modern authentication
> - Implement an authentication method
> - Certificate-based Microsoft Entra ID authentication
> - Implement passwordless authentication

Basic and modern authentication

There are two general forms of authentication: basic and modern. It is important to understand the differences between modern authentication and basic authentication:

- **Basic authentication**   When a client performs basic authentication, it transmits Base64-encoded credentials from the client to the server. These credentials are protected from interception within a Transport Layer Security (TLS)-encrypted session. TLS is the successor protocol to Secure Sockets Layer (SSL). Basic authentication is also termed proxy authentication when the client sends credentials to an Office 365–related service in Microsoft 365, and the service proxies those credentials to an identity provider on behalf of the client. Depending on the organization's configuration, the identity provider can be Microsoft Entra ID or an on-premises Active Directory instance if passed-through Active Directory Federation Services is configured. In the last few years, Microsoft has deprecated basic authentication, making it unavailable for new tenants and requiring special steps to keep it available to existing tenants.

- **Modern authentication**   Instead of just user name and password-based authentication, modern authentication supports technologies such as multifactor authentication, smart card authentication, certificate-based authentication, and SAML-based third-party identity providers.

Modern authentication provides a more secure authentication and authorization than basic authentication methods. Modern authentication can be used with Microsoft 365 hybrid deployments that include Exchange Online and Teams. All Office and Microsoft 365 tenancies created after August 2017, including Exchange Online, have modern authentication enabled by default. Modern authentication includes a combination of the following authentication and authorization methods, as well as secure access policies:

- **Authentication methods** Multifactor authentication, Client Certificate Authentication, and Active Directory Authentication Library (ADAL)
- **Authorization methods** Microsoft's implementation of Open Authorization (OAuth)
- **Conditional access policies** Mobile application management (MAM) and Microsoft Entra ID Conditional Access

> *MORE INFO* **HYBRID MODERN AUTHENTICATION**
>
> You can learn more about hybrid modern authentication at the following address: *https://learn.microsoft.com/microsoft-365/enterprise/hybrid-modern-auth-overview.*

Implement an authentication method

Microsoft 365 supports multiple authentication methods. When considering how users will authenticate, you must decide which authentication methods will be supported. For example, if you want to implement self-service password reset or Azure multifactor authentication, you must provide an additional method, as shown in Figure 4-1.

FIGURE 4-1 Multiple methods of verifying identity during authentication

Microsoft Entra ID and Microsoft 365 support the following authentication methods:

- **Password**   The password assigned to a Microsoft Entra ID account is an authentication method. Although you can perform passwordless authentication, you cannot disable the password as an authentication method.

- **Security questions**   These are available only with Microsoft Entra ID self-service password reset and can be used only with accounts not assigned administrative roles. Questions are stored on the user object within Microsoft Entra ID and cannot be read or modified by an administrator. Security questions should be used in conjunction with some other security method. Microsoft Entra ID includes the following predefined questions; in addition, you can create custom questions:

  - In what city did you meet your first spouse/partner?
  - In what city did your parents meet?
  - In what city does your nearest sibling live?
  - In what city was your father born?
  - In what city was your first job?
  - In what city was your mother born?
  - What city were you in on New Year's 2000?
  - What is the last name of your favorite teacher in high school?
  - What is the name of a college you applied to but didn't attend?
  - What is the name of the place in which you held your first wedding reception?
  - What is your father's middle name?
  - What is your favorite food?
  - What is your maternal grandmother's first and last name?
  - What is your mother's middle name?
  - What is your oldest sibling's birthday month and year? (e.g., November 1985)
  - What is your oldest sibling's middle name?
  - What is your paternal grandfather's first and last name?
  - What is your youngest sibling's middle name?
  - What school did you attend for sixth grade?
  - What was the first and last name of your childhood best friend?
  - What was the first and last name of your first significant other?
  - What was the last name of your favorite grade school teacher?
  - What was the make and model of your first car or motorcycle?
  - What was the name of the first school you attended?
  - What was the name of the hospital in which you were born?
  - What was the name of the street of your first childhood home?

- What was the name of your childhood hero?
- What was the name of your favorite stuffed animal?
- What was the name of your first pet?
- What was your childhood nickname?
- What was your favorite sport in high school?
- What was your first job?
- What were the last four digits of your childhood telephone number?
- When you were young, what did you want to be when you grew up?
- Who is the most famous person you have ever met?

- **Email address** This is used only for Microsoft Entra ID self-service password resets and should be separate from the user's Microsoft 365 Exchange Online email address.

- **Microsoft Authenticator app** This is available for Android and iOS. It either notifies the user through the mobile app and asks them to enter the number displayed on the logon prompt into the mobile app or periodically asks them to enter a set of changing numbers displayed on the mobile app.

- **OATH hardware tokens** Microsoft Entra ID supports using OATH-TOTP SHA-1 tokens of both the 30- and 60-second variety. Secret keys can have a maximum of 128 characters. Once acquired, a token must be uploaded in comma-separated format, including the UPN, serial number, secret key, time interval, manufacturer, and model.

- **Mobile phone** The user can either enter a code sent to their mobile phone via text message into a dialog to complete authentication or place a phone call to provide a personal authentication PIN. Phone numbers must include the country code.

- **App password** Many nonbrowser apps do not support multifactor authentication. An app password enables these users to continue to authenticate using these apps when multifactor authentication is not supported. An app password can be generated for each app, allowing each app password to be individually revoked.

This information is summarized in Table 4-1.

TABLE 4-1 Authentication methods and usage

Authentication method	Where it can be used
Password	Multifactor authentication and self-service password reset
Security question	Self-service password reset only
Email address	Self-service password reset only
Microsoft Authenticator app	Multifactor authentication and self-service password reset
OATH hardware token	Multifactor authentication and self-service password reset
Mobile phone	Multifactor authentication and self-service password reset
Voice call	Multifactor authentication and self-service password reset
App password	Multifactor authentication, in some cases

> **MORE INFO** **WHAT ARE AUTHENTICATION METHODS?**
>
> You can learn more about what authentication methods are supported by Microsoft 365 and Microsoft Entra ID at *https://learn.microsoft.com/azure/active-directory/authentication/concept-authentication-methods*.

You should also enable multiple authentication methods for multifactor authentication and self-service password reset. Doing so enables the user to fall back to a different authentication method if their chosen one is unavailable. For example, if a user cannot access their mailbox and needs to perform a self-service password reset, you can allow them to answer several security questions to validate their identity.

You configure the authentication methods users can use to perform self-service password reset on the **Password Reset – Authentication Methods** blade in Microsoft Entra ID.

Unless there is a good reason otherwise, you should enable as many authentication methods for self-service password resets as possible and require two methods to perform a reset. This strategy gives users maximum flexibility while still ensuring a high level of security.

> **MORE INFO** **AUTHENTICATION METHODS**
>
> You can learn more about authentication methods at *https://learn.microsoft.com/azure/active-directory/authentication/concept-authentication-methods*.

Certificate-based Microsoft Entra ID authentication

Certificate-based authentication eliminates the need for a username and password combination when authenticating against Exchange Online and other Microsoft 365 services. Certificate-based authentication is supported on Windows, Android, and iOS devices, and has the following requirements:

- Supported only for Federated environments for browser applications or where native clients use modern authentication through the Active Directory Authentication Library (ADAL). Exchange Active Sync (EAS) for Exchange Online (EXO) is exempt from the Federation requirement and can be used with both federated and managed accounts.

- The organization's root certificate authority (CA) and any intermediate CAs must be integrated with Microsoft Entra ID.

- Each organizational CA must publish a certificate revocation list (CRL) in a location accessible to the internet.

- The Windows, Android, or iOS device must have access to an organizational CA configured to issue client certificates.

- The Windows, Android, or iOS device must have a valid certificate installed.
- Exchange ActiveSync clients require that the client certificate include the user's routable email address in the **Subject Alternative Name** field.

To add an organizational CA that Microsoft Entra ID trusts, you must first ensure that the CA is configured with a CRL publication location accessible on the internet and then export the CA certificate. After you export the CA certificate, which will include the internet-accessible location where the CRL is published, you use the `New-AzureADTrustedCertificateAuthority` PowerShell cmdlet to add the organizational CA's certificate to Microsoft Entra ID. You can view a list of trusted CAs for your organization's Microsoft Entra ID instance using the `Get-AzureADTrustedCertificateAuthority` cmdlet.

> **MORE INFO** **CERTIFICATE-BASED MICROSOFT ENTRA ID AUTHENTICATION**
>
> You can learn more about certificate-based Microsoft Entra ID authentication at *https://learn.microsoft.com/azure/active-directory/authentication/certificate-based-authentication-federation-get-started*.

Implement passwordless authentication

Passwordless authentication allows you to replace authentication using a password with authentication requiring "something you have" and "something you know." An example might be a biometric, such as your face or fingerprint, combined with a code generated by an authenticator device.

Microsoft currently offers three passwordless authentication options:

- **Windows Hello for Business** This method uses biometric authentication technologies included with Windows computers, such as Windows Hello compatible-cameras for facial recognition or Windows Hello-compatible fingerprint readers. Most appropriate for users who are the only people who regularly interact with a specific Windows computer.
- **Security key sign-in allows access via FIDO2 security keys** This method is appropriate for users who sign in to shared machines, such as those in a call center. Because it requires the physical FIDO2 security key, this is also an excellent method of protecting privileged identities because it can, in turn, be secured in a safe for which another person has the access code.
- **Phone sign-in through the Microsoft Authenticator app** The Microsoft Authenticator app runs on iOS and Android phones and supports identity verification via biometrics or PIN-based authentication. When using this method, a user will be prompted on the screen to select a specific number displayed among a list of options on the Microsoft Authenticator app and perform identity verification via biometrics or a PIN.

Deploying passwordless authentication requires the following administrative roles:

- **Global Administrator**   This role allows the combined registration experience to be implemented in the directory.
- **Authentication Administrator**   This role can implement and manage authentication methods for individual user accounts.
- **User**   Although not an administrative role, this account must configure an authenticator app on a device or enroll a security device for their specific accounts once passwordless authentication is enabled.

To enable passwordless phone sign-in authentication, perform the following steps:

1. In the **Microsoft Entra ID** section of the admin portal, click **Security**.
2. On the **Security** page, click **Authentication Methods**.
3. On the **Authentication Methods** page, select the authentication method you want to enable, toggle the slider to **On**, and then choose whether you want to enable the authentication method for some or all Microsoft Entra ID users by choosing **All Users** or **Select Users**.

> **MORE INFO   PASSWORDLESS MICROSOFT ENTRA ID AUTHENTICATION**
>
> You can learn more about passwordless authentication at *https://learn.microsoft.com/azure/active-directory/authentication/concept-authentication-passwordless*.

To enable passwordless phone sign-on, users must have the latest version of the Microsoft Authenticator installed on their devices. Their devices should run iOS 8.0 or greater or Android 6.0 or greater. Because these operating systems are quite dated now, it is unlikely you will encounter mobile platforms that do not support Microsoft Authenticator. Users will also need to be enrolled for multifactor authentication. When these conditions have been met, an authenticator sign-in policy must be configured. You can do this when a PowerShell connection is established to the Microsoft 365 tenancy by issuing the following command:

```
New-AzureADPolicy -Type AuthenticatorAppSignInPolicy -Definition
'{"AuthenticatorAppSignInPolicy":{"Enabled":true}}'
-isOrganizationDefault $true -DisplayName AuthenticatorAppSignIn
```

To enable phone sign-in on the app, choose the dropdown arrow next to the account name and select **Enable Phone Sign-On**. If an icon with a key appears next to the Microsoft 365 account name, the phone sign-on for the account has been configured successfully.

> **MORE INFO   PASSWORDLESS PHONE SIGN-ON**
>
> You can learn more about configuring passwordless phone sign-on at *https://learn.microsoft.com/azure/active-directory/authentication/howto-authentication-passwordless-phone*.

Skill 4.2: Managing passwords

While people often talk of a future world in which passwords are no longer used, even when passwordless authentication is implemented, Microsoft 365 and Microsoft Entra ID provide a fallback option allowing users to authenticate using a password. This means that you need to consider how often users update their passwords and the nature of those passwords for your Microsoft Entra ID and Microsoft 365 environment.

> **This section covers the following topics:**
> - Manage password policies
> - Resetting passwords

Manage password policies

Password policies determine how often users must update their passwords. Microsoft 365 user passwords are configured to never expire by default, as shown in Figure 4-2. Password policies for Microsoft 365 are configured in the Microsoft 365 admin center.

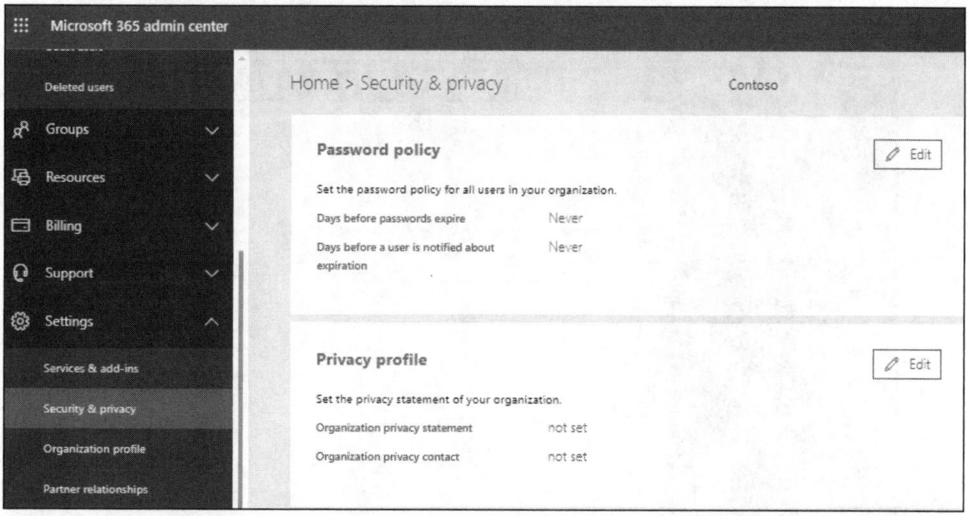

FIGURE 4-2 Default Microsoft 365 password policy

Users assigned the Global Administrator role can modify the password policy. After configuring passwords to expire, you can configure the number of days before passwords expire and the number of days before a user is notified that their password will expire. Figure 4-3 shows a maximum password age of 90 days and how a user will be notified 14 days before expiration. You can configure a maximum password age of up to 730 days.

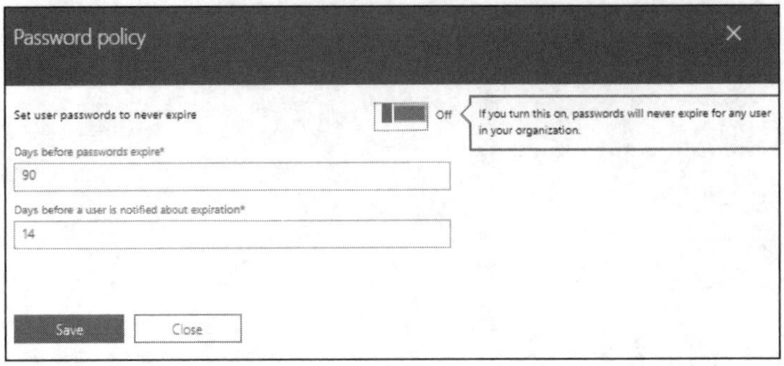

FIGURE 4-3 Configuring a Microsoft 365 password policy

You can configure a password expiration policy for all users by performing the following steps:

1. In the Microsoft 365 admin center, select **Security & Privacy** under **Settings**, as shown in Figure 4-4.

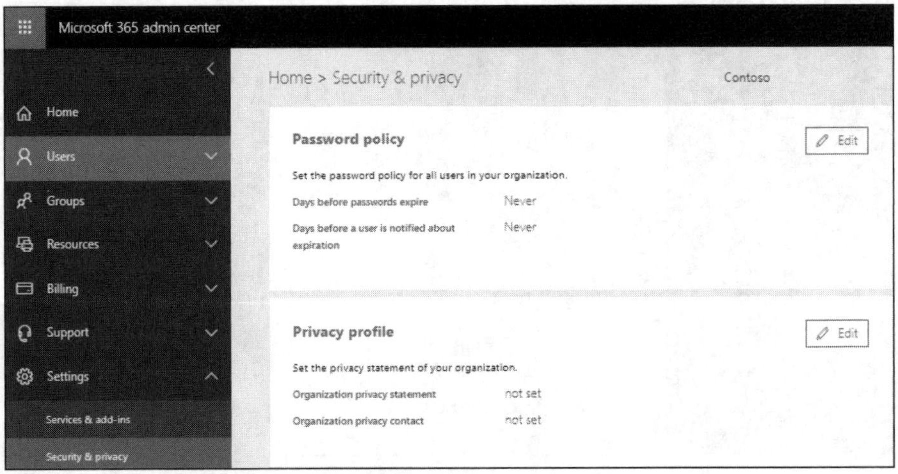

FIGURE 4-4 Security & Privacy settings

2. Next to **Password Policy**, select **Edit**.

3. On the **Password Policy** page shown in Figure 4-5, you can choose to have passwords never expire (**Set User Passwords To Never Expire**) or configure passwords to expire after a specific number of days (**Days Before Passwords Expire**). You can also configure the number of days before a user will be informed that their password will expire (**Days Before A User Is Notified About Expiration**).

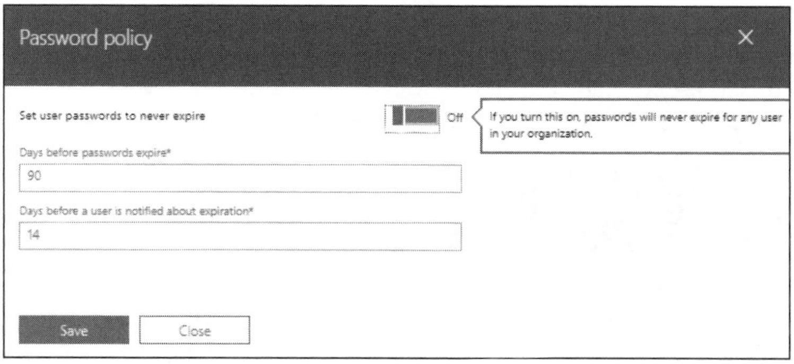

FIGURE 4-5 The Password Policy page

> **MORE INFO**   **PASSWORD EXPIRATION POLICIES**
>
> You can learn more about password expiration policies at *https://learn.microsoft.com/ microsoft-365/admin/manage/set-password-expiration-policy.*

Resetting passwords

The only thing people forget more often than where they put their keys is their password. As someone who supports Microsoft 365, it's more likely than not that if you haven't enabled self-service password reset, or even if you have, you will have to reset user passwords semi-regularly.

To reset a Microsoft 365 user password, perform the following steps:

1. In the Microsoft 365 admin center, select the user whose password you want to reset in the list of active users by selecting the checkbox next to the user's name.

2. On the user's properties page, select the **Reset Password** button, as shown in Figure 4-6.

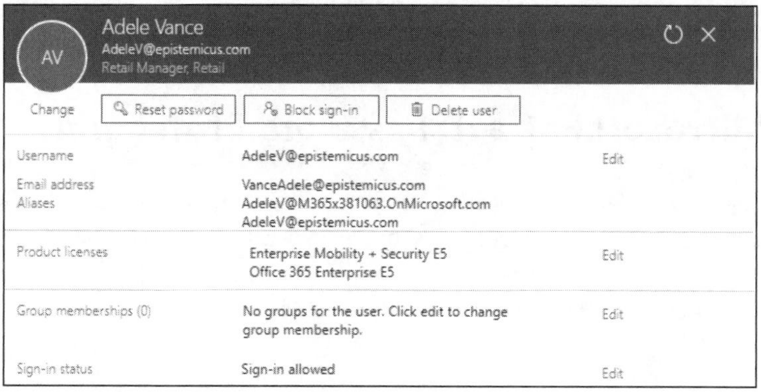

FIGURE 4-6 Reset Password button

3. On the **Reset Password** page shown in Figure 4-7, choose whether to autogenerate a password (**Auto-Generate Password**) or create a password (**Let Me Create The Password**) and select whether the password needs to be changed when the user signs in next (**Make This User Change Their Password When They First Sign In**).

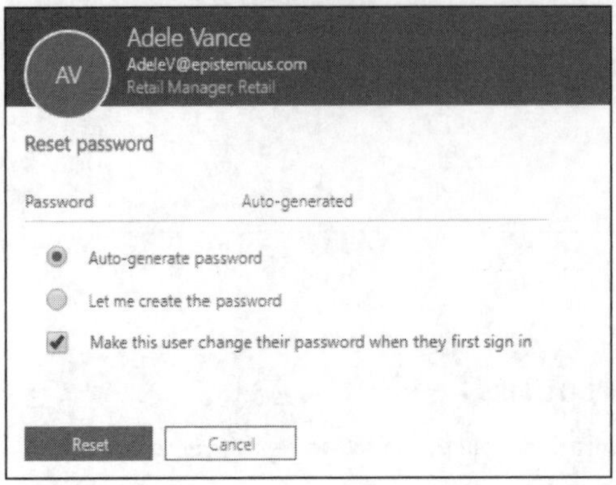

FIGURE 4-7 Password reset

4. Provide the new password to the user through a secure channel, such as in person or over the phone. Do not send the password in an email, and make sure you have some way of verifying that the person you are resetting the password for is actually that individual and not an AI deepfake or an elite Tasmanian hacker impersonating Mavis from accounting.

You can also reset a user's password through PowerShell using the `Set-MsolUserPassword` cmdlet with this syntax:

```
Set-MsolUserPassword -UserPrincipalName <UPN> -NewPassword <NewPassword>
-ForceChangePassword $True
```

> **MORE INFO** **RESET USER PASSWORDS**
>
> You can learn more about resetting Microsoft 365 user passwords at *https://docs.microsoft. com/en-us/microsoft-365/admin/add-users/reset-passwords*.

Skill 4.3: Microsoft Entra ID Password Protection

Microsoft Entra ID Password Protection allows you to block users from using a set of known passwords. A challenge for many organizations is that most users aren't particularly creative when constructing passwords, so the chances that someone in your organization is using one of the most popular known passwords is relatively high.

> **This section covers the following topics:**
> - Configuring banned password lists
> - Microsoft Entra ID Smart Lockout

Configure banned password lists

Microsoft Entra ID also uses a global banned password list that will restrict users in your organization from using a commonly used password. Another aspect of managing authentication is implementing a custom banned password list. A user in your organization cannot use any password on the banned password list. You can only implement a custom banned password list if your organization has a Microsoft Entra ID P1 or P2 license. Common character substitution within banned passwords is enabled by default.

There are multiple lists of commonly used passwords that you can download free from the internet and add to the Microsoft Entra ID banned password list to prevent users from using them. You can also import lists of all passwords exposed in data breaches to ensure that users cannot use those passwords.

> **MORE INFO** **MICROSOFT ENTRA ID PASSWORD PROTECTION**
>
> You can learn more about Microsoft Entra ID Password Protection at *https://learn.microsoft.com/azure/active-directory/authentication/concept-password-ban-bad*.

Microsoft Entra ID Smart Lockout

The Microsoft Entra ID Smart Lockout technology enables you to lock out attackers trying to brute-force user passwords. Based on machine learning, Smart Lockout can discern when sign-ins are coming from authentic users and treat those sign-ins differently from those that appear to come from attackers or other unknown sources.

Smart Lockout locks out an account for 60 seconds after 10 failed sign-in attempts. If subsequent failed sign-in attempts occur after the 60 seconds expire, the duration of the lockout period increases. Smart Lockout tracks only when different passwords are used, which is the pattern during a brute-force attack, so if a user enters the same incorrect password 10 times, that will only count as one bad password toward the 10 that trigger account lockout.

Microsoft Entra ID Smart Lockout is enabled by default on Microsoft 365 Entra ID tenancies. You can configure a custom Smart Lockout threshold in the Microsoft Entra admin center's Authentication Methods section.

> **MORE INFO** **MICROSOFT ENTRA ID SMART LOCKOUT**
>
> You can learn more about Microsoft Entra ID Smart Lockout at *https://learn.microsoft.com/azure/active-directory/authentication/howto-password-smart-lockout*.

Skill 4.4: Multifactor authentication (MFA)

MFA requires that a person use multiple authentication methods when signing in to a resource. Today, this mostly involves being prompted by a specially configured authenticator app after performing the initial sign-in, but other methods are available.

This section covers the following topics:

- Enable MFA
- Administer MFA users
- Account lockout
- Block/unblock users
- Fraud alert settings
- OATH tokens
- Phone call settings
- Report MFA utilization

Enable MFA

When users perform multifactor authentication, the user usually provides their username and password credentials and then provides one of the following:

- **A code generated by an authenticator app**   This can be the Microsoft Authenticator app or a third-party authenticator app, such as the Google Authenticator app.
- **A response provided to the Microsoft Authenticator app**   When this method is used, Microsoft Entra ID provides an on-screen code to the user authenticating the app; this code must also be selected on an application registered with Microsoft Entra ID.
- **A phone call to a number registered with Microsoft Entra ID**   The user needs to provide a preconfigured PIN that they will be instructed to enter by the automated service that performs the phone call. Microsoft provides a default greeting during authentication phone calls, so you don't have to record one for your organization.
- **An SMS message sent to a mobile phone number registered with Microsoft Entra ID**   The user provides the code sent in the message as a second factor during authentication.

When designing your solution, you'll need to ensure that users can access the appropriate MFA technology. This might require you to come up with a method of ensuring that all users in your organization already have the Microsoft Authenticator app installed on their mobile devices before you enable MFA on their accounts.

> ***MORE INFO*** **PLAN FOR MULTIFACTOR AUTHENTICATION**
>
> **You can learn more about designing a multifactor authentication solution for Microsoft 365 deployments at *https://learn.microsoft.com/en-us/microsoft-365/admin/security-and-compliance/multi-factor-authentication-microsoft-365*.**

To enable MFA on a Microsoft Entra ID tenancy and configure MFA for specific users, perform the following steps:

1. In the **Microsoft Entra ID** area of the Azure portal, navigate to **Users** and then click **All Users**.
2. **Click More** > **Multifactor Authentication**.
3. After selecting this option, MFA will be enabled for the tenancy, and you'll be provided with a list of users similar to that shown in Figure 4-8.

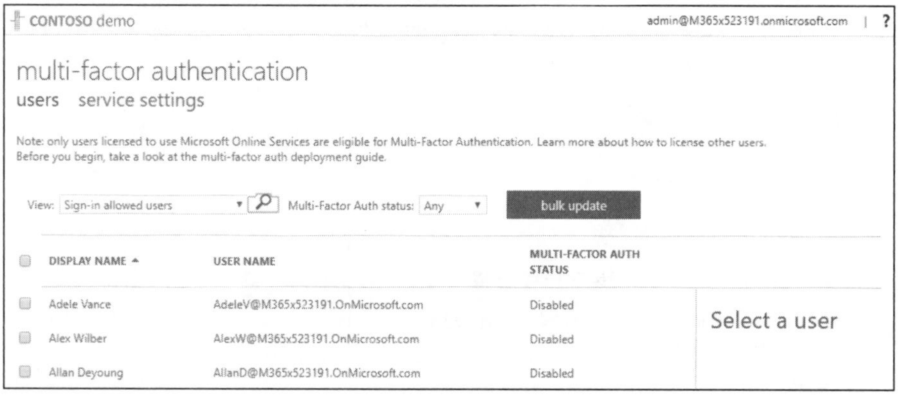

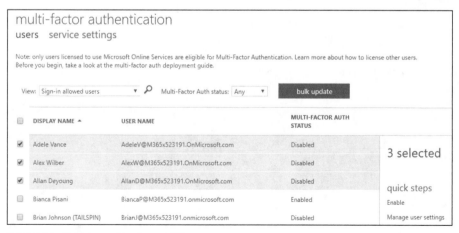

FIGURE 4-8 Set up users for Azure MFA

4. Select the users you want to set up for MFA, as shown in Figure 4-9, and then click **Enable**.

FIGURE 4-9 Select users for Azure MFA

5. On the **About Enabling Multi-Factor Auth** dialog shown in Figure 4-10, click **Enable Multi-Factor Auth**.

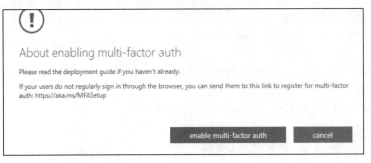

FIGURE 4-10 Enabling multifactor authorization

6. The next time users sign in, they will be prompted to enroll in multifactor authentication and will be presented with a dialog similar to that shown in Figure 4-11, asking them to provide additional information.

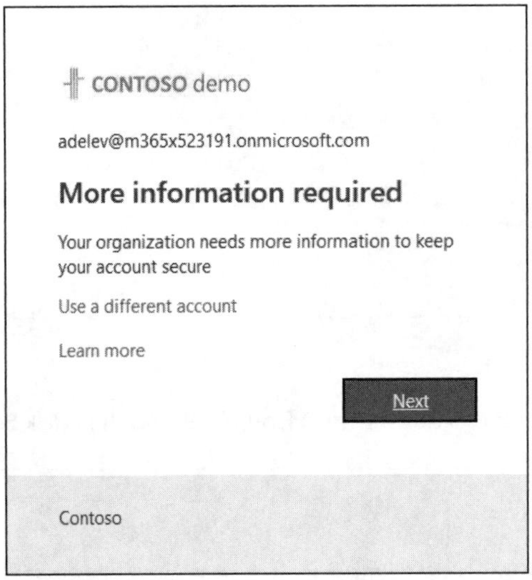

‖ **CONTOSO** demo

adelev@m365x523191.onmicrosoft.com

More information required

Your organization needs more information to keep your account secure

Use a different account

Learn more

Next

Contoso

FIGURE 4-11 More information required

7. Choose between providing a mobile phone number or an office phone number or configuring a mobile app using the dropdown option shown in Figure 4-12.

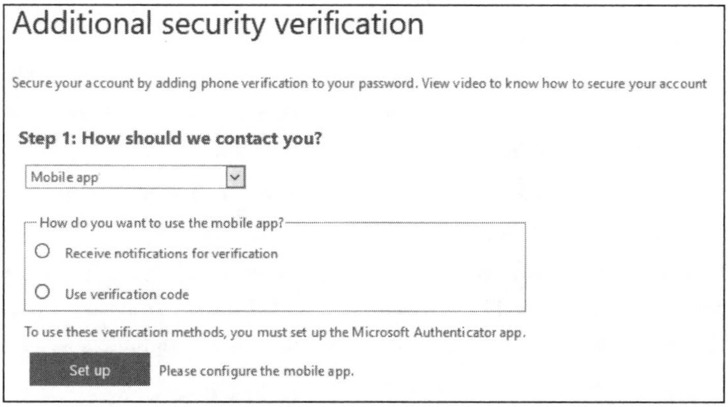

Additional security verification

Secure your account by adding phone verification to your password. View video to know how to secure your account

Step 1: How should we contact you?

| Mobile app | ∨ |

How do you want to use the mobile app?

○ Receive notifications for verification

○ Use verification code

To use these verification methods, you must set up the Microsoft Authenticator app.

| Set up | Please configure the mobile app.

FIGURE 4-12 Contact preferences

8. When you specify one of these options, you are presented with a QR code. You can add a new account within the app by scanning the QR code. Once you have configured the application, you must confirm that the configuration has been completed successfully by approving a sign-in through the app, as shown in Figure 4-13.

Approve sign-in?

Contoso
AdeleV@M365x523191.OnMicrosoft
.com

DENY   APPROVE

FIGURE 4-13 Verify on the app

9. Once this is done, you'll be prompted to provide additional security information in the form of a phone number, as shown in Figure 4-14.

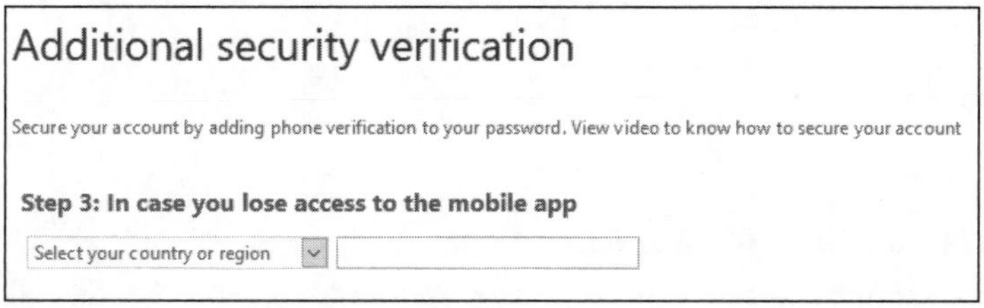

Additional security verification

Secure your account by adding phone verification to your password. View video to know how to secure your account

Step 3: In case you lose access to the mobile app

| Select your country or region | ∨ | |

FIGURE 4-14 Verify on the app

You can configure the following multifactor authentication service settings, as shown in Figure 4-15.

- **App Passwords** Allow or disallow users from using app passwords for non-browser apps that do not support multifactor authentication.

- **Trusted IP Addresses** Configure a list of trusted IP addresses where MFA will be skipped when federation is configured between the on-premises environment and the Microsoft 365 Microsoft Entra ID tenancy.

- **Verification Options** Specify which verification options are available to users, including phone calls, text messages, app-based verification, or hardware token.

- **Remember Multi-Factor Authentication** Decide whether to allow users to have MFA authentication remembered for a specific period of time on a device so that MFA does not need to be performed each time the user signs on. The default is 14 days.

multi-factor authentication
users   service settings

app passwords (learn more)

○ Allow users to create app passwords to sign in to non-browser apps
○ Do not allow users to create app passwords to sign in to non-browser apps

trusted ips (learn more)

☐ Skip multi-factor authentication for requests from federated users on my intranet
Skip multi-factor authentication for requests from following range of IP address subnets

192.168.1.0/27
192.168.1.0/27
192.168.1.0/27

verification options (learn more)

Methods available to users:
☑ Call to phone
☑ Text message to phone
☑ Notification through mobile app
☑ Verification code from mobile app or hardware token

remember multi-factor authentication (learn more)

☐ Allow users to remember multi-factor authentication on devices they trust
Days before a device must re-authenticate (1-60): 14

FIGURE 4-15 MFA service settings

MORE INFO **SET UP MULTIFACTOR AUTHENTICATION**

You can learn more about multifactor authentication at *https://learn.microsoft.com/azure/active-directory/authentication/concept-mfa-howitworks*.

Administer MFA users

Once you configure MFA for users, there might be certain times when you want to force users to provide updated contact methods, you might want to revoke all app passwords, or you might want to revoke MFA on all remembered devices. You can do this by performing the following steps:

1. With an account assigned the Global Administrator role, open the Microsoft Entra admin center and select the **All Users** node. Select the user to manage MFA.

2. On the user's properties page, select **Authentication Methods**.

3. On the **Authentication Methods** page, select the action to be performed. You can choose between **Require MFA-Reregistration** or **Revoke MFA Sessions**.

> **MORE INFO** **SETTING UP MULTIFACTOR AUTHENTICATION**
>
> You can learn more about setting up multifactor authentication at *https://learn.microsoft.com/azure/active-directory/authentication/concept-system-preferred-multifactor-authentication*.

Account lockout

Account lockout settings for MFA, shown in Figure 4-16, allow you to configure the conditions under which MFA lockout will occur. On this page, you can configure the number of MFA denials triggering the account lockout process, how long before the account lockout counter is reset, and the number of minutes until the account is unblocked. For example, if the account lockout counter is reset after 10 minutes, and the number of MFA denials to trigger account lockout is set to 5, then 5 denials in 10 minutes will trigger a lockout. However, 5 denials over 30 minutes would not trigger a lockout because the account lockout counter would reset during that period.

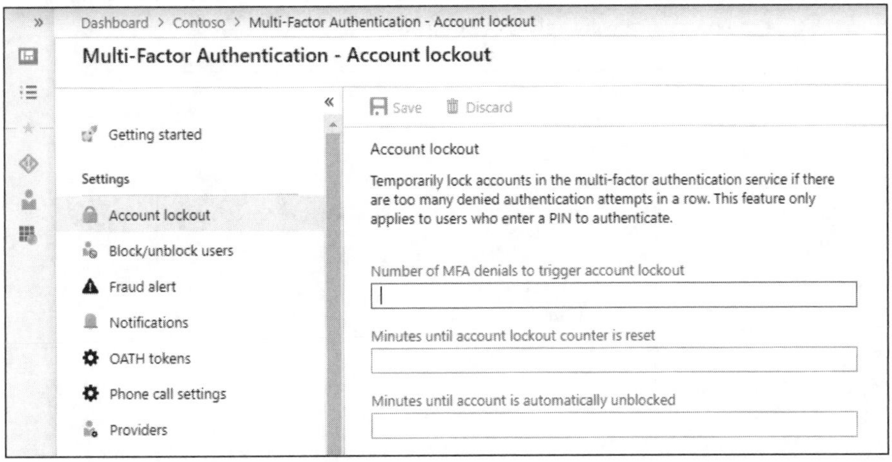

FIGURE 4-16 Account lockout settings

Block/unblock users

The Block/Unblock Users page setting shown in Figure 4-17 allows you to block specific users of an on-premises MFA server from being able to receive an MFA request. Any requests sent to a user on the blocked-users list will automatically be denied. Users on this list remain blocked for 90 days, after which they are removed from the blocked-users list. To unblock a blocked user, click **Unblock**.

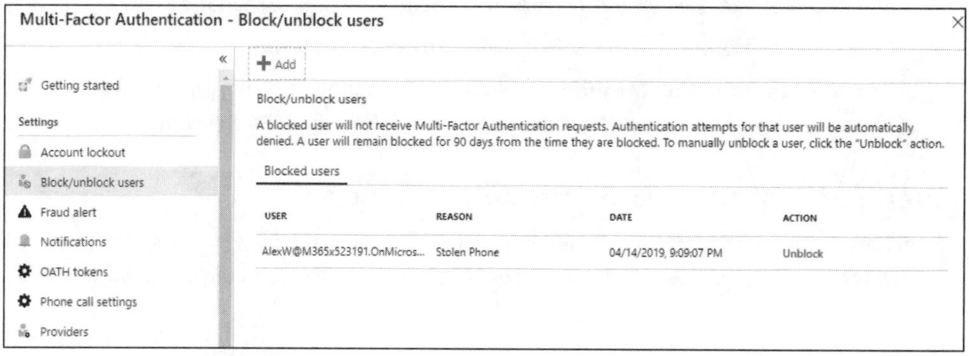

FIGURE 4-17   Block/Unblock Users

Fraud alert settings

Figure 4-18 shows that fraud alert settings allow you to configure whether users can report fraudulent verification requests. A fraudulent verification request might occur when an attacker has access to a user's password but does not have access to an alternative MFA method. Users become aware of this by receiving an MFA prompt through their app, an SMS, or a phone call when they haven't attempted to authenticate against a Microsoft 365 workload. When a user reports fraud, you can choose to have their account automatically blocked for 90 days, which indicates that the password will likely be compromised.

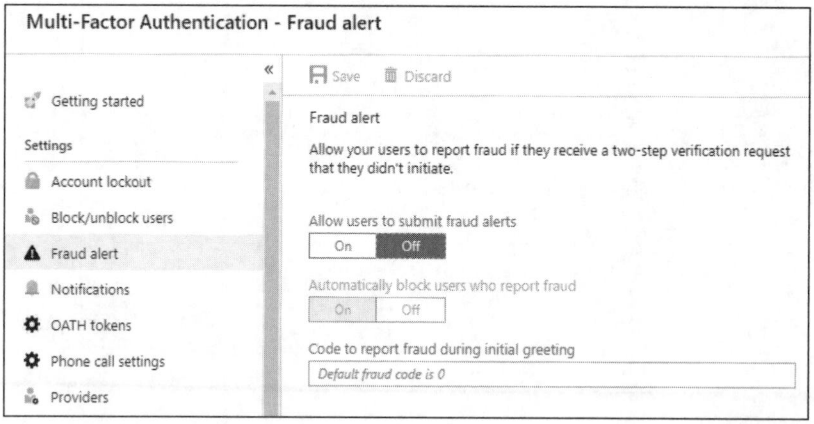

FIGURE 4-18   Fraud alert

OATH tokens

The OATH Tokens page shown in Figure 4-19 allows you to upload a specially formatted CSV file containing the details and keys of the OATH tokens you want to use for multifactor authentication. The specially formatted CSV file should include a formatted header row, as shown here, with the **UPN** (user principal name), **Serial Number**, **Secret Key**, **Time Interval**, **Manufacturer**, and **Model**. Each file is associated with a specific user. If a user has multiple OATH tokens, these should be included in the file associated with their account.

FIGURE 4-19   OATH tokens

Phone call settings

Phone call settings allow you to configure the caller ID number displayed when the user is contacted for MFA authentication. This number must be a United States number. You can also configure custom voice messages using the Phone Call Settings page shown in Figure 4-20. The voice messages must be in .wav or .mp3 format, must be no larger than 5 MB, and should be shorter than 20 seconds.

FIGURE 4-20   Phone Call Settings

Report MFA utilization

Azure MFA provides several reports that you can use to understand how MFA is being used in your organization, including:

- **Blocked User History** Provides a history of requests to block or unblock users.
- **Usage And Fraud Alerts** Provides information on a history of fraud alerts submitted by users. Also, this report provides information on the overall MFA usage.
- **Usage For On-Premises Components** Provides information on the utilization of MFA through the Network Policy Server extension, Active Directory Federation Services, and on-premises MFA server.
- **Bypassed User History** Provides information on requests to bypass MFA by a specific user.
- **Server Status** Provides status data of MFA servers associated with your organization's Microsoft Entra ID tenancy.

EXAM TIP

Remember the steps to automatically lock out users who incorrectly answer MFA prompts.

Skill 4.5: Self-service password reset

Self-service password reset is challenging to deploy in an on-premises environment but relatively straightforward to deploy in an environment that uses Microsoft Entra ID as a source of identity authority. A self-service password reset allows users to reset their passwords when they forget them rather than contacting the service desk and having an IT staff member perform the task for them.

Password reset registration

As you can see in Figure 4-21, you can configure self-service password reset so that users must sign up for the service when they first authenticate and then periodically renew their information, with the default renewal period being every 180 days.

FIGURE 4-21 The Password Reset – Registration blade

You can require users to provide multiple forms of authentication when performing a self-service password reset. When a user signs up for self-service password reset, they can configure the following alternate methods of authentication:

- Mobile app notification
- Mobile app code
- Email
- Mobile phone
- Office phone
- Security questions

> **MORE INFO**   **CONFIGURE SELF-SERVICE PASSWORD RESET**
>
> You can learn more about configuring self-service password reset at *https://learn.microsoft. com/azure/active-directory/authentication/tutorial-enable-sspr.*

Enable self-service password reset

To enable self-service password reset, perform the following steps:

1. In the **Microsoft Entra admin center**, select the **All Users** node and then select **Password Reset**.

2. On the **Password Reset – Properties** page, select **All**, as shown in Figure 4-22, to enable the self-service password reset for all Microsoft 365 users.

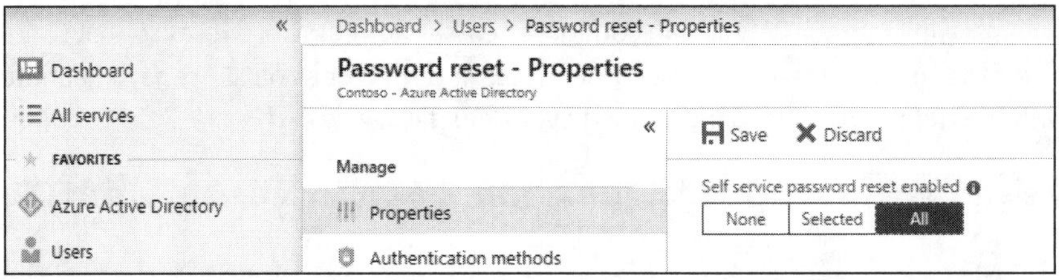

FIGURE 4-22   Enabling self-service password reset

Once self-service password reset is enabled, users will be prompted for additional information the next time they sign in, which will be used to verify their identity if they use the self-service password reset tool. Users can reset their passwords by navigating to the website at *https://passwordreset.microsoftonline.com* shown in Figure 4-23 and completing the form.

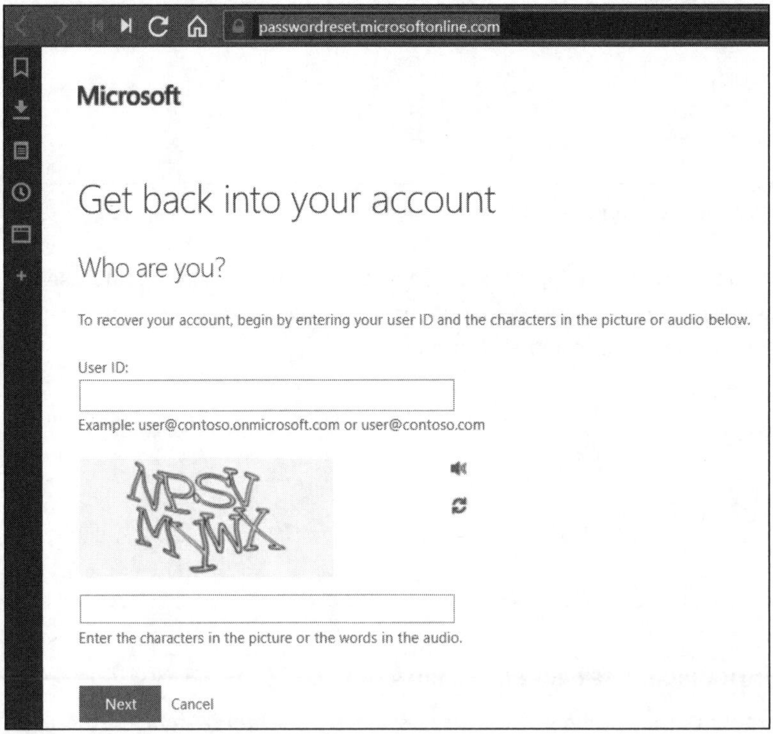

FIGURE 4-23   Resetting a password

Skill 4.6: Microsoft Entra ID Identity Protection

Microsoft Entra ID Identity Protection allows you to automate the detection and remediation of identity-based risks, including the following:

- **Atypical travel**   When a user's account sign-in indicates they have performed unusual shifts in location. This could include a user signing in from Sydney and then Los Angeles in a two-hour period when the flight between the two cities takes about seven times that amount of time.

- **Anonymous IP address**   When a user signs in from an anonymous IP address. While users might use an anonymizing VPN to access organizational resources, attackers also use tools such as TOR nodes to launch compromise attempts.

- **Unfamiliar sign-in properties**   When a user's sign-in properties differ substantially from those observed in the past.

- **Malware-linked IP address**   When the IP address the user is signing in from is known to be part of a malware botnet or has exhibited other malicious network activity in the past.

- **Leaked credentials**   When the user's credentials have been discovered in a data breach, such as those recorded on haveibeenpwned.com.

- **Microsoft Entra ID threat intelligence**   When the sign-in behavior correlates with known attack patterns identified by Microsoft's internal or external threat intelligence sources.

Enabling Microsoft Entra ID Identity Protection requires a Microsoft Entra ID P2 license.

Microsoft Entra ID Identity Protection allows you to configure two types of risk policy: a sign-in risk policy and a user-risk policy:

- **Sign-in risk**   These policies analyze signals from each sign-in and determine how likely the person associated with the user account did not perform the sign-in. If a sign-in is determined to be risky, administrators can specify whether to block access or allow access but require multifactor authentication.

- **User-risk**   These policies are based on identifying deviations from the user's normal behavior, such as the user signing in from an unusual location at a time that substantially differs from when they usually sign in. User risk policies allow administrators to block access, allow access, or allow access but require a password change when the policy is triggered.

To enable user risk and sign-in risk policies, perform the following steps:

1. In the **Microsoft Entra admin center**, select **Protection**, then select **Risky Activities**, select **Identity Protection**, and then select select **User Risk Policy**.

2. On the **User Risk Remediation Policy** blade, shown in Figure 4-24, configure the following settings:

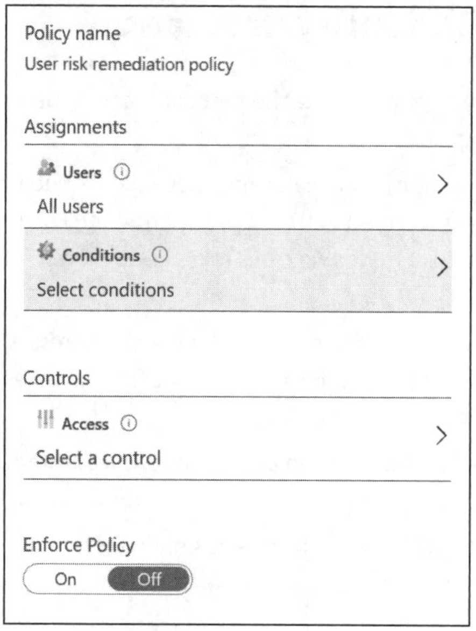

FIGURE 4-24   User Risk Remediation Policy

- **Assignments**   Determines which users the user risk remediation policy applies to.
- **Conditions**   Allows you to determine at which risk level the policy applies. You can choose between **Low And Above**, **Medium And Above**, or **High**.
- **Controls**   Access level for a user risk policy. You can choose between **Block**, **Allow**, and **Allow And Require Password Change**.
- **Enforce Policy**   The policy can be switched **On** or **Off**.

3. Click **Sign-In Risk Policy**. On the **Sign-In Risk Remediation Policy** blade, configure the following settings and click **Save**:

- **Assignments**   Determines which users the user risk remediation policy applies to.
- **Conditions**   Allows you to determine at which risk level the policy applies. You can choose between **Low And Above**, **Medium And Above**, or **High**.
- **Controls**   Access for a user risk policy. You can choose between **Block**, **Allow**, and **Allow And Require Multi-Factor Authentication**.
- **Enforce Policy**   The policy can be switched **On** or **Off**.

Skill 4.7: Conditional access policies

Microsoft Entra ID conditional access uses the properties of a user account, device, and location to determine what access a user will have to organizational resources. For example, you can configure conditional access to require a user to perform multifactor authentication if they are accessing a sensitive application from an unusual location or to block a user from access if they are not using a Microsoft Entra ID hybrid–joined computer.

This section covers the following topics:

- Preparing for conditional access
- Create a conditional access policy
- What If tool

Preparing for conditional access

When designing a conditional access solution, take the following steps into account:

- **Engage the right stakeholders**   Rather than enabling conditional access for everyone on a whim, determine which stakeholders within your organization you should consult with when it comes to planning conditional access. The stakeholders' needs will determine your approach to conditional access. For example, you might not be able to implement multifactor authentication as a part of a conditional access policy if stakeholders have concerns about requiring users to all have devices capable of responding to multifactor authentication challenges.

- **Plan communications**   When shifting to a conditional access posture, it will be necessary to explain to users why they may be required to perform multifactor authentication to access some resources and why they may be blocked from access at other times. New security procedures are far less likely to encounter resistance from users if they are explained before implementation rather than justified in an apologetic email sent from the IT department after enough complaints have reached the service desk.

- **Plan a pilot**   When you've decided on the details of the conditional access policies you want to implement, conduct a pilot where you apply those policies to a subset of users and solicit their feedback. Vocal users are the best ones to include in a pilot because they won't be shy about providing feedback. Also, consider including the users who contact the service desk most often because they are the most likely group to encounter problems when conditional access policies are deployed organization-wide.

Figure 4-25 shows that conditional access policies use assignments and access controls. Assignments are the conditions that determine when the policy will apply—for example, which users are included, which applications or actions are relevant, and which conditions will trigger the policy. Access controls specify what occurs when conditions are met.

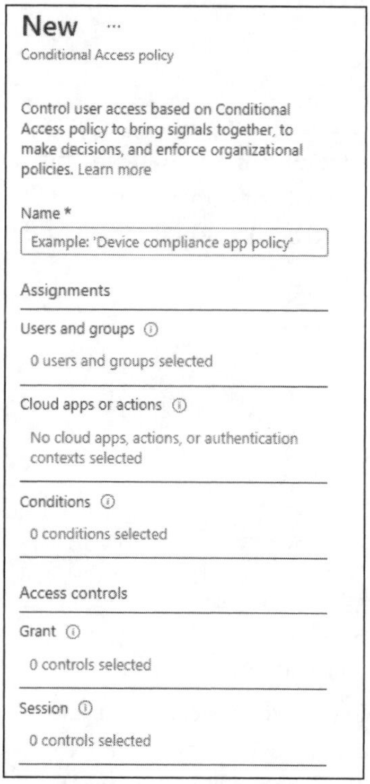

FIGURE 4-25 Conditional Access Policy assignments

Conditional access policies allow you to require additional steps to be taken when a certain set of circumstances occur. For example, you could configure a conditional access policy to require MFA to occur if a user attempts to access a specific resource in Azure or if a user is accessing Azure from an unusual location. Conditional access policies can also be used to block access to Azure resources when certain conditions are met, such as when someone attempts to access an application from a region where IP address ranges have been blocked.

Conditional access policies will only be enforced after the first-factor authentication has been completed. Conditional access policies require a Microsoft Entra ID P2 or equivalent subscription. Commonly used conditional access policies include:

- Require MFA for all users with administrative roles
- Require MFA before performing Azure management tasks

- Block sign-ins for legacy authentication protocols
- Require a trusted location when registering for Azure MFA
- Block access from specific locations
- Require organization-managed devices for certain applications

Conditional access policies can be applied based on user circumstances that include (but are not limited to) the following:

- **IP address location**   An administrator can designate certain IP address ranges as trusted, such as the public IP addresses associated with the organization's internet gateway devices. Administrators can also specify regional IP address ranges as being blocked from access, such as those belonging to people trying to access resources from Tasmania.
- **Device**   Whether the user attempts to access Microsoft Entra ID resources from a trusted device or a new untrusted device.
- **Application**   Whether the user attempts to access a specific Microsoft Entra ID application.
- **Group membership**   Whether the user is a member of a specific group.

In addition to the simple option to block access, conditional access policies can be configured to:

- Require multifactor authentication
- Require a device to be marked as compliant
- Require the device to be Hybrid Microsoft Entra ID joined
- Require an approved client app
- Require an app protection policy

> *MORE INFO*   **DESIGN CONDITIONAL ACCESS**
>
> You can learn more about designing conditional access at *https://learn.microsoft.com/azure/active-directory/conditional-access/plan-conditional-access*.

Create a conditional access policy

To create a conditional access policy, perform the following steps:

1.   In the **Microsoft Entra admin center**, select **Protection**, and then select **Conditional Access**.
2.   On the **Conditional Access | Overview** page, select **Create New Policy**.

3. On the **New Conditional Access Policy** page, provide the following information:

- **Name**   A name for the conditional access policy.
- **Users And Groups**   Users and groups the policy applies to.
- **Cloud Apps Or Actions**   Which cloud apps or user actions the policy applies to. Policies can apply to some or all cloud apps. You can also specify specific user actions that will trigger the conditional access policy, such as attempting to access a specific Azure resource (such as a virtual machine).
- **Conditions**   The conditions associated with the policy: user risk, sign-in risk, device platforms, locations, client apps, and device state.
- **Access Controls**   Select which additional controls are required to grant access. This allows you to require MFA, a compliant device, a Hybrid Microsoft Entra ID joined device, an approved client app, an app protection policy, or that the user performs a password change.
- **Session**   Allows you to specify the behavior of specific cloud applications. Options include **Conditional Access App Control**, **Sign-In Frequency**, and **Persistent Browser Session**.
- **Enable Policy**   Can be set to **Report Only**, which you should use to determine how the policy will function before enforcing, enabling, or disabling it.

4. Click **Create** to create the policy.

> **MORE INFO**   **CONDITIONAL ACCESS POLICIES**
>
> You can learn more about conditional access policies at *https://learn.microsoft.com/azure/active-directory/conditional-access/overview*.

What If tool

You can use the conditional access What If tool to determine how conditional access policies will function without implementing the policies on a pilot group of users. To run the What If tool, perform the following steps:

1. In the **Microsoft Entra admin center**, select **Protection**, and then select **Conditional Access**.
2. In the left pane of the **Conditional Access** page, select **Policies**.
3. On the **Policies** page, select **What If**.

4. In the **What If** pane, configure the following settings, and then select **What If** to view the simulated results of applying the policy.

- **User**   Select a user for which to run the What If tool. You can select only one user at a time.

- **Cloud Apps, Actions, Or Authentication Context**   By default, all cloud apps are selected, but you can choose a specific cloud app when attempting to ascertain how conditional access policies will mediate access.

- **IP Address**   Enables you to specify a public IPv4 address to simulate location conditions.

- **Country**   Instead of specifying a specific public IPv4 address, you can specify a country.

- **Device Platform**   Enables you to specify the device platform being used. Options include **Android**, **iOS**, **Windows**, and **macOS**.

- **Client Apps**   The default settings will evaluate for browser, mobile apps, and desktop clients, but you can limit it to any or all of these options.

- **Device State**   Enables you to specify whether the device is hybrid AD joined or marked as compliant.

- **Sign-In Risk**   Here, you can specify the sign-in risk level you want to evaluate.

- **User Risk**   Enables you to specify the user risk level you want to evaluate.

After selecting **What If**, you'll be informed which policies do and do not apply to the user. The set of relevant controls is listed for all the policies that do apply to the user. For all the policies that do not apply, there is a list of reasons why the conditions of that policy were not triggered.

> *MORE INFO*   **WHAT IF TOOL**
>
> You can learn more about the conditional access What If tool at *https://learn.microsoft.com/azure/active-directory/conditional-access/what-if-tool*.

EXAM TIP

Remember the licensing requirement of conditional access policies.

Skill 4.8: Resolving authentication issues

Beyond telling a user they've probably entered the wrong password, resolving authentication issues often involves checking existing telemetry, such as audit and sign-in logs, to determine what activity has occurred. Checking these will also allow you to determine whether the authentication issue is specific to one clever user or whether the issues are more widely spread.

> **This section covers the following topics:**
> - Audit logs
> - Sign-in event logs
> - Self-service password reset activity

Audit logs

Several methods allow you to monitor authentication for your organization's Microsoft 365 tenancy. Microsoft Entra ID's reporting architecture includes the following elements:

- **Sign-ins**   Provides you with information about user sign-in activity and the use of managed applications
- **Audit logs**   Enables you to view information about changes that have occurred within Microsoft Entra ID, such as adding or removing user accounts
- **Risky sign-ins**   Provides you with data about sign-in activity that has been flagged as suspicious by Microsoft's security mechanisms
- **Users flagged for risk**   Provides you with a list of users that Microsoft's security mechanisms suggest might have compromised accounts

Users who have been assigned the global administrator, security administrator, security reader, or report reader Microsoft Entra ID role can view data in Microsoft Entra ID reports. Users without membership in these roles can view audit activities related to their accounts.

Each event recorded in the audit logs provides the following data:

- Data and time of the event
- Service that logged the event
- Name and category of the event logged
- Activity status (success or failure)
- The target of the action (which user, group, and so on)
- Which security principal initiated the action

You can filter audit logs using the following fields:

- Service
- Category
- Activity
- Status
- Target
- Initiated by (Actor)
- Date Range

> **MORE INFO** **AUDIT ACTIVITY REPORTS**
>
> You can learn more about audit activity reports at *https://learn.microsoft.com/azure/*
> *active-directory/reports-monitoring/concept-audit-logs*.

Sign-in event logs

Sign-in event logs provide user information and managed application authentication activity.
Figure 4-26 shows the basic sign-in events log.

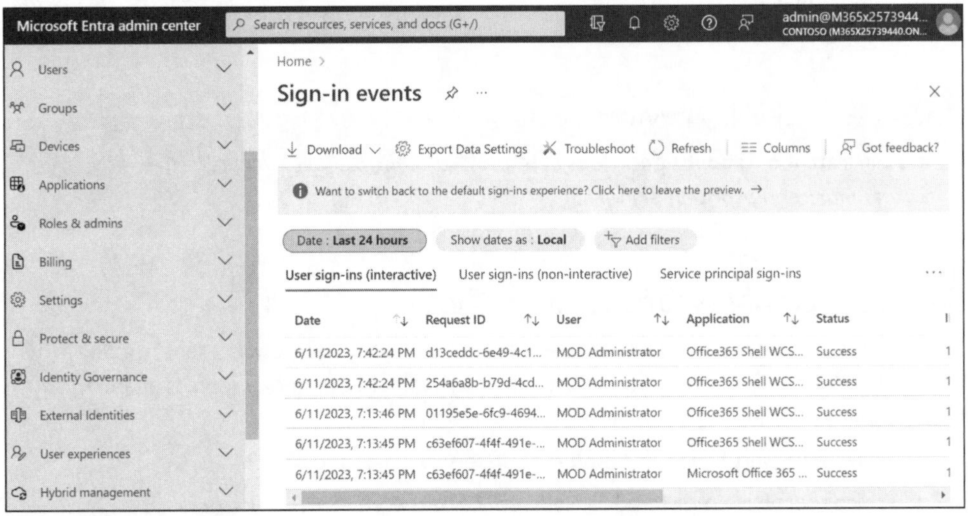

FIGURE 4-26 Sign-in log

This log enables you to answer the following questions:

- What patterns are present in a user's sign-in activities?
- How many users associated with the Microsoft 365 tenancy have signed in over the last week?
- How many sign-ins have been successful, and how many have failed?

The sign-in log provides the following information by default:

- Sign-in date
- User account
- Application the user has authenticated against
- Sign-in status (success or failure)
- Risk-detection status
- Multifactor authentication status

The following fields can filter the sign-in log.

- User
- Application
- Status
- Conditional Access
- Date

> **MORE INFO** **SIGN-IN ACTIVITY REPORTS**
>
> You can learn more about sign-in logs at *https://learn.microsoft.com/azure/active-directory/ reports-monitoring/concept-sign-ins.*

Self-service password reset activity

You can view the self-service password reset events in the audit log under Identity in the Microsoft Entra admin center. You can use the Activity filter to generate reports enabling you to determine the following information:

- How many users have registered for self-service password reset?
- Which users have registered for self-service password reset?
- What information are users providing when registering for self-service password reset?
- How many users reset their passwords using self-service password reset in the previous seven days?
- What methods are being used for authentication when performing self-service password reset?

- Is there any suspicious activity occurring during the self-service password reset process?
- Which authentication methods generate the most problems during the self-service password reset process?

> **MORE INFO   SELF-SERVICE PASSWORD RESET REPORTS**
>
> You can learn more about self-service password reset reports at *https://learn.microsoft.com/ azure/active-directory/authentication/howto-sspr-reporting*.

Chapter summary

- Modern authentication supports technologies such as multifactor authentication, smart card authentication, certificate-based authentication, and SAML-based third-party identity providers.
- Microsoft 365 supports a variety of authentication methods for self-service password reset and MFA, including passwords, security questions, email addresses, the Microsoft Authenticator app, OATH hardware tokens, SMS, voice calls, and app passwords.
- When configuring self-service password reset, enable multiple authentication methods and require two separate authentication methods to be used before allowing password reset.
- Smart Lockout is a technology that enables you to lock out attackers trying to brute-force user passwords.
- A user in your organization cannot use any password on the Azure custom banned list.
- Certificate-based authentication is supported for Federated environments where Microsoft Entra ID trusts an organizational CA, and the CRL is published in an internet-accessible location.
- Microsoft Entra ID's reporting architecture enables you to monitor sign-ins, risky sign-ins, users flagged for risk, and Azure administrator activity.
- Multifactor authentication methods include phone calls, text messages, notifications through mobile apps, or verification codes from mobile apps or hardware tokens.

Thought experiment

In this thought experiment, demonstrate your skills and knowledge of the topics covered in this chapter. You can find answers to this thought experiment in the next section.

You are the Microsoft 365 administrator for Tailwind Traders. You are currently in the process of configuring authentication and authorization. You can access a list of the 100 passwords most commonly seen in data breaches. You want to ensure your organization's users do not use any of these passwords. You also want to empower users who forget their password to resolve the problem themselves.

After several account compromise events in the past, you want to get an idea of which users are most likely to have compromised accounts. Similarly, users who receive 2FA notifications on their Microsoft Authenticator app should have a way of reporting this event so that your team can investigate.

Your final task in managing authentication and authorization involves an on-premises accounting application. You want users who are signed into Microsoft 365 to be able to access this application using their Microsoft 365 credentials without requiring them to reauthenticate.

With this information in mind, answer the following questions:

1. Which Microsoft Entra ID authentication feature can you use to ensure that users do not use passwords on the list of 100 most commonly used passwords?

2. How can you ensure users regain access to Microsoft 365 workloads if they forget their password without contacting the service desk?

3. Which report should you consult to determine whether a user will likely have a compromised account?

4. Which MFA feature should you enable so users can report suspicious MFA notifications?

Thought experiment answers

This section contains the solution to the thought experiment. Each answer explains why the answer choice is correct.

1. Populate and enable the Microsoft Entra ID custom banned passwords list with the passwords on the 100 most commonly used list.

2. Configure self-service password reset. This feature must be enabled, and the user or group should be included in the scope of the feature.

3. Consult the users flagged for risk reports to determine which users will likely have compromised accounts.

4. Enable the fraud alert option to allow users to notify you if they receive notifications for authorization on their Microsoft Authenticator app when they haven't attempted authentication.

CHAPTER 5

Manage security and threats using Microsoft 365 Defender

Microsoft 365 Defender allows you to manage the security of your Microsoft 365 workloads and the security of client devices onboarded to your organization's tenancy. This chapter teaches you how to assess your tenancy security posture and manage incidents, alerts, and threats. You'll also learn how to protect collaboration through email, Microsoft Teams, and SharePoint and configure client protection through Endpoint protection functionality.

Topics in this chapter:

- Skill 5.1: Security reports and alerts
- Skill 5.2: Collaboration protection
- Skill 5.3: Endpoint protection

Skill 5.1: Security reports and alerts

Security reports and alerts allow you to quickly ascertain the strength of your organization's Microsoft 365 security posture and the threats against your tenancy and devices to which you should pay attention.

> **This section covers the following skills:**
> - Secure Score
> - Incidents
> - Alerts
> - Threat analytics

Secure Score

Microsoft Secure Score provides a numerical score against which you can assess how many recommended security measures have been implemented across your Microsoft 365 tenancy. The Secure Score is a percentage calculated by points awarded for the actions and configuration settings enabled against the points awarded for completing all possible actions you could take, given the licenses you hold. Figure 5-1 displays a hypothetical organization's Secure Score where of the total points that could be awarded for security configuration, tasks earning 76.52 percent of those points have been completed.

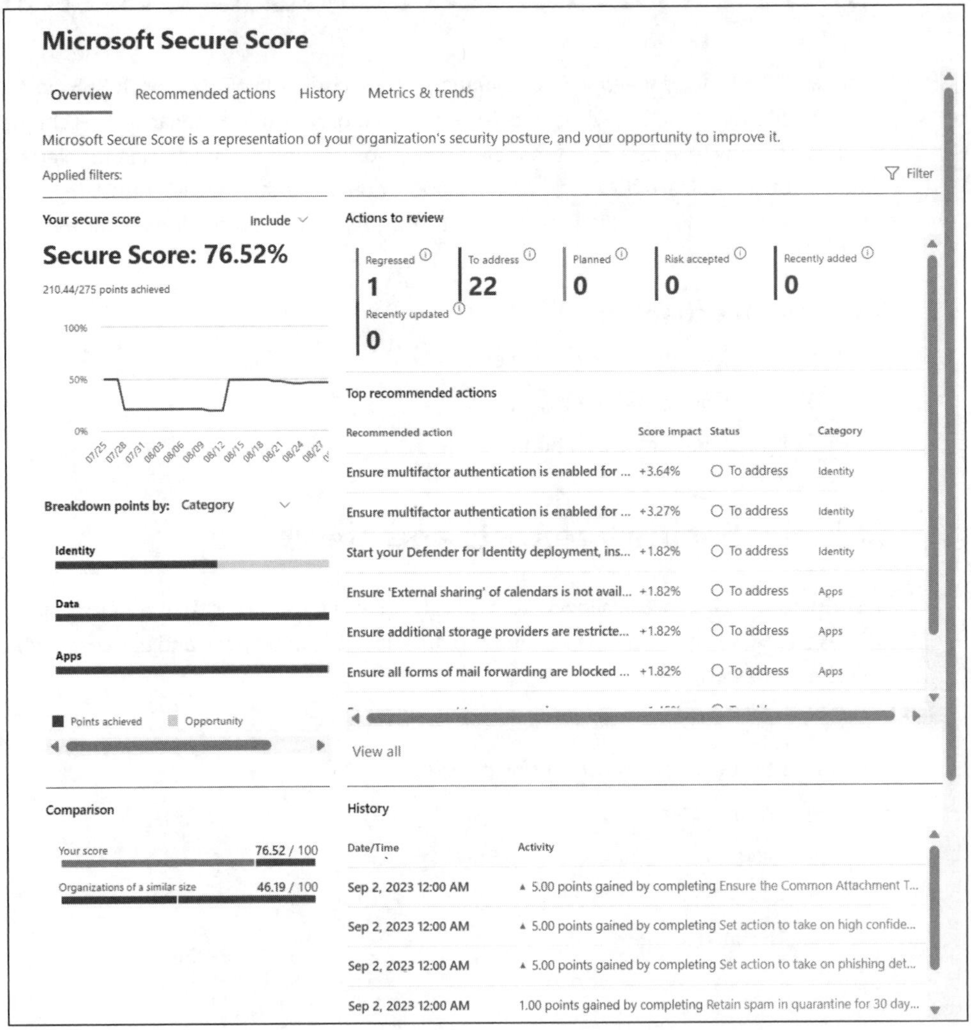

FIGURE 5-1 Microsoft Secure Score

You can increase your organization's Secure Score by performing the following tasks:

- Configuring recommended security features
- Performing security-related tasks
- Addressing the recommended action with a third-party application or software or an alternate mitigation

Each recommended action is worth a maximum of 10 points. Some recommended actions only assign points when fully completed. Some recommended actions provide partial points if they're completed for some devices or users. Recommendations will be provided for products for which you have licenses. Having licenses does not increase a Secure Score unless the recommendations related to that product are enacted. Organizations might have a different number of points that can be awarded depending on what products are licensed for that organization.

If you enable Microsoft Entra ID security defaults, your Secure Score will include points for the following activities:

- Ensure all users can complete multifactor authentication for secure access (9 points)
- Require MFA for administrative roles (10 points)
- Enable policy to block legacy authentication (7 points)

At the time of publication, Secure Score can provide recommendations for the following products with more likely to be included over time:

- App governance
- Citrix ShareFile
- Microsoft Defender for Endpoint
- Microsoft Defender for Identity
- Microsoft Defender for Office
- Microsoft Entra ID
- DocuSign
- Exchange Online
- GitHub
- Microsoft Defender for Cloud Apps
- Microsoft Information Protection
- Microsoft Teams
- Okta
- Salesforce
- ServiceNow
- SharePoint Online
- Zoom

The following Microsoft Entra ID roles have read and write access and can make changes, directly interact with Secure Score, and assign read-only access to other users:

- Global Administrator
- Security Administrator
- Exchange Administrator
- SharePoint Administrator

Recommended actions

The **Recommended Actions** tab shown in Figure 5-2 provides you with a ranked list of activities you can perform to increase your organization's Secure Score.

Microsoft Secure Score

Overview | **Recommended actions** | History | Metrics & trends

Actions you can take to improve your Microsoft Secure Score. Score updates may take up to 24 hours.

⬇ Export   70 items | 🔍 Search   ⬚ Filter   ☰ Group by ⌄

	Rank	Recommended action	Score impact	Points achieved	Status	Regressed	Have license?	Cate
☐	1	Ensure multifactor authentication is enabled for all users in adn	+3.64%	1.25/10	◯ To address	No	Yes	Ider
☐	2	Ensure multifactor authentication is enabled for all users	+3.27%	0.25/9	◯ To address	No	Yes	Ider
☐	3	Start your Defender for Identity deployment, installing Sensors	+1.82%	0/5	◯ To address	No	Yes	Ider
☐	4	Ensure 'External sharing' of calendars is not available	+1.82%	0/5	◯ To address	No	Yes	App
☐	5	Ensure additional storage providers are restricted in Outlook or	+1.82%	0/5	◯ To address	No	Yes	App
☐	6	Ensure all forms of mail forwarding are blocked and/or disablec	+1.82%	0/5	◯ To address	No	Yes	App
☐	7	Ensure user consent to apps accessing company data on their b	+1.45%	0/4	◯ To address	No	Yes	Ider
☐	8	Create an app discovery policy to identify new and trending clc	+1.09%	0/3	◯ To address	No	Yes	App
☐	9	Ensure mailbox auditing for all users is Enabled	+1.09%	0/3	◯ To address	No	Yes	App
☐	10	Ensure Exchange Online Spam Policies are set to notify adminis	+1.09%	0/3	◯ To address	No	Yes	App
☐	11	Only invited users should be automatically admitted to Teams r	+0.73%	0/2	◯ To address	Yes	Yes	App
☐	12	Configure which users are allowed to present in Teams meeting	+0.73%	0/2	◯ To address	No	Yes	App
☐	13	Enable Azure AD Identity Protection sign-in risk policies	+2.55%	5.44/7	◯ To address	No	Yes	Ider

FIGURE 5-2 Secure Score recommended actions

Selecting an item allows you to see a description of the item and provides a link to the relevant *learn.microsoft.com* documentation on how to implement the recommendation. Figure 5-3 describes the **Ensure External Sharing Of Calendars Is Not Available** security recommendation.

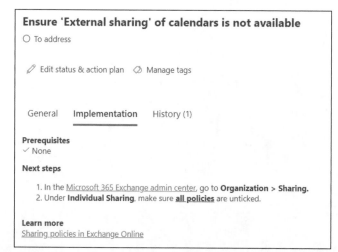

FIGURE 5-3 External sharing of calendars setting

You can choose a status and provide notes related to the action by selecting **Edit Status & Action Plan**. On this page, shown in Figure 5-4, you can provide one of the following responses:

- **To Address**   Indicate that the recommended action is necessary and plan to address it in the future. This state also applies to partially detected detected but not fully completed actions.

- **Planned**   You have specific plans in place to complete the recommended action.

- **Risk Accepted**   Instead of remediating, you can choose to accept the risk (or the remaining risk) and not enact the recommended action. Points will not be measured for this status.

- **Resolved Through Third Party** and **Resolved Through Alternate Mitigation**
  Allows you to indicate that a third-party application, software, or internal tool has already addressed the recommended action. Points will be assigned points will be assigned so that your Secure Score better reflects your overall security posture.

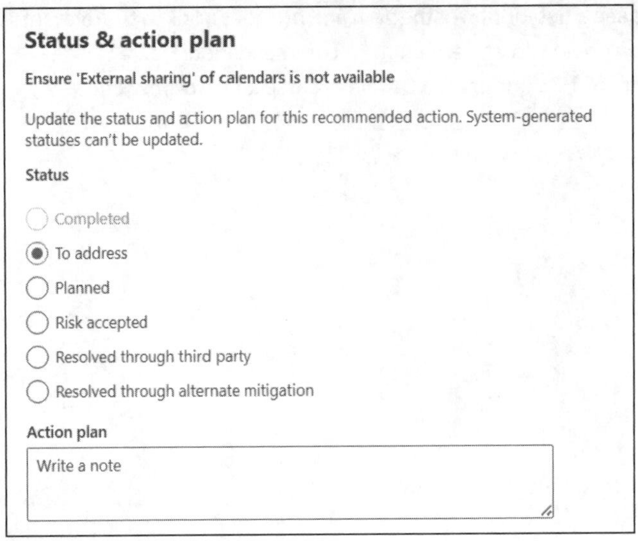

Status & action plan

Ensure 'External sharing' of calendars is not available

Update the status and action plan for this recommended action. System-generated statuses can't be updated.

Status

- ○ Completed
- ◉ To address
- ○ Planned
- ○ Risk accepted
- ○ Resolved through third party
- ○ Resolved through alternate mitigation

Action plan

Write a note

FIGURE 5-4 Status & Action Plan

Secure Score roles

The following Microsoft Entra ID roles have read-only access and cannot edit the status or notes for a recommended action or edit score zones or custom comparisons:

- Helpdesk Administrator
- User Administrator
- Service Support Administrator
- Security Reader
- Security Operator
- Global Reader

You can access your organization's Secure Score by selecting the **Secure Score** item in the Microsoft 365 Defender portal.

> **MORE INFO**   **MICROSOFT SECURE SCORE**
>
> You can learn more about Microsoft Secure Score at *https://learn.microsoft.com/en-us/ microsoft-365/security/defender/microsoft-secure-score*.

Incidents

When Microsoft Defender for Endpoint detects a threat, alerts will be created that you can investigate. Alerts that leverage the same attack techniques or appear to come from the same attacker will be aggregated into a singular entity termed an *incident*.

Incidents queue

The incidents queue collects incidents flagged from managed devices. The default queue will display incidents from the previous 30 days, with the most recent incident displayed at the top of the queue. Incidents in the queue are assigned one of the following severities:

- **High (Red)**   These threats are associated with advanced persistent threats (APT). These incidents are high risk because they are likely to inflict severe device damage.
- **Medium (Orange)**   These threats are less frequently observed in the organization. They include events such as anomalous registry changes, execution of suspicious files, and behaviors typical of stages within known attack chains.
- **Low (Yellow)**   These are threats associated with common malware and intrusion tools that do not necessarily indicate that an advanced threat is targeting an organization, but a less-skilled attacker might be active.
- **Informational (Gray)**   Informational incidents are generally not harmful to the network but are worth keeping an eye on.

Incidents are also categorized based on the stage of the cybersecurity kill chain they are in. These stages are as follows:

- **Reconnaissance**   Attacker is gathering information.
- **Weaponization**   The attacker has created a weapon, such as a malware payload, to exploit vulnerabilities identified during the reconnaissance phase.
- **Delivery**   The attacker delivers the weapon to target systems or devices.
- **Exploitation**   Code is executed to leverage the vulnerability.
- **Installation**   The malware or exploit gains persistence on the target system and might involve the creation of backdoor access to provide additional means of surreptitious access.
- **Command and Control**   The compromised system connects to the attacker's control servers. This allows the attacker to have remote administration privileges over the compromised system and might allow for data exfiltration or deployment of additional hostile software.
- **Actions on Objectives**   The attacker performs the planned activities, possibly including further exfiltration, data destruction, and encryption for a ransomware attack.

Manage incidents

Managing incidents involves assigning the incident, associating appropriate metadata tags with the incident, configuring the incident status and classification, and providing any necessary incident notes. The **Manage Incident** page is displayed in Figure 5-5. You can manage an incident by choosing the incident in the **Incidents** queue and selecting **Manage Incident**.

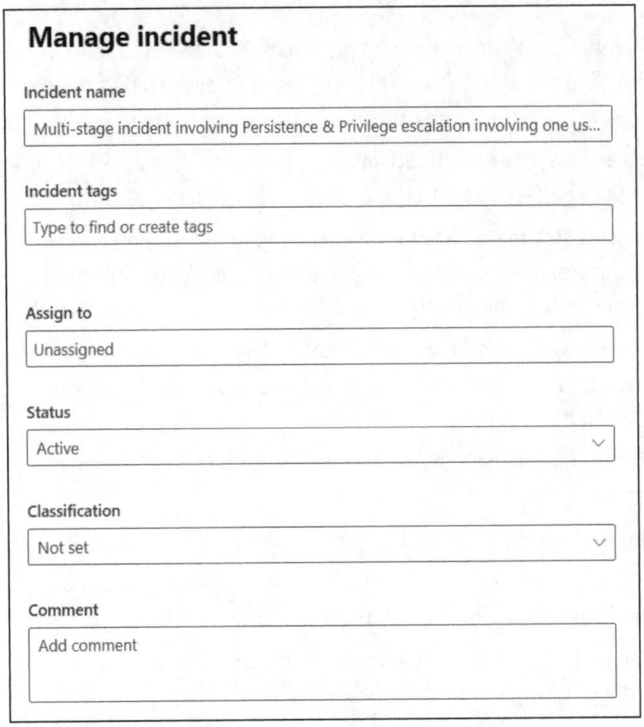

FIGURE 5-5 Manage Incident

Incident management tasks accomplish the following goals:

- **Assign Incidents**   If you assign an incident, you assign ownership of the incident and any associated alerts.
- **Incidents Status**   Allows you to categorize an incident as **Active** or **Resolved**.

- **Classification** Allows you to set the classifications shown in Figure 5-6.

  - **Not Set** No classification is configured for the incident.

  - **True Positive** Allows you to choose between **Multi-Staged Attack**, **Malware**, **Malicious User Activity**, **Unwanted Software**, **Phishing**, **Compromised Account**, or **Other**.

  - **Informational, Expected Activity** Allows you to choose between **Security Testing**, **Confirmed Activity**, **Line Of Business Application**, or **Other**.

  - **False Positive** Allows you to choose between **Not Malicious**, **Not Enough Data To Validate**, and **Other**.

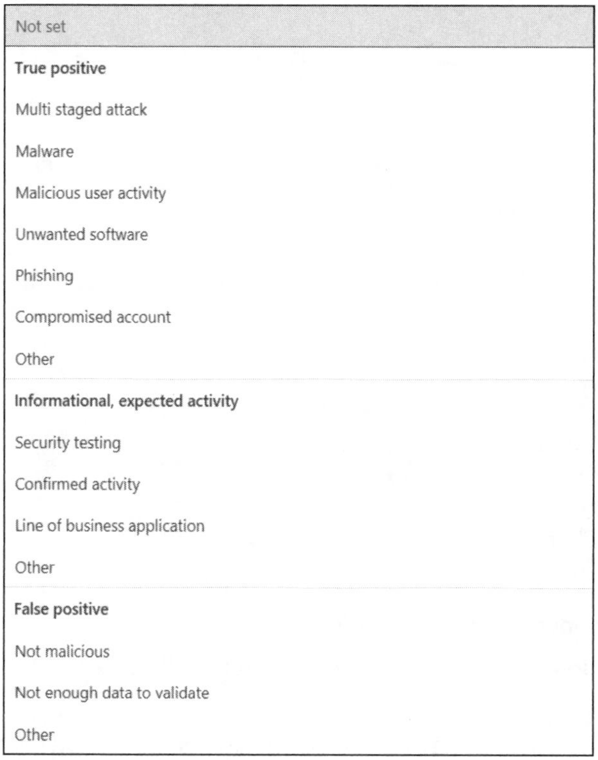

Not set
True positive
Multi staged attack
Malware
Malicious user activity
Unwanted software
Phishing
Compromised account
Other
Informational, expected activity
Security testing
Confirmed activity
Line of business application
Other
False positive
Not malicious
Not enough data to validate
Other

FIGURE 5-6 Incident classification

MORE INFO **MANAGE MICROSOFT DEFENDER FOR ENDPOINT INCIDENTS**

You can learn more about managing incidents at *https://learn.microsoft.com/en-us/microsoft-365/security/defender-endpoint/manage-incidents*.

Investigate incidents

Investigating an incident involves opening the incident and reviewing related information, including alerts, devices, investigations, evidence, and the incident graph. Figure 5-7 shows an incident with the **Attack Story** tab selected.

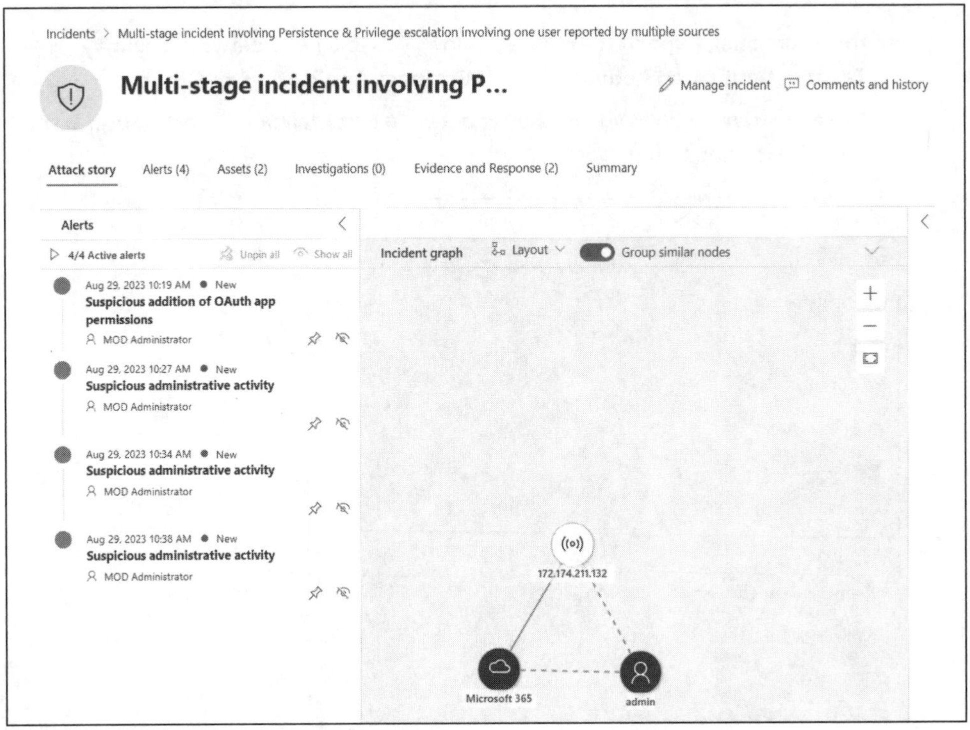

FIGURE 5-7 Attack Story tab

The **Alerts** tab will group incidents using the following reasons:

- **Automated Investigation** Automatic processes triggered the linked alert while investigating the original alert.
- **File Characteristics** The files associated with the alert have similar characteristics.
- **Manual Association** An administrator has manually linked the alerts.
- **Proximate Time** The alerts were triggered on the same device within a short time-frame.
- **Same File** The files associated with the alert are identical.
- **Same URL** The URL that triggered the alert is identical.

Microsoft Defender for Endpoint automatically examines each of the incidents' supported events and suspicious entities. You will receive an autoresponse option and information about the important files, processes, services, and more. Each entity analyzed will be marked as **Infected**, **Remediated**, or **Suspicious**.

The incident graph provides a visual representation of the attack. It might indicate where the attacker gained access, connections to compromised indications, and the activity recorded on each managed device.

> **MORE INFO** **INVESTIGATE INCIDENTS**
>
> You can learn more about investigating incidents at *https://learn.microsoft.com/en-us/ microsoft-365/security/defender-endpoint/investigate-incidents*.

Alerts

The **Alerts** queue in Defender for Endpoint provides you with a place to review notifications of malicious events, the attributes of those events, and contextual information you need to know about the event to understand its properties. You can view the **Alerts** queue by selecting **Alerts** under **Incidents & Alerts** in the Microsoft 365 Defender portal. The **Alerts** queue is displayed in Figure 5-8.

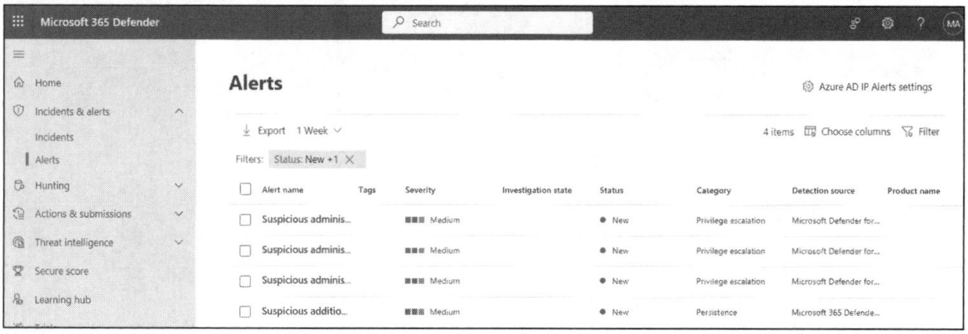

FIGURE 5-8 Alerts

You can manage alerts by selecting an alert in the **Alerts** queue. Doing so opens the **Alert Management** pane, which shows the following information (see Figure 5-9):

- **Alert Story**   Provides information on why the alert was triggered and related events before and after the triggering event.
- **Manage Alert**   Allows you to link the alert to another incident, assign, suppress, or classify the alert, change the alert status, add comments, and view the alert's history.

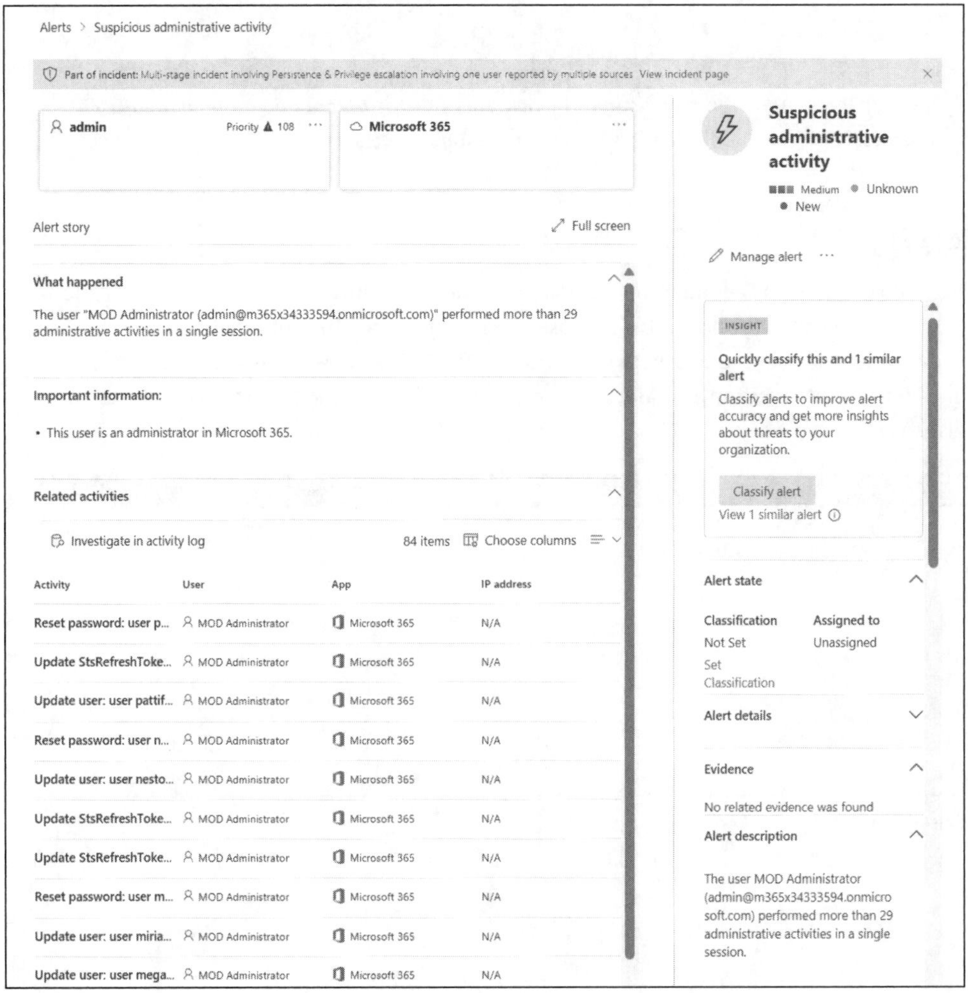

FIGURE 5-9   Alert Management pane.

When you create an alert suppression rule, you can choose between suppressing alerts on a specific device and suppressing alerts within your organization:

- **Suppress Alert On This Device**   Alerts with the same alert title and on that specific device only will be suppressed. All other alerts on that device will not be suppressed.
- **Suppress Alert In My Organization**   Alerts with the same alert title on any device managed by the organization will be suppressed.

> *MORE INFO*   **ALERTS QUEUE**
>
> You can learn more about the Alerts queue at *https://learn.microsoft.com/microsoft-365/security/defender-endpoint/alerts-queue-endpoint-detection-response.*

Threat analytics

Threat analytics is a set of reports from Microsoft's security research team that covers threats relevant to your organization including:

- Active threat actors and their campaigns
- Popular and new attack techniques
- Critical vulnerabilities
- Common attack surfaces
- Prevalent malware

Reports provide detailed analyses of specific threats and extensive guidance on how to protect against them. The report will also incorporate data from your network, allowing you to determine whether the threat is active and whether you have applicable defenses in place.

The Threat Analytics dashboard is located under the Threat Intelligence item in the Microsoft 365 Defender portal, as shown in Figure 5-10. This dashboard provides the following information:

- **Latest Threats**   Provides a list of the most recently published threat reports. Includes the number of devices in your organization with active and resolved alerts.
- **High-Impact Threats**   Provides a list of the threats that have had the highest impact on your organization. This section ranks threats by the number of managed devices that have active alerts.
- **Threat Summary**   Displays the overall impact of tracked threats by showing the number of threats with active and resolved alerts.

FIGURE 5-10 Threat Analytics

Each report allows you to view charts that will provide you with information that allows you to assess the potential impact of a specific threat. These charts include the following categories:

- **Devices With Alerts** Displays the number of distinct managed devices impacted by the threat. A device is categorized as **Active** if at least one alert is associated with that threat. A device is categorized as **Resolved** if all alerts associated with the threat on the device have been resolved.

- **Devices With Alerts Over Time** Displays the number of distinct managed devices with **Active** and **Resolved** alerts over time. You can use this chart do assess how rapidly your organization responds to alerts associated with threats.

- **Security Configuration Status** Displays the number of managed devices that have applied recommended security settings that mitigate the threat. Devices will be marked as **Secure** if all the tracked settings are applied.
- **Vulnerability Patching Status** Displays the number of managed devices that have applied security updates that remediate vulnerabilities exploited by the threat.

> *MORE INFO* **THREAT ANALYTICS**
>
> You can learn more about threat analytics at *https://learn.microsoft.com/en-us/microsoft-365/security/defender-endpoint/threat-analytics*.

Skill 5.2: Collaboration protection

Microsoft Defender for Office 365 is a security service that integrates into the Office 365 products in your organization's Microsoft 365 tenancy and protects against email threats, links (URLs), attachments, or collaboration tools.

> **This section covers the following skills:**
> - Defender for Office Policies and Rules
> - Configuration Analyzer
> - Managing threats with Defender for Office
> - Managing attack simulations
> - Blocked users

Defender for Office Policies and Rules

Defender for Office Policies determines which security settings are applied within Microsoft 365 tenancies to workloads related to Office 365. Individual policies are separated into two broad categories: Exchange Online Protection (EOP) policies and Microsoft Defender for Office 365 Policies.

EOP policies include

- Anti-spam policies
- Anti-malware policies
- EOP anti-phishing policies

Microsoft Defender for Office 365 policies include

- Anti-phishing policies (same spoof settings as EOP anti-phishing policies)
- Impersonation settings
- Advanced phishing thresholds
- Safe Links policies
- Safe Attachments policies

As shown in Figure 5-11, two built-in policies—**Standard Protection** and **Strict Protection**— apply medium- and strict-level security settings, respectively, across all policy categories. The collected policy settings should be appropriate for most organizations. If these policies do not meet your needs, you can create customized policies.

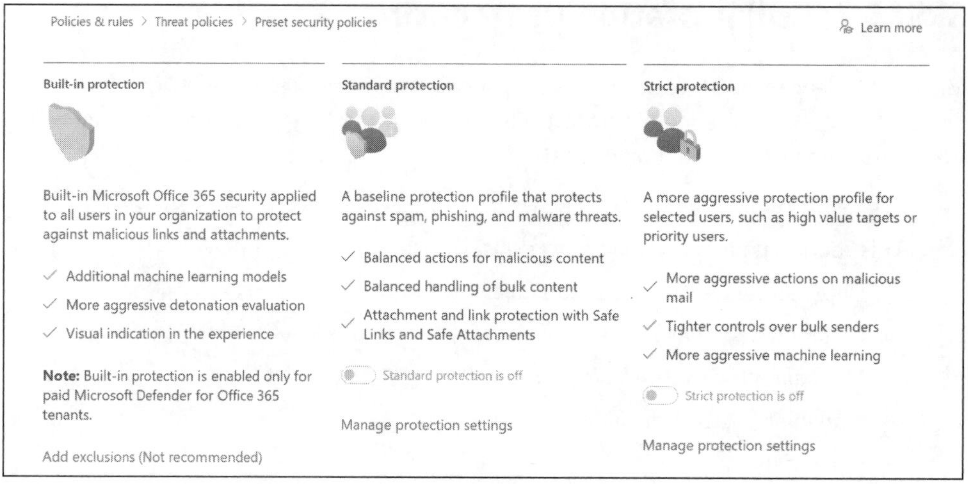

Policies & rules > Threat policies > Preset security policies   🔑 Learn more

Built-in protection

Built-in Microsoft Office 365 security applied to all users in your organization to protect against malicious links and attachments.

✓ Additional machine learning models

✓ More aggressive detonation evaluation

✓ Visual indication in the experience

Note: Built-in protection is enabled only for paid Microsoft Defender for Office 365 tenants.

Add exclusions (Not recommended)

Standard protection

A baseline protection profile that protects against spam, phishing, and malware threats.

✓ Balanced actions for malicious content

✓ Balanced handling of bulk content

✓ Attachment and link protection with Safe Links and Safe Attachments

⬤ Standard protection is off

Manage protection settings

Strict protection

A more aggressive protection profile for selected users, such as high value targets or priority users.

✓ More aggressive actions on malicious mail

✓ Tighter controls over bulk senders

✓ More aggressive machine learning

⬤ Strict protection is off

Manage protection settings

FIGURE 5-11   Preset Security Policies

Configure preset security policies

The Standard and Strict built-in collected policies cover a range of settings for EOP policies and Microsoft Defender for Office 365 policies. Configuring the Standard and Strict policies involves assigning those policies to a set of users, groups, or domains. To configure one of the preset policies in Microsoft Defender for Office 365 to apply to a particular scope, perform the following steps:

1. Determine which users, groups, or domains you want to include with the Standard and Strict security presets.

2. In the Microsoft Security portal, select **Email & Collaboration** > **Policies And Rules** > **Threat Policies**. This will open the **Threat Policies** page shown in Figure 5-12.

Policies & rules > Threat policies

Threat policies

Templated policies

 Preset Security Policies   Easily configure protection by applying all policies at once using our recommended protection templates

Configuration analyzer   Identify issues in your current policy configuration to improve your security

Policies

Anti-phishing   Protect users from phishing attacks, and configure safety tips on suspicious messages.

Anti-spam   Protect your organization's email from spam, including what actions to take if spam is detected

Anti-malware   Protect your organization's email from malware, including what actions to take and who to notify if malware is de

Safe Attachments   Protect your organization from malicious content in email attachments and files in SharePoint, OneDrive, and Tea

Safe Links   Protect your users from opening and sharing malicious links in email messages and Office apps

Rules

Tenant Allow/Block Lists   Manage allow or block entries for your organization.

Email authentication settings   Settings for Authenticated Received Chain (ARC) and DKIM in your organization.

Advanced delivery   Manage overrides for special system use cases.

Enhanced filtering   Configure Exchange Online Protection (EOP) scanning to work correctly when your domain's MX record doesn't r

Quarantine policies   Apply custom rules to quarantined messages by using default quarantine policies or creating your own

FIGURE 5-12 Threat Policies

3. Select **Preset Security Policies**. On the **Preset Security Policies** page, select **Manage Protection Settings** under either **Standard Protection** or **Strict Protection**, depending on which preset policy you want to apply to the users, groups, or domains you are working with.

4. On the **Exchange Online Protection** page, choose between **All Recipients**, **Specific Recipients**, **None**, or **Exclude These Recipients**. Figure 5-13 shows **Specific Recipients** selected and displays the text entry boxes where you can select individual users, groups, or domains. Choose **Next**.

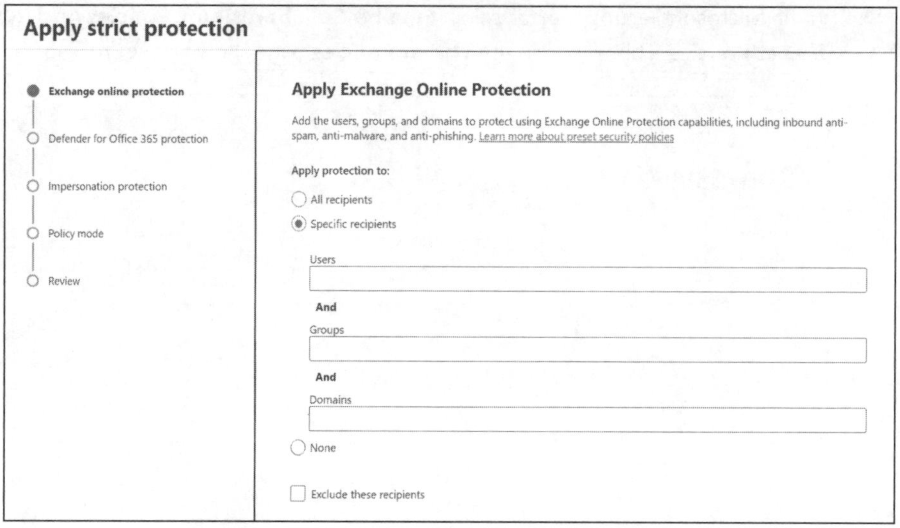

FIGURE 5-13 Apply policy to specific recipients

5. On the **Apply Defender for Office 365 Protection** page, choose between **All Recipients**, **Specific Recipients**, **None**, or **Exclude These Recipients**. Figure 5-14 shows **Specific Recipients** selected and displays the text entry boxes where you can select individual users, groups, or domains. Choose **Next**.

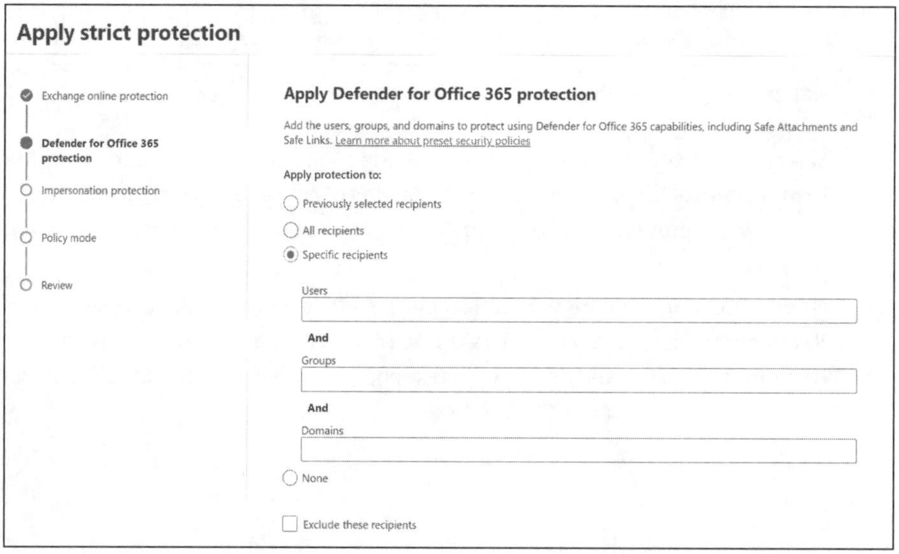

FIGURE 5-14 Defender for Office 365 Protection

6. On the **Impersonation Protection** page, select **Next**.

7. On the **Protected Custom Users** page, specify the internal and external addresses of people likely to be impersonated by attackers, as shown in Figure 5-15.

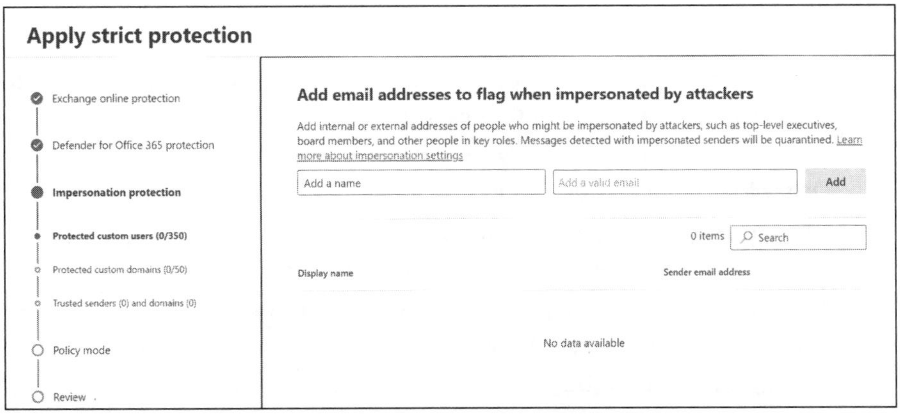

FIGURE 5-15   Impersonation Protection

8. On the **Protected Custom Domains** page, add domains to flag when impersonated by attackers. Messages detected with impersonated sender domains will be quarantined.

9. On the **Add Trusted Email Addresses And Domains To Not Flag As Impersonation** page shown in Figure 5-16, provide a list of senders you want to ensure are not flagged as impersonation.

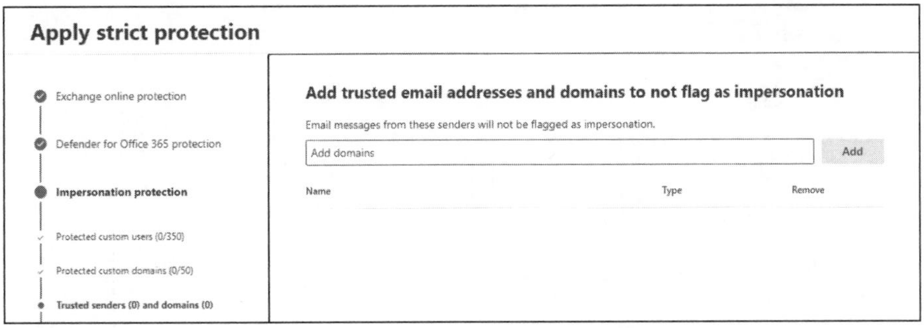

FIGURE 5-16   Impersonation protection for trusted senders and domains

10. On the **Policy Mode** page, enable or disable the policy. Select **Next** and then select **Confirm** to enact the policy.

> **MORE INFO   HARDEN MICROSOFT 365 TENANT SECURITY**
>
> You can learn more about hardening Microsoft 365 tenant security at *https://learn.microsoft.com/en-us/microsoft-365/security/office-365-security/tenant-wide-setup-for-increased-security.*

Anti-phishing policy

You can configure custom anti-phishing policies to protect users from phishing attacks. You can also use these policies to provide safety tips to users on messages that have suspicious characteristics. Office 365's default anti-phishing policy, Office 365 Anti-Phishing Default, provides a basic level of protection. To create a custom anti-phishing policy, perform the following steps:

1. In the Microsoft 365 Defender portal, select **Email & Collaboration** > **Policies & Rules** > **Threat Policies** > **Anti-Phishing**.

2. On the **Anti-Phishing** page, select **Create** to start the new Anti-Phishing Policy wizard. On the **Policy Name** page, provide a policy name and description and select **Next**.

3. On the **Users, Groups, And Domains** page, select which users, groups, and domains should be included or excluded by the policy and then select **Next**.

4. On the **Phishing Threshold & Protection** page shown in Figure 5-17, provide the following information and select **Next**:

   - **Enable Users To Protect**   Specify which users to protect.

   - **Enable Domains To Protect**   Specify which custom domains to protect.

   - **Add Trusted Senders And Domains**   Specify which senders and domains should not be flagged as phishing.

   - **Enable Spoof Intelligence**   Select how you will filter email from senders from spoofing domains.

FIGURE 5-17   Phishing Threshold & Protection

5. On the **Actions** page, configure the following settings and choose **Next**:

- **If A Message Is Detected As User Impersonation**   Choose between redirecting the message to a specific email address, sending the message to the junk folder, quarantining the message, delivering the message, adding other addresses to the Bcc line, deleting the message, or taking no action.

- **If The Message Is Detected As Spoofed**   Quarantine the message or move it to the junk folder.

- **If The Message Is Detected As Spoof By Spoof Intelligence**   Quarantine the message or move the message to the junk folder.

- **Enable Specific Safety Tips & Indicators Related To Phishing, Impersonation, And Unauthenticated Senders**.

6. Review the policy settings and choose **Submit**.

Anti-spam policy

Anti-spam policies allow you to protect your organization from unsolicited commercial email. By configuring a custom policy, you can be granular about how unsolicited commercial email is treated for specific users, groups, or domains. For example, you might want to block spam for all users except those in the Sales department who consider spam an excellent source of sales leads. Or you might want to allow messages that trigger the spam filters to be sent by Sales team members. By default, Microsoft 365 includes three anti-spam policies, including one for outbound email messages. To configure a custom inbound anti-spam policy, perform the following steps:

1. In the Microsoft 365 Defender portal, select **Email & Collaboration** > **Policies & Rules** > **Threat Policies** > **Anti-Spam**.

2. On the **Anti-Spam Policies** page, select **Create Policy**. Choose **Inbound Policy** for messages coming into the organization.

3. Provide a policy name and description and choose **Next**.

4. On the **Users, Groups, And Domains** page, select the users, groups, and domains to which this policy will apply.

5. On the **Bulk Email Threshold & Spam Properties** page shown in Figure 5-18, config-ure the following settings and choose **Next**:

- **Bulk Email Threshold**   Set a numerical value with a higher value, meaning more bulk emails will be delivered. The default value is **7**.

- **Image Links To Remote Websites**   Specify whether including images in messages should raise the spam score.

- **Numeric IP Address In URL**   Specify whether including numerical IP addresses in messages should raise the spam score.

- **URL Redirect To Other Port**   Specify whether including port addresses in mes-sages should raise the spam score.

- **Links To .biz or .info Websites**   Specify whether including *.biz* or *.info* websites in messages should raise the spam score.

- **Empty Messages**   Mark a message as spam if the contents of the message are empty.

- **Embedded Tags In HTML**   Mark a message as spam if embedded tags in HTML are present in the message body.

- **JavaScript Or VBScript In HTML**   Mark a message as spam if JavaScript or VBScript is present in HTML in the message body.

- **Form Tags In HTML**   Mark a message as spam if HTML Form tags are present in the message body.

- **Frame Or iframe Tags In HTML**   Mark a message as spam if HTML frame or iframe tags are present in the message body.

- **Web Bugs In HTML**   Mark a message as spam if HTML web bugs are present in the message body.

- **Object Tags In HTML**   Mark a message as spam if HTML object tags are present in the message body.

- **Sensitive Words**   Email contains words deemed sensitive.

- **SPF Record: Hard Fail**   Message is sent from an IP address not included in the mail domain's Sender Protection Framework (SPF) information.

- **Sender ID Filtering Hard Fail**   Message fails a sender ID and SPF check.

- **Backscatter**   Allows you to block messages with forged return-path or reply to information.

- **Contains Specific Languages**   Allows you to block messages containing text in specific languages.

- **From These Countries**   Allows you to block messages from specific countries.

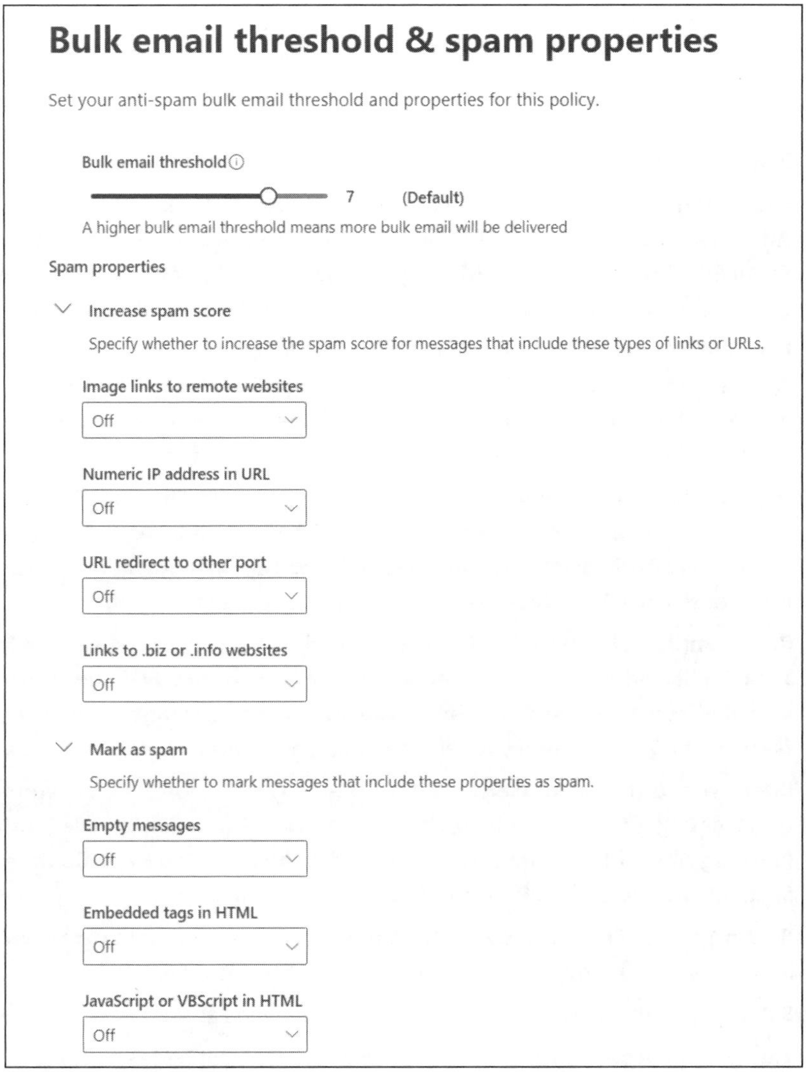

Bulk email threshold & spam properties

Set your anti-spam bulk email threshold and properties for this policy.

Bulk email threshold ⓘ

●————————————○———— 7   (Default)

A higher bulk email threshold means more bulk email will be delivered

Spam properties

⌄   Increase spam score

Specify whether to increase the spam score for messages that include these types of links or URLs.

Image links to remote websites

| Off | ⌄ |

Numeric IP address in URL

| Off | ⌄ |

URL redirect to other port

| Off | ⌄ |

Links to .biz or .info websites

| Off | ⌄ |

⌄   Mark as spam

Specify whether to mark messages that include these properties as spam.

Empty messages

| Off | ⌄ |

Embedded tags in HTML

| Off | ⌄ |

JavaScript or VBScript in HTML

| Off | ⌄ |

FIGURE 5-18   Bulk Email Threshold

6.   On the **Message Actions** page, configure the following settings and choose **Next**.

- **Spam**   Choose **Move Messages To The Junk Email Folder**, **Add An X-Header**, **Add Text To The Start Of The Subject Line**, **Redirect Message To An Email Address**, **Delete Message**, or **Place The Message In Quarantine**. If you choose **Place The Message In Quarantine**, select a quarantine policy.

- **High Confidence Spam**   Choose **Move Messages To The Junk Email Folder**, **Add An X-Header**, **Add Text To The Start Of The Subject Line**, **Redirect Message To An Email Address**, **Delete Message**, or **Place The Message In Quarantine**. If you choose **Place The Message In Quarantine**, select a quarantine policy.

- **Phishing**   Choose **Move Messages To The Junk Email Folder**, **Add An X-Header**, **Add Text To The Start Of The Subject Line**, **Redirect Message To An Email Address**, **Delete Message**, or **Place The Message In Quarantine**. If you choose **Place The Message In Quarantine**, select a quarantine policy.

- **High Confidence Phishing**   Choose **Move Messages To The Junk Email Folder**, **Add An X-Header**, **Add Text To The Start Of The Subject Line**, **Redirect Message To An Email Address**, **Delete Message**, or **Place The Message In Quarantine**. If you choose **Place The Message In Quarantine**, select a quarantine policy.

- **Bulk Complaint Level (BCL) Met Or Exceeded**   Choose **Move Messages To The Junk Email Folder**, **Add An X-Header**, **Add Text To The Start Of The Subject Line**, **Redirect Message To An Email Address**, **Delete Message**, or **Place The Message In Quarantine**. If you choose quarantine, select a quarantine policy.

- **Inter Organizational Messages To Take Action On**   Choose which interorganizational messages to take action on. Options are **None**, **High-Confidence Phishing**, **Phishing And High-Confidence Phishing**, **All Phishing And High-Confidence Spam Messages**, and **All Phishing And Spam Messages**.

- **Retain Spam In Quarantine For This Many Days**   Provide a value for how long a message remains in quarantine before being automatically deleted.

- **Safety Tips**   Provide safety tips for messages identified as spam.

- **Zero-Hour Purge**   Purge messages from mailboxes identified as phishing or spam messages.

7.   On the **Allow & Block** list, specify which senders and domains should always have messages delivered and which senders and domains should always have messages blocked. Choose **Next** and then choose **Create**.

To create an outbound anti-spam policy, perform the following steps:

1. In the Microsoft 365 Defender portal, select **Email & Collaboration** > **Policies & Rules** > **Threat Policies** > **Anti-Spam**.

2. On the **Anti-Spam Policies** page, select **Create Policy**. Choose **Outbound Policy For Messages Being Sent Outside The Organization**.

3. Provide a policy name and description and choose **Next**.

4. On the **Users, Groups, And Domains** page, select the users, groups, and domains to which this policy will apply and choose **Next**.

5. On the **Protection Settings** page, configure the following settings, as shown in Figure 5-19, and choose **Next**.

   - **Set An External Message Limit**   Sets a limit on the number of email messages to external recipients an individual subject to this policy can send.

   - **Set An Internal Message Limit**   Sets a limit on the number of email messages to internal recipients an individual subject to this policy can send.

   - **Set A Daily Message Limit**   Sets a daily message limit for individuals that fall within the scope of this policy.

   - **Restriction Placed On Users Who Reach The Message Limit**   Allows you to set what restriction will be placed, with the option being restriction until the next day, to restrict the user from sending email, or just to raise an alert.

   - **Automatic Forwarding Rules**   Allows you to set how automatic forwarding functions.

   - **Send A Copy Of Suspicious Outbound Messages Or Messages That Exceed These Limits**   Allows you to send a copy of suspicious messages to a specific user or group of users.

   - **Notify These Users And Groups If A Sender Is Blocked Due To Sending Outbound Spam**   Configures who will be notified when a sender is blocked.

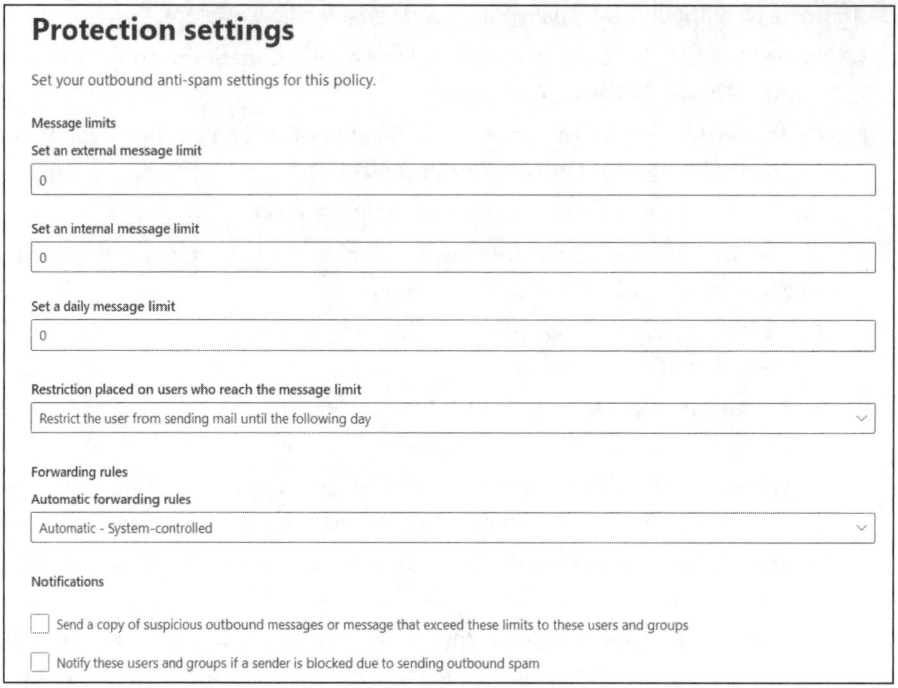

Protection settings

Set your outbound anti-spam settings for this policy.

Message limits

Set an external message limit

```
0
```

Set an internal message limit

```
0
```

Set a daily message limit

```
0
```

Restriction placed on users who reach the message limit

```
Restrict the user from sending mail until the following day          ⌄
```

Forwarding rules

Automatic forwarding rules

```
Automatic - System-controlled          ⌄
```

Notifications

☐ Send a copy of suspicious outbound messages or message that exceed these limits to these users and groups

☐ Notify these users and groups if a sender is blocked due to sending outbound spam

FIGURE 5-19   Message sending protection

6. Review the configured settings and choose **Create**.

Anti-malware policy

Anti-malware policies allow you to configure how Microsoft 365 protects your organization from malware transmitted through email messages. By default, existing policies will already provide adequate protection against threats of this type. If necessary, you can create a custom anti-malware policy by performing the following steps:

1. In the Microsoft 365 Defender portal, select **Email & Collaboration** > **Policies & Rules** > **Threat Policies** > **Anti-Malware**.

2. On the Microsoft 365 Defender portal's **Anti-Malware** page, select **Create**. Provide a name and description of the policy, and select **Next**.

3. On the **Users, Groups, And Domains** page, select the users, groups, domains, and policy exclusions.

4. On the **Protection Settings** page shown in Figure 5-20, configure the following settings and choose **Next**:

   - **Enable Common Attachments Filters**   Allows you to choose a set of file types and extensions to filter automatically. You can automatically reject messages containing these attachments or place them in quarantine.

- **Enable Zero-Hour Auto Purge For Malware** Automatically removes malware from any messages delivered to Exchange Online mailboxes.

- **Quarantine Policy** For messages placed in quarantine, set the policy. Options are `AdminOnlyAccessPolicy`, `DefaultFullAccessPolicy`, and `DefaultFullAccessWithNotificationPolicy`.

- **Notification** Can be set to notify administrators about undelivered messages from internal senders or undelivered messages from external senders and allows customized notification text.

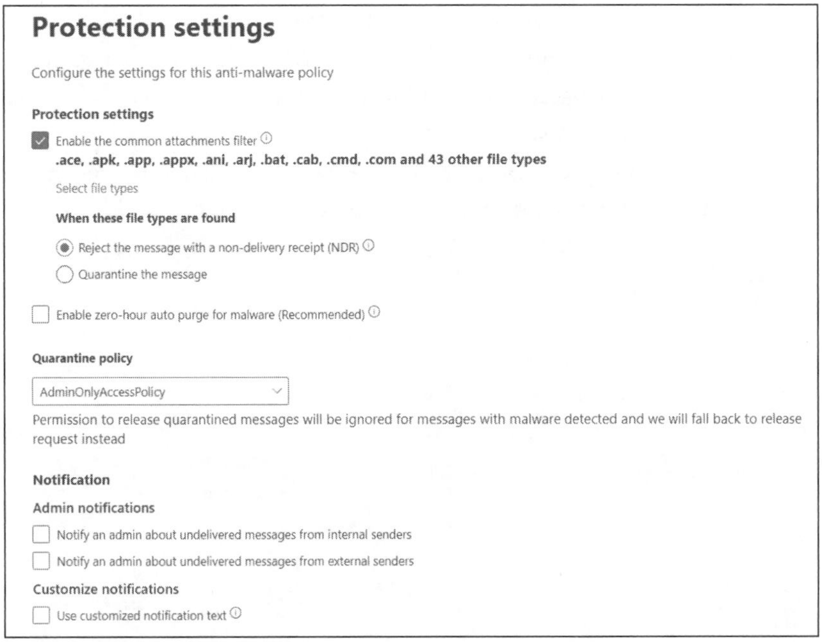

FIGURE 5-20 Attachments filter settings

5. On the **Review** page, review the selected settings and choose **Submit**.

Safe Attachments policy

Safe Attachments policies protect an organization from malicious content in email attachments. They also apply to files stored in SharePoint and OneDrive and distributed through Microsoft Teams. By default, existing policies already provide adequate protection against threats of this type. If necessary, you can create a custom safe attachments policy by performing the following steps:

1. In the Microsoft 365 Defender portal, select **Email & Collaboration** > **Policies & Rules** > **Threat Policies** > **Safe Attachments**.

2. On the **Safe Attachments** page of the Microsoft 365 Defender portal, choose **Create**. Provide a name and description of the policy and then select **Next**.

3. On the **Users, Groups, And Domains** page, select the policy's users, groups, domains and exclusions.

4. On the **Settings** page shown in Figure 5-21, configure the following **Safe Attachments** settings and then choose **Next**:

- **Off** Attachments are not scanned.

- **Monitor** Deliver the message even if malware is detected.

- **Block** Block current and future messages and attachments where malware is detected.

- **Dynamic Delivery** Deliver the message without attachments. Reattach files after they have been scanned and determined to be safe.

- **Quarantine Policy** Configure a quarantine policy for messages. Quarantine options are `AdminOnlyAccessPolicy`, `DefaultFullAccessPolicy`, and `DefaultFullAccessWithNotificationPolicy`.

- **Redirect Messages With Detected Attachments** Configure a redirect for messages with attachments identified as malware to a specific email address.

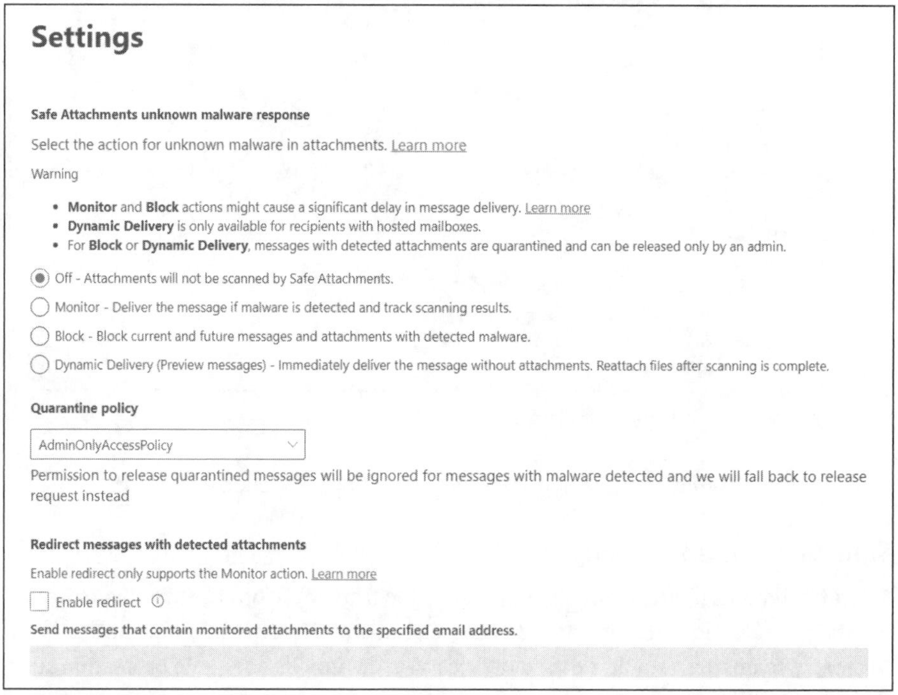

Settings

Safe Attachments unknown malware response

Select the action for unknown malware in attachments. Learn more

Warning

- **Monitor** and **Block** actions might cause a significant delay in message delivery. Learn more
- **Dynamic Delivery** is only available for recipients with hosted mailboxes.
- For **Block** or **Dynamic Delivery**, messages with detected attachments are quarantined and can be released only by an admin.

◉ Off - Attachments will not be scanned by Safe Attachments.

◯ Monitor - Deliver the message if malware is detected and track scanning results.

◯ Block - Block current and future messages and attachments with detected malware.

◯ Dynamic Delivery (Preview messages) - Immediately deliver the message without attachments. Reattach files after scanning is complete.

Quarantine policy

AdminOnlyAccessPolicy ⌄

Permission to release quarantined messages will be ignored for messages with malware detected and we will fall back to release request instead

Redirect messages with detected attachments

Enable redirect only supports the Monitor action. Learn more

☐ Enable redirect ⓘ

Send messages that contain monitored attachments to the specified email address.

FIGURE 5-21 Attachment protection

5. On the **Review** page, review the selected settings and choose **Submit**.

Safe Links policy

Safe Links policies protect an organization from malicious links in email messages and Office apps, including Teams. By default, existing policies will already provide adequate protection against threats of this type. If necessary, you can create a custom Safe Links policy by performing the following steps:

1. In the Microsoft 365 Defender portal, select **Email & Collaboration** > **Policies & Rules** > **Threat Policies** > **Safe Links**.

2. On the Microsoft 365 Defender portal's **Safe Links** page, choose **Create**. Provide a policy name and description and select **Next**.

3. On the **Users, Groups, And Domains** page, select the policy's users, groups, domains, and exclusions.

4. On the **URL & Click Protection Settings** page shown in Figure 5-22, configure the following settings and choose **Next**:

   - **Email**   Allows you to enable Safe Links. You can configure the following settings: URLs are rewritten by default, and users will be blocked from accessing unsafe sites. You can enable this setting to check email messages sent within the organization. You can also scan suspicious links and links pointing to files. You can also wait for URL scanning to complete before delivering a message. The final option is that URLs are not rewritten but are checked.

   - **Do Not Rewrite The Following URLs**   Specify which URLs should not be rewritten.

   - **Teams**   Allows you to enable safe links for Microsoft Teams.

   - **Office 365 Apps**   Allows you to have safe links checked for Office 365 apps such as Word and Excel where documents might contain URLs.

   - **Click Protection Settings**   Allows you to track user clicks and display organizational branding on notification and warning pages so that users understand the warning is provided by your local services and is not a random warning page on the internet.

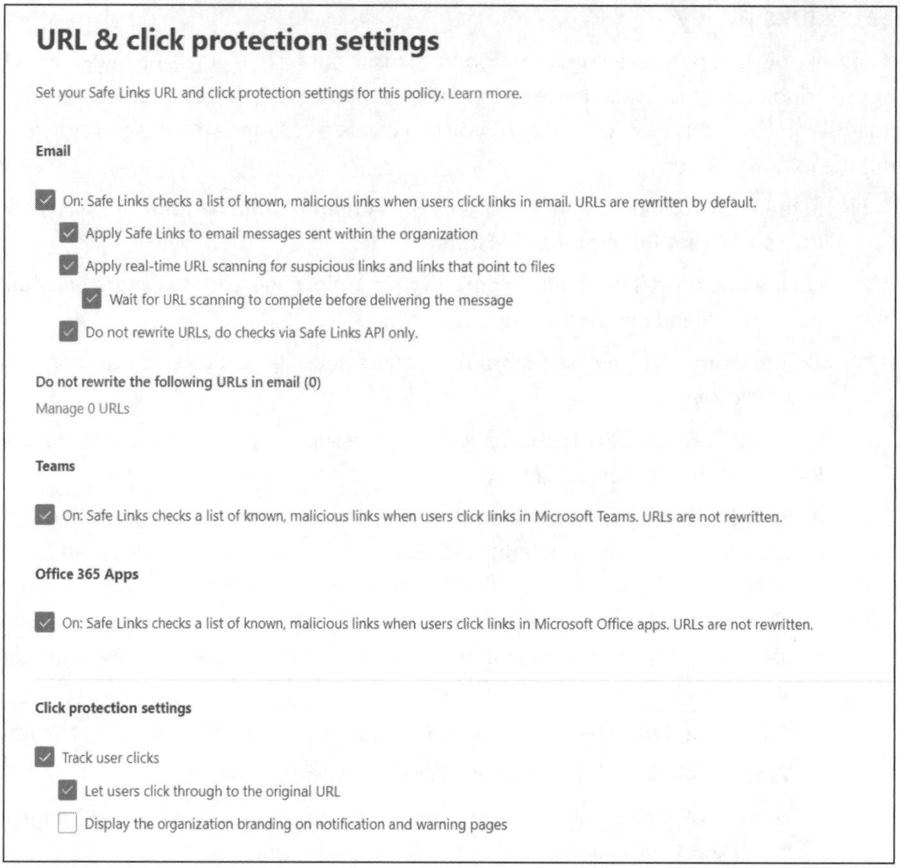

URL & click protection settings

Set your Safe Links URL and click protection settings for this policy. Learn more.

Email

☑ On: Safe Links checks a list of known, malicious links when users click links in email. URLs are rewritten by default.

　☑ Apply Safe Links to email messages sent within the organization

　☑ Apply real-time URL scanning for suspicious links and links that point to files

　　☑ Wait for URL scanning to complete before delivering the message

　☑ Do not rewrite URLs, do checks via Safe Links API only.

Do not rewrite the following URLs in email (0)

Manage 0 URLs

Teams

☑ On: Safe Links checks a list of known, malicious links when users click links in Microsoft Teams. URLs are not rewritten.

Office 365 Apps

☑ On: Safe Links checks a list of known, malicious links when users click links in Microsoft Office apps. URLs are not rewritten.

Click protection settings

☑ Track user clicks

　☑ Let users click through to the original URL

　☐ Display the organization branding on notification and warning pages

FIGURE 5-22 URL & Click Protection Settings

5. On the **Notification** page, choose between displaying a default notification or creating a customized notification. Select **Next**.

6. On the **Review** page, review the selected settings and choose **Submit**.

Tenant Allow/Block Lists rules

Tenant Allow/Block Lists rules allow you to allow or block domains, addresses, spoofed senders, URLs, and files for your organization.

To create a Tenant Allow/Block Lists rule for domains and addresses, perform the following steps:

1. In the Microsoft 365 Defender portal, select **Email & Collaboration** > **Policies & Rules** > **Threat Policies** > **Tenant Allow/Block Lists**.

2. To create a domain and addresses block list, choose **Block** on the **Domains & Addresses** section of the **Tenant Allow/Block Lists** page.

3. In the **Block Domains & Addresses** section shown in Figure 5-23, provide up to 20 email addresses and domains. Choose when to remove the block entry, with the options being **1 Days**, **7 Days**, **30 Days**, **Never Expire**, and **Specific Date**. Choose **Add**.

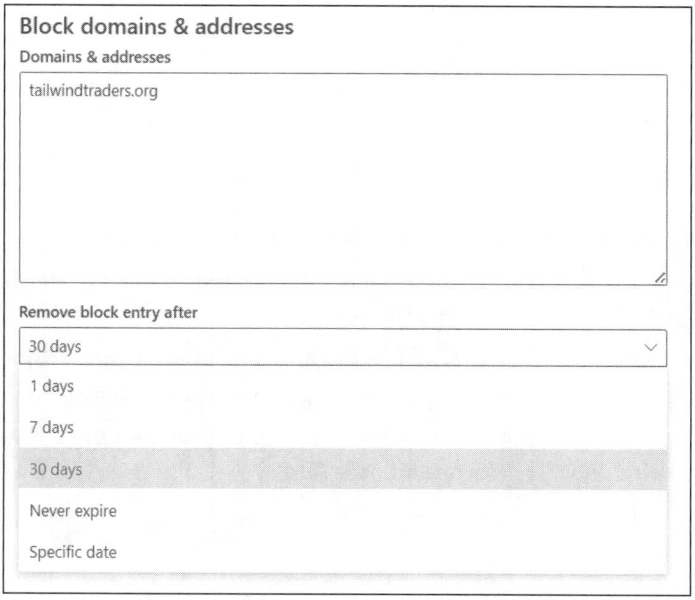

Block domains & addresses

Domains & addresses

tailwindtraders.org

Remove block entry after

30 days

1 days

7 days

30 days

Never expire

Specific date

FIGURE 5-23   Block Domains & Addresses

To create a tenant allow/block lists rule for spoofed senders, perform the following steps:

1. In the Microsoft 365 Defender portal, select **Email & Collaboration** > **Policies & Rules** > **Threat Policies** > **Tenant Allow/Block Lists**.

2. In the **Spoofed Senders** section of the **Tenant Allow/Block Lists** page, choose **Add**.

3.   On the Add **New Domain Pairs** dialog, provide a domain name, IP address ranges, or individual email addresses, as shown in Figure 5-24. You can also choose to block **Internal** or **External** spoofing and whether you want to **Allow** or **Block** the spoofed address. Choose **Add** when you have completed the list.

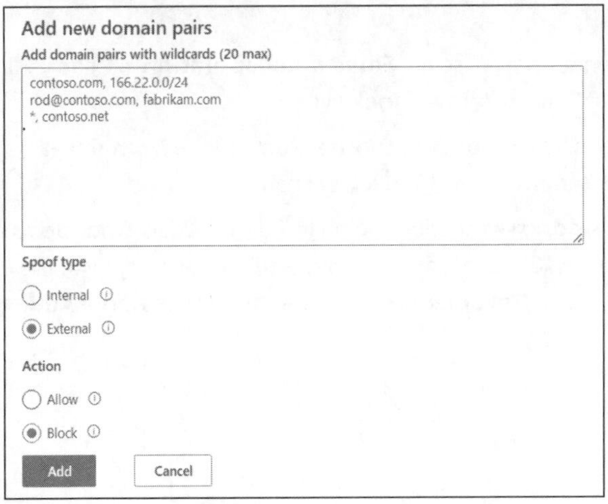

Add new domain pairs

Add domain pairs with wildcards (20 max)

contoso.com, 166.22.0.0/24
rod@contoso.com, fabrikam.com
*, contoso.net

Spoof type

○ Internal ⓘ

◉ External ⓘ

Action

○ Allow ⓘ

◉ Block ⓘ

[Add]   [Cancel]

FIGURE 5-24   Block spoofed senders

To create a tenant allow/block lists rule for URLs, perform the following steps:

1.   In the Microsoft 365 Defender portal, select **Email & Collaboration** > **Policies & Rules** > **Threat Policies** > **Tenant Allow/Block Lists**.

2.   In the **URLs Senders** section of the **Tenant Allow/Block Lists** page, choose **Block**.

3.   On the **Block URLs** page shown in Figure 5-25, provide URLs with wildcards and specify the period after which the block should be removed. The options are **1 Days**, **7 Days**, **30 Days**, **Never Expire**, and **Specific Date**. Choose **Add**.

Block URLs

Add URLs with wildcards (20 max) ⓘ

*.contoso.com

Remove block entry after

Never expire   ⌄

Optional note (100 characters max)

100 characters left

[Add]   [Cancel]

FIGURE 5-25   Block URLs

You can block files based on the file hash. Because you're using a file hash, you can block a file based on its cryptographic signature, even if it has been given a different name. You can use the certutil.exe command line utility to create a file hash using SHA256.

To create a tenant allow/block lists rule for files, perform the following steps:

1. In the Microsoft 365 Defender portal, select **Email & Collaboration** > **Policies & Rules** > **Threat Policies** > **Tenant Allow/Block Lists**.

2. In the **Files** section of the **Tenant Allow/Block Lists** page, choose **Block**.

3. On the **Block Files** page shown in Figure 5-26, provide up to 20 SHA256 file hashes and configure when to remove the block entry. The options are **1 Days**, **7 Days**, **30 Days**, **Never Expire**, and **Specific Date**. Choose **Add**.

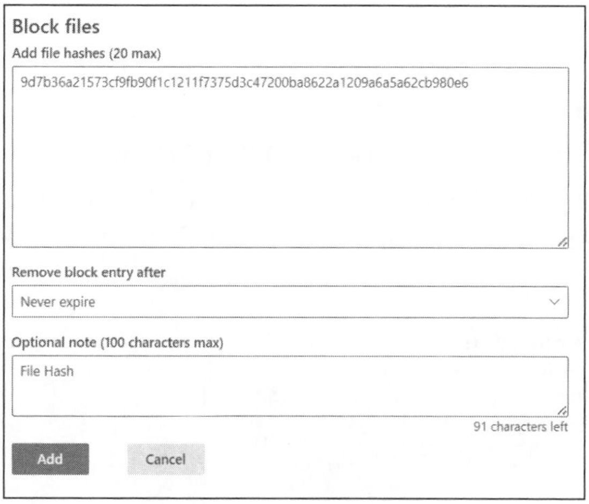

Block files

Add file hashes (20 max)

9d7b36a21573cf9fb90f1c1211f7375d3c47200ba8622a1209a6a5a62cb980e6

Remove block entry after

Never expire

Optional note (100 characters max)

File Hash

91 characters left

Add   Cancel

FIGURE 5-26   Block files by SHA256 hash

Email authentication settings rules

Email authentication settings rules allow you to configure settings for Authenticate Received Chain (ARC) and DomainKeys Identified Mail (DKIM) in your organization. Authentication Received Chain (ARC) is an authentication method that preserves authentication results across intervening devices and technologies. Domain Keys Identified Mail (DKIM) is an authentication process that can help protect both senders and recipients from forged and phishing email.

To configure email authentication settings for ARC, perform the following steps:

1. In the Microsoft 365 Defender portal, select **Email & Collaboration** > **Policies & Rules** > **Select Threat Policies** > **Email Authentication Settings**.

2. In the **ARC** section of the **Email Authentication Settings** page, choose **Add**.

3. On the **Add Trusted ARC Sealers** page, add trusted signing domains. The domain name you enter must match the domain shown in the domain "d" tag in the ARC-Seal and ARC-Message-Signature headers. You can locate this information in the email headers if you are unsure.

To export DKIM settings for your tenancy's authenticated domains, perform the following steps:

1. In the Microsoft 365 Defender portal, select **Email & Collaboration** > **Policies & Rules** > **Select Threat Policies** > **Email Authentication Settings**.

2. In the **DKIM** section of the **Email Authentication Settings** page, select the domain for which you want to export the DKIM information and choose **Export**.

Advanced delivery rules

Advanced delivery rules allow you to manage overrides for special system use cases. These rules allow you to specify dedicated mailboxes that are used by security teams to collect and analyze unfiltered messages that Exchange Online Protection would otherwise block. Email delivered to these mailboxes bypasses EOP and is delivered unfiltered. You can configure a SecOps mailbox and third-party phishing simulations.

1. In the Microsoft 365 Defender portal, select **Email & Collaboration** > **Policies & Rules** > **Threat Policies** > **Advanced Delivery**.

2. On the **SecOps Mailbox** page, specify which mailbox will be used for SecOps tasks.

3. On the **Phishing Simulations** page shown in Figure 5-27, provide the **Sending Domain Entry** and **Sending IP** that will allow the phishing simulation traffic to be sent to target users. Select **Save**.

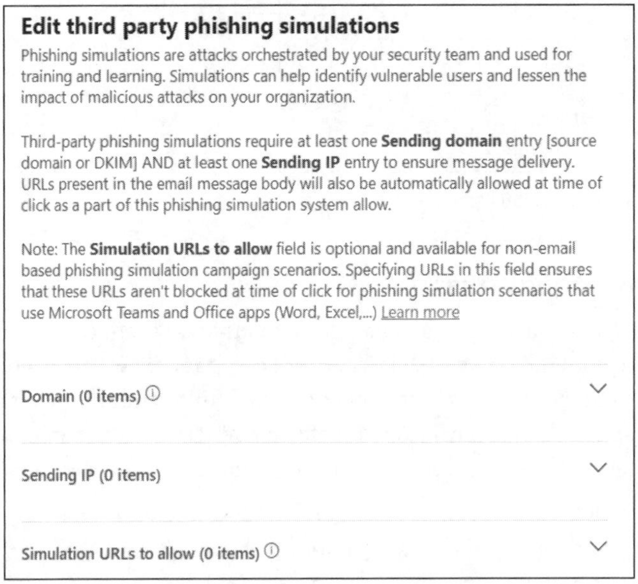

Edit third party phishing simulations

Phishing simulations are attacks orchestrated by your security team and used for training and learning. Simulations can help identify vulnerable users and lessen the impact of malicious attacks on your organization.

Third-party phishing simulations require at least one **Sending domain** entry [source domain or DKIM] AND at least one **Sending IP** entry to ensure message delivery. URLs present in the email message body will also be automatically allowed at time of click as a part of this phishing simulation system allow.

Note: The **Simulation URLs to allow** field is optional and available for non-email based phishing simulation campaign scenarios. Specifying URLs in this field ensures that these URLs aren't blocked at time of click for phishing simulation scenarios that use Microsoft Teams and Office apps (Word, Excel,...) Learn more

Domain (0 items) ⓘ   ⌄

Sending IP (0 items)   ⌄

Simulation URLs to allow (0 items) ⓘ   ⌄

FIGURE 5-27 Phishing simulations

Enhanced filtering rules

You can use Enhanced Filtering for Connectors to filter incoming emails based on the source of messages that arrive over the connector. Enhanced Filtering skips the source IP addresses of the connector and traces the routing path to determine the actual source of the incoming messages. Existing connectors must be present and configured to enable enhanced filtering for connectors.

Quarantine policies rules

Quarantine policies allow you to configure how messages are handled by quarantine. There are three default quarantine policies:

- **DefaultFullAccessPolicy**   This policy allows the message recipient to release the message from quarantine, block the sender, delete the message, and preview the message. No notification is provided.
- **AdminOnlyAccessPolicy**   This policy only allows users with Administrative permissions access to quarantined messages.
- **DefaultFullAccessWithNotificationPolicy**   This policy allows the message recipient to release the message from quarantine, block the sender, delete the message, and preview the message. Notifications are enabled.

To create a new quarantine policy, perform the following steps:

1. In the Microsoft 365 Defender portal, select **Email & Collaboration** > **Policies & Rules** > **Threat Policies** > **Quarantine Policy**.
2. On the **Quarantine Policy** page, choose **Add Custom Policy**. Provide a policy name and choose **Next**.
3. On the **Recipient Message Access** page shown in Figure 5-28, choose the following settings and select **Next**.
   - **Limited Access**   Allows recipients to view quarantined messages, but they cannot release messages from quarantine.
   - **Set Specific Access**   Allows you to choose between allowing a recipient to release a message from quarantine and allowing the recipient to request the release of a message from quarantine. Also allows you to let the recipient delete the message, preview the message, or block the message sender.

Recipient message access

Specify what access you would like recipients to have when this quarantine policy is applied to a message. Learn more about recipient message access

Recipient message access *

◯ **Limited access**
Recipients can view quarantined messages, but they cannot release messages from the quarantine state

⦿ **Set specific access (Advanced)**
Specify exactly what recipients can do with quarantined messages

Select release action preference

Allow recipients to request a message to be released from quarantine ⌄

Select additional actions recipients can take on quarantined messages

☐ Delete

☐ Preview

☐ Block sender

FIGURE 5-28 Quarantine Recipient Message Access

4. On the **Quarantine Notification** page, choose whether to enable notifications and select **Next**.

5. On the **Summary** page, choose **Submit**.

Configuration analyzer

You can use the Configuration analyzer tool to determine where the settings in existing applied policies are below the **Standard Protection** and **Strict Protection** profile settings in the pre-set security policies. This tool can be used to analyze the following policies:

- Anti-spam policies
- Anti-malware policies
- EOP anti-phishing policies

The Configuration analyzer page has three main sections, as shown in Figure 5-29:

- **Standard Recommendations**   Compare your existing security policy settings to those defined by the **Standard Collected** policy. The analyzer allows you to adjust your settings values to align them at the same level as in **Standard Protection**.

- **Strict Recommendations**   Compare your existing security policy settings to those defined by the **Strict Collected** policy. You can adjust your settings values to align them at the same level as in **Strict Protection**.

- **Configuration Drift Analysis And History**   Audit and track policy changes over time.

Policies & rules > Threat policies > Configuration analyzer

Configuration analyzer

The configuration analyzer can help identify issues in your current configuration, and help improve your policies for better security. Learn more.

Standard recommendations   Strict recommendations   Configuration drift analysis and history

| Anti-spam | Anti-phishing | Anti-malware |
| 5 | 11 | 1 |

◯ Refresh   17 items   Search   Filter

Recommendations	Policy	Policy group/setting name	Policy type
☐ Quarantine message	Default	High confidence spam detection action	Anti-spam
☐ Quarantine message	Default	Phishing email detection action	Anti-spam
☐ Change 7 to 6	Default	Bulk email threshold	Anti-spam
☐ Change 15 to 30	Default	Quarantine retention period	Anti-spam
☐ Change False to True	Default	Enable end-user spam notifications	Anti-spam
☐ Change False to True	Office365 AntiPhish Default	Add users to protect	Anti-phishing
☐ Change False to True	Office365 AntiPhish Default	Automatically include the domains I own	Anti-phishing

FIGURE 5-29   Configuration Analyzer

MORE INFO   **CONFIGURATION ANALYZER FOR PROTECTION POLICIES**

You can learn more about the configuration analyzer for protection policies at *https://learn.microsoft.com/microsoft-365/security/office-365-security/configuration-analyzer-for-security-policies*.

Managing threats with Defender for Office

You manage threats for Defender for Office using the Threat Explorer. You can open Threat Explorer in the Microsoft 365 Defender portal by selecting **Email & Collaboration** and then choosing **Explorer**. Threat Explorer is shown in Figure 5-30.

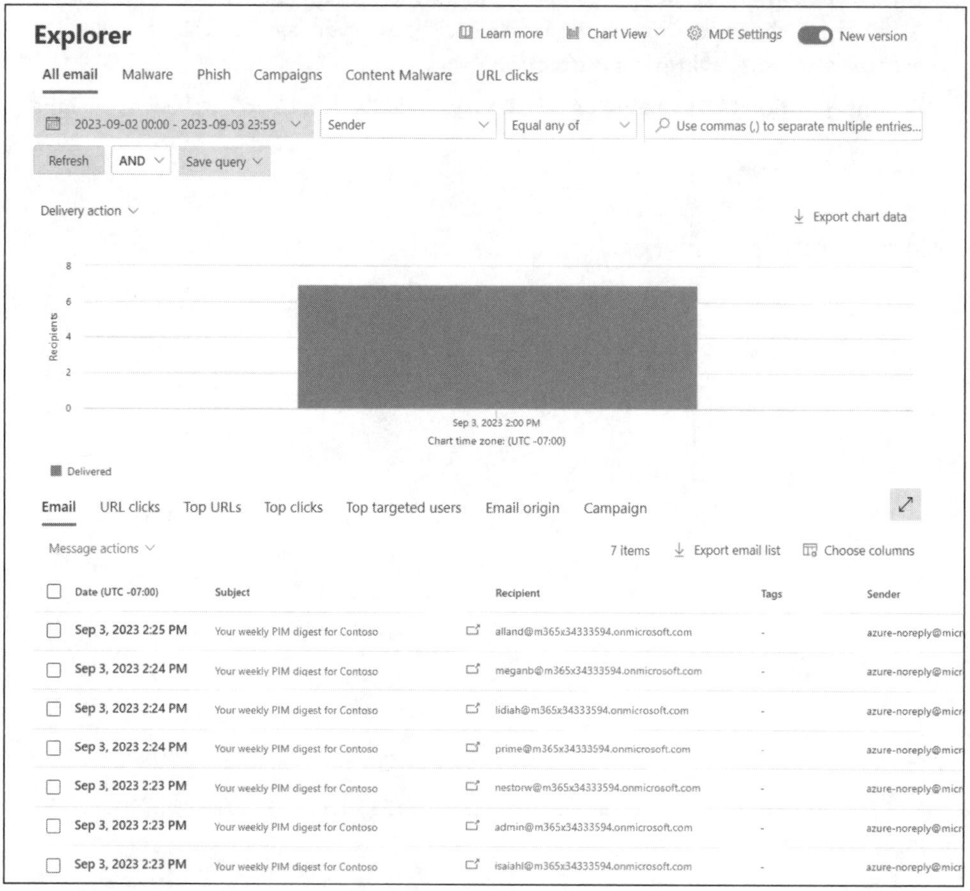

FIGURE 5-30 Threat Explorer

The tabs in Threat Explorer provide the following information:

- **All Email**   This tab displays all emails categorized as malicious, including phishing or malware content. This page also displays information about non-malicious email, including spam, bulk email, and routine message traffic.

- **Malware**   This tab displays all email messages identified as containing malware. The report provides information about the sender, recipients, sender domain, subject, detection, top malware families, and the top targeted users.

- **Phish** This tab displays all email messages categorized as phishing attempts. The page includes data by sender, recipients, sender domain, sender IP, URL domain, and click verdict (whether a user interacted with the phishing email).

- **Campaigns** Identifies and categorizes coordinated phishing and malware email attacks. Provides information on campaign source IP addresses, sender email domains, message properties, message recipients, and attack payloads in the messages.

- **Content Malware** View information by malware family, detection technology (how the malware was detected), and workload (OneDrive, SharePoint, or Teams).

- **URL Clicks** Displays all end user URL clicks in emails, Microsoft Teams messages, and Office 365 apps like OneDrive and SharePoint.

> **MORE INFO   DEFENDER FOR OFFICE SECURITY OPERATIONS**
>
> You can learn more about using Defender for Office to manage the security of collaboration workloads at *https://learn.microsoft.com/en-us/microsoft-365/security/office-365-security/mdo-sec-ops-guide*.

Managing attack simulations

Attack simulation training allows you to run simulated attacks against users in your organization to determine which ones might need remedial advice to avoid clicking on suspicious links or questionable attachments. To initiate attack simulation training, you need an account with Microsoft 365 Global Administrator or Security Administrator permissions or be assigned to one of the following roles.

- **Attack Simulator Administrators** Create and manage all aspects of attack simulation campaigns.

- **Attack Simulator Payload Authors** Create attack payloads that an admin can start later.

Attack simulation training requires that all email is hosted in Exchange Online, and you cannot run the process against on-premises deployments of Exchange. Running an attack simulation involves performing the following steps:

1. Choose a social engineering technique.
2. Choose a payload.
3. Select the target audience.
4. Assign training.
5. Launch details and review.

Choose a social engineering technique

You can choose to simulate the following social engineering techniques when performing an attack simulation as shown in Figure 5-31:

- **Credential Harvest**   In this scenario, the attacker sends the recipient a message that contains a URL. If the recipient clicks the URL, they're taken to a website that shows a dialog asking the user for their username and password. The website might be styled to appear legitimately related to your organization.

- **Malware Attachment**   In this scenario, the attacker sends the recipient a message that contains an attachment. If the recipient opens the attachment, the code executes on the user's device.

- **Link In Attachment**   In this scenario, the attacker sends the recipient a message containing a URL inside an attachment, such as a Word document or Excel spreadsheet. If the recipient opens the attachment and clicks the URL, they're taken to a website that asks the user for their username and password. For example, the website might be styled to appear legitimately related to your organization, such as an internal SharePoint site.

- **Link To Malware**   In this scenario, the attacker sends the recipient a message that contains a link to an attachment on a well-known file-sharing site such as OneDrive or SharePoint Online. If the recipient clicks the URL, the attachment opens, and arbitrary code is run on the user's device.

- **Drive-By-URL**   In this scenario, the attacker sends the recipient a message that contains a URL. If the recipient clicks the URL, they're taken to a website that tries to run background code to gather information about the recipient or deploy arbitrary code on their device.

- **OAuth Consent Grant**   In this scenario, an attacker creates a malicious Azure application designed to use the user's privileges to gain access to sensitive data. The application sends an email request that contains a URL. If the recipient clicks the URL, the consent grant mechanism of the application asks for access to the data.

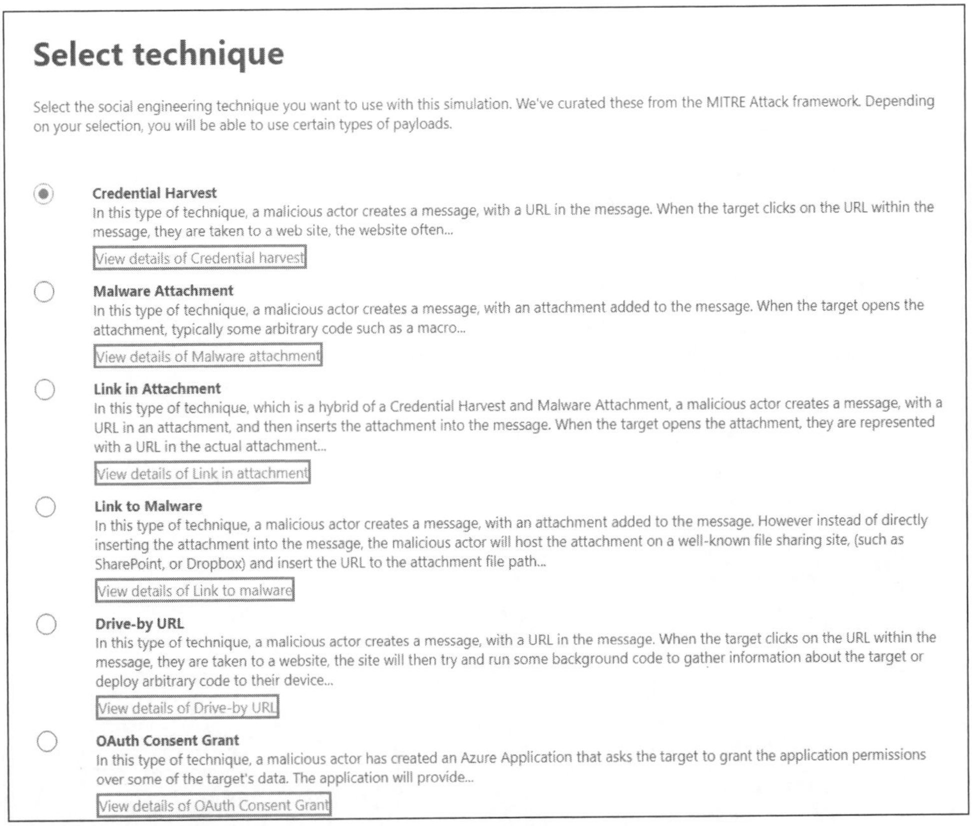

Select technique
Select the social engineering technique you want to use with this simulation. We've curated these from the MITRE Attack framework. Depending on your selection, you will be able to use certain types of payloads.
Credential Harvest
In this type of technique, a malicious actor creates a message, with a URL in the message. When the target clicks on the URL within the message, they are taken to a web site, the website often...
View details of Credential harvest
Malware Attachment
In this type of technique, a malicious actor creates a message, with an attachment added to the message. When the target opens the attachment, typically some arbitrary code such as a macro...
View details of Malware attachment
Link in Attachment
In this type of technique, which is a hybrid of a Credential Harvest and Malware Attachment, a malicious actor creates a message, with a URL in an attachment, and then inserts the attachment into the message. When the target opens the attachment, they are represented with a URL in the actual attachment...
View details of Link in attachment
Link to Malware
In this type of technique, a malicious actor creates a message, with an attachment added to the message. However instead of directly inserting the attachment into the message, the malicious actor will host the attachment on a well-known file sharing site, (such as SharePoint, or Dropbox) and insert the URL to the attachment file path...
View details of Link to malware
Drive-by URL
In this type of technique, a malicious actor creates a message, with a URL in the message. When the target clicks on the URL within the message, they are taken to a website, the site will then try and run some background code to gather information about the target or deploy arbitrary code to their device...
View details of Drive-by URL
OAuth Consent Grant
In this type of technique, a malicious actor has created an Azure Application that asks the target to grant the application permissions over some of the target's data. The application will provide...
View details of OAuth Consent Grant

FIGURE 5-31 Attack techniques

Create an attack simulation

To launch a simulated phishing attack, perform the following steps:

1. In the Microsoft 365 Defender portal, select **Email & Collaboration** > **Attack Simulation Training**.
2. On the **Simulations** tab shown in Figure 5-32, choose **Launch A Simulation**.

Attack simulation training
Learn more
What's New?
Share
Overview
Simulations
Training
Automations
Content library
Settings
A list of all your simulations and their status.
Draft 0
Scheduled 0
In progress 0
Completed 0
Failed 0
Cancelled 0
Show excluded simulations
Launch a simulation
0 items
Refresh
Search
Choose columns
Filter

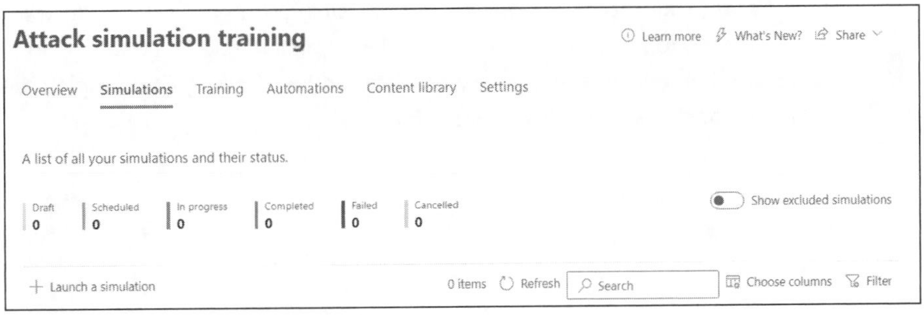

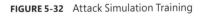

FIGURE 5-32 Attack Simulation Training

3. On the **Select Technique** page, choose which type of social engineering you will use with this specific campaign. The example we will explore here is **Credential Harvest**. Choose **Next**.

4. On the **Name Simulation** page, provide a name for the simulation.

5. On the **Select Payload And Login Page**, choose from the existing options and choose **Next**. Figure 5-33 shows an **Acrobat Document Share** payload selected.

Select payload and login page

Select payload for this simulation technique. You can create or collect your own payloads to add this list. Note that if you create a new payload, you will be redirected to a payload creation wizard. You can also map a login page for Credential Harvest or Link in Attachment technique to a payload from the preview tab.

Global payloads   Tenant payloads

▷ Send a test   1 of 100 selected   🔍 Search   ⅂⅂ Filter

Payload Name	Language	Predicted Compromise Rate (%)
☐ Voicemail from Polin Marshall	English	32
☐ Black Friday Offer	English	20
☐ Declined sendgrid payment	English	34
☐ Suspended Mailgun account	English	38
☑ Acrobat Document Share	English	21
☐ PR TIMES Magazine	Other	20
☐ Facebook identity check	English	34
☐ 2 Failed Messages	English	39
☐ Email Quarantined Notification	English	37

FIGURE 5-33   Select Payload And Login Page

6. On the **Target Users** page, choose whether to include all users in the organization or just specific users and groups. Select **Next**. If you choose all users in the organization, you can select specific exclusions.

7. On the **Assign Training** page, you can choose training content to also be forwarded to the target users. You can choose to assign default training, selected training, no training, or a custom URL. You can also select a due date for the training to be completed. After you have made these selections, choose **Next**.

8. On the **Select Phish Landing Page**, choose which page is displayed if the user is successfully phished. These landing pages can contain "learning moments," which explain to the user why their choice to interact with the phishing email would lead to deleterious results if this were not a simulation. This page is shown in Figure 5-34. Select **Next**.

Select Phish landing page

Select landing page that provides a learning moment to the user after getting phished. Learn more

⦿ Use landing pages from library
◯ Use a custom URL

Payload Indicators

☐ Add payload indicators to email. They help users to learn how to identify the phishing email.

Global landing pages   Tenant landing pages

↻ Refresh   5 items   🔍 Search   ⦓ Filter   ⊞ Choose columns

	Name ⌄	Language ⌄	Default Language ⌄	Status ⌄
☐	Microsoft Landing Page Template 1	German, English.. +10	English	✓ Ready
☐	Microsoft Landing Page Template 2	German, English.. +10	English	✓ Ready
☐	Microsoft Landing Page Template 3	German, English.. +10	English	✓ Ready
☐	Microsoft Landing Page Template 4	German, English.. +10	English	✓ Ready
☐	Microsoft Landing Page Template 5	German, English.. +10	English	✓ Ready

FIGURE 5-34 Phishing landing page

9. On the **Select End User Notification** page, choose what end user notifications occur as a result of this campaign. Your options are to not deliver notifications, deliver default notifications, or create a custom notification. Select **Next**. You can then select what information about the simulation, training assignments, training reminders, and positive reinforcements the user will receive as part of the campaign.

10. On the **Launch Details** page, choose when to schedule the **Attack Simulation**. Choose **Next**.

11. On the **Review** page, review the simulation. You can send a test or select **Submit** to launch the attack simulation campaign.

MORE INFO   ATTACK SIMULATION TRAINING

You can learn more about attack simulation training at *https://learn.microsoft.com/microsoft-365/security/office-365-security/attack-simulation-training-get-started*.

Create an attack payload

Attack payloads include the content of the email and associated malware and websites related to the campaign. Payloads are segmented into three general categories, available in the **Content Library** in the following sections shown in Figure 5-35:

- **Global Payloads**   Contains the built-in, non-modifiable payloads.
- **Tenant Payloads**   Contains the custom payloads that you've created.
- **MDO Recommendations**   Payloads recommended by Defender for Office 365 have a considerable impact when used by attackers. This list is refreshed monthly.

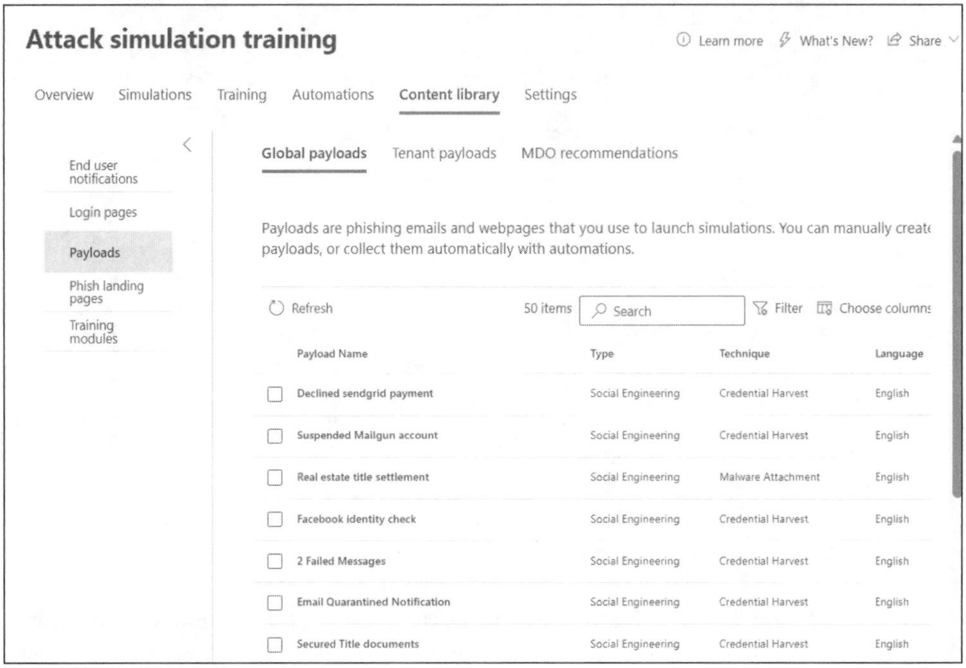

FIGURE 5-35   Attack simulation payloads

Creating a custom payload involves making selections related to the nature of the payload. As artificial intelligence is further integrated into Microsoft 365 Defender, attack payloads will appear increasingly realistic to those targeted by simulation campaigns. To create a custom payload, perform the following steps:

1. In the Microsoft 365 Defender portal, choose **Email & Collaboration** > **Attack Simulation Training**, select the **Content Library** tab, and then select **Payloads** and the **Tenant Payloads** tab.

2. On the **Tenant Payloads** tab, select **Create A Payload** to start the new payload wizard.

3. The only value you can currently select on the **Select Type** page is **Email**. Choose **Next**.

4. On the **Select Technique** page, choose a technique related to the payload. The available options are the same as on the **Select Technique** page in the new simulation wizard:

   - **Credential Harvest**
   - **Malware Attachment**
   - **Link In Attachment**
   - **Link To Malware**
   - **Drive-By URL**
   - **OAuth Consent Grant**

5. On the **Payload Name** page, configure the following settings and select **Next**:

   - **Name**   Enter a unique, descriptive name for the payload.
   - **Description**   Enter an optional detailed description for the payload.

6. Most of the settings on the **Configure Payload** page will be determined by the selection you made on the **Select Technique** page. Available settings depend on the chosen technique and include the following:

   - **Sender Details Section**   Provide information about the fictional sender for the campaign, including **Name**, **Display Name**, **From Email**, **Email Subject**, and whether an external tag is applied.
   - **Attachment Details Section**   Provide information on the attachment's name and type, **Docx** or **HTML**.
   - **Link For Attachment**   Select one of the prepopulated URLs.
   - **Phishing Link Section**   Select one of the prepopulated URLs.
   - **Attachment Content Section**   Allows you to create a custom login page.
   - **Theme**   Allows you to choose a theme for the content of the phishing email. The theme determines the type of email in which the simulated attack will be hidden. Options include **Account Activation, Account Verification, Billing, Clean Up Mail, Document Received, Expense, Fax, Finance Report, Incoming Messages, Invoice, Item Received, Login Alert, Mail Received, Other, Password, Payment, Payroll, Personalized Offer, Quarantine, Remote Work, Review Message, Security Update, Service Suspended, Signature Required, Upgrade Mailbox Storage, Verify Mailbox**, or **Voicemail**.
   - **Brand**   Allows you to have the attack simulation appear related to a specific brand. Options include **American Express, Capital One, DHL, DocuSign, Dropbox, Facebook, First American, Microsoft, Netflix, Scotiabank, SendGrid, Stewart Title, Tesco, Wells Fargo, Syrinx Cloud**, or **Other**.

- **Industry** Allows you to have the attack simulation appear related to a specific industry. The available values are **Banking**, **Business Services**, **Consumer Services**, **Education**, **Energy**, **Construction**, **Consulting**, **Financial Services**, **Government**, **Hospitality**, **Insurance**, **Legal**, **Courier Services**, **IT**, **Healthcare**, **Manufacturing**, **Retail**, **Telecom**, **Real Estate**, or **Other**.

- **Current Event** Allows you to have the content of the email mention a current event to seem topical and relevant to the target.

- **Controversial** Allows you to have the content of the email include a controversial topic to appear more engaging to the target.

- **Language** Allows you to specify which language the target email and any associated websites are presented in. The available values are **English**, **Spanish**, **German**, **Japanese**, **French**, **Portuguese**, **Dutch**, **Italian**, **Swedish**, **Chinese (Simplified)**, **Norwegian Bokmål**, **Polish**, **Russian**, **Finnish**, **Korean**, **Turkish**, **Hungarian**, **Hebrew**, **Thai**, **Arabic**, **Vietnamese**, **Slovak**, **Greek**, **Indonesian**, **Romanian**, **Slovenian**, **Croatian**, **Catalan**, or **Other**.

- **Email Message Section** Allows you to construct the email format by making more choices about the elements that constitute the email content.

7. On the **Add Indicators** page, you can add indicators that should hint to the recipient that the email is a phishing message.

8. On the **Review** page, you can review the settings you chose for the email. You can send a test message to send a test version of the email to yourself to preview what the payload looks like when it arrives through email. You can also select **Submit** to complete the creation of the new payload.

> **MORE INFO** **ATTACK SIMULATION PAYLOADS**
>
> You can learn more about attack simulation payloads at *https://learn.microsoft.com/microsoft-365/security/office-365-security/attack-simulation-training-payloads*.

Gain insights from attack simulations

Once you've performed an attack simulation, you can use insights and reports to determine how the targets of the simulated attack responded to that attack. You can view information about this on the **Attack Simulation Training Overview** tab and within simulation reports for in-progress or completed simulations on the **Recent Simulations** card (an element of a particular page displaying collected information). The **Recent Simulations** card shown in Figure 5-36 displays the three most recent simulations created or run.

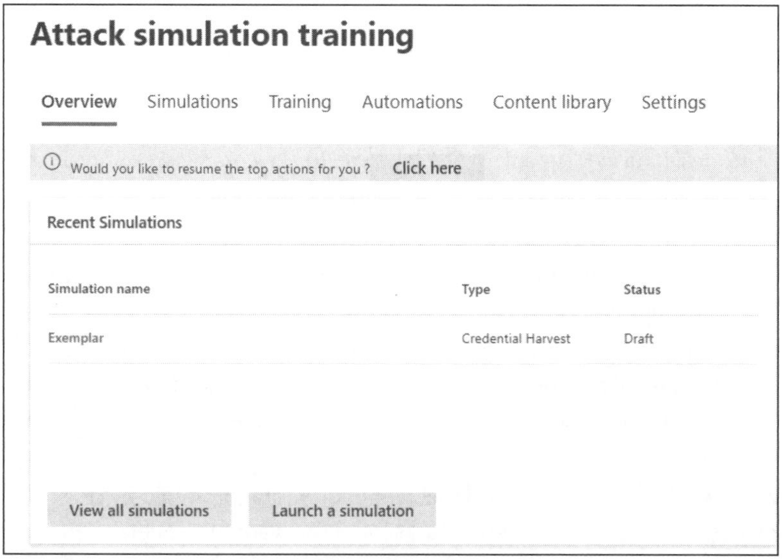

Attack simulation training

Overview   Simulations   Training   Automations   Content library   Settings

ⓘ Would you like to resume the top actions for you ?   **Click here**

Recent Simulations

Simulation name	Type	Status
Exemplar	Credential Harvest	Draft

View all simulations   Launch a simulation

FIGURE 5-36   List of recent simulations

The **Overview** tab of the **Attack Simulations Training** page on the Microsoft 365 Defender portal includes the following cards:

- **Simulation Coverage Card**   This card shows the percentage of users in your organization who have received a simulation (**Simulated Users**) versus users who haven't received a simulation (**Non-Simulated Users**).

- **Training Completion Card**   Displays the percentages of users who have received training through the simulations. Displays information on training completed, training in-progress, and training incomplete.

- **Repeat Offenders Card**   Displays information about users compromised by consecutive simulations. These are the users you want to target with remedial training and who represent a vulnerability to your organization because of their willingness to interact with content that can be used to compromise your organization's security.

- **Behavior Impact On Compromise Rate Card**   This card displays how your users responded to your simulations as compared to the historical data in Microsoft 365. Allows you to view predicted compromise rates against what actually happened when you ran the simulations.

The Attack Simulation Report provides detailed information on a specific attack simulation that isn't available in the summary cards on the overview page. This report includes the following tabs:

- **Training Efficacy**   Displays how your users responded to specific simulations as compared to the historical data in Microsoft 365. Allows you to view predicted compromise rates against what actually happened when you ran each simulation.

- **User Coverage**   Displays the percentage of users in your organization who have received specific simulations (**Simulated Users**) versus users who haven't received specific simulations (**Non-Simulated Users**).

- **Training Completion**   Displays the number of **Completed**, **In Progress**, and **Incomplete** simulations. Allows you to view username, email address, date of last simulation, last simulation result, name of most recent training completed, date completed, and all assigned training.

- **Repeat Offenders**   This tab will display details about users compromised by consecutive simulations. You can determine which attacks these users are susceptible to and how often they have succumbed to the attack.

Each simulation report includes the following information:

- **Simulation Impact**   Displays how many users succumbed to the simulation and the total number of users targeted by the simulation. Depending on the nature of the simulation, this report also displays the following:
  - Number of users that entered credentials and did not enter credentials
  - Number of users that opened attachments and did not open attachments

- **All User Activity**   Displays information on the statistics related to the possible outcomes of the attack simulation.

- **Training Complete**   Displays information related to training completion for the training included in a specific simulation.

- **Recommended Actions**   Displays Secure Score recommendation actions and the impact the action will have on your Secure Score.

> **MORE INFO   ATTACK SIMULATION TRAINING INSIGHTS**
>
> You can learn more about attack simulation training insights at *https://learn.microsoft.com/ microsoft-365/security/office-365-security/attack-simulation-training-insights*.

Blocked users

If a user exceeds the outbound sending limits of the service or outbound spam policies, the following rules come into effect:

- The user is restricted from sending emails. They are still able to receive email.
- The user is added to the **Restricted Entities** page in the Microsoft 365 Defender portal.

If the user attempts to send an email, they will be sent a non-delivery report informing them that they are not recognized as a valid sender. When a user exceeds the outbound email or outbound spam threshold, the user will be added to the **Restricted Entities** page in the Microsoft 365 Defender portal.

To remove a user from the **Restricted Entities** page, perform the following steps:

1. In the Microsoft 365 Defender portal, navigate to **Email & Collaboration** and select **Review** > **Restricted Entities**.

2. On the **Restricted Entities** page, select the user to unblock by selecting the checkbox for the entity and then selecting the **Unblock** action that appears on the page.

3. In the **Unblock User** flyout menu, verify that the account isn't compromised and select **Next**.

4. On the **Unblock User** page, consider the recommendations and use the links in the **Multi-Factor Authentication** and **Change Password** sections to enable MFA and reset the user's password.

5. When you're finished on the **Unblock User** page, select **Submit**.

> *MORE INFO* **BLOCKED USERS**
>
> You can learn more about removing blocked users at *https://learn.microsoft.com/en-us/ microsoft-365/security/office-365-security/removing-user-from-restricted-users-portal- after-spam.*

Skill 5.3: Endpoint protection

Defender for Endpoint allows you to protect endpoint devices, including PCs, laptops, phones, routers, firewalls, and access points.

> **This section covers the following skills:**
> - Defender for Endpoint
> - Onboarding devices
> - Manage Defender for Endpoint settings

Defender for Endpoint

Defender for Endpoint leverages the following combination of device functionality and cloud services:

- **Endpoint behavioral sensors**   Processes behavioral telemetry from the operating system and forwards it to an isolated instance of Microsoft Defender for Endpoint hosted in the cloud.

- **Cloud security analytics**   Examines behavioral signals to detect advanced threats and provide recommended responses.

- **Threat intelligence**   Threat intelligence takes research from Microsoft's security teams and partners to identify attacker tools and methods. Alerts will be generated when these tools and methods are detected in collected sensor data.

> **MORE INFO**   **OVERVIEW OF DEFENDER FOR ENDPOINT**
>
> You can learn more about Defender for Endpoint at *https://learn.microsoft.com/ microsoft-365/security/defender-endpoint/microsoft-defender-endpoint*.

Onboarding devices

Before Defender for Endpoint can collect telemetry from a client device, that device needs to be connected through a process known as onboarding. You can use the following methods to onboard Windows client devices to Defender for Endpoint.

- Onboard using Intune
- Onboard using Configuration Manager
- Onboard using Group Policy
- Onboard using a local script

Defender for Endpoint can use one of the following architectures, which will influence the method you leverage when onboarding devices:

- Cloud-native
- Co-management
- On-premises

> **MORE INFO**   **ONBOARDING WINDOWS CLIENTS**
>
> You can learn more about onboarding Windows clients at *https://learn.microsoft.com/ microsoft-365/security/defender-endpoint/onboard-windows-client*.

Onboard using Intune

If you already have devices enrolled in Microsoft Intune, you can use Intune to onboard the devices into Microsoft Identity for Defender. Defender for Endpoint supports OMA-URIs (Open Mobile Alliance Uniform Resource Identifier) for policies to manage endpoint devices such as client computers running Windows 10 and Windows 11. OMA-URI is a standardized set of URI strings used to manage endpoint device settings.

To configure the connection between Intune and Defender for Endpoint, perform the following steps:

1. From the Microsoft Intune admin center, choose **Endpoint Security** > **Microsoft Defender For Endpoint**. When Defender for Endpoint is not configured, the connection status will be shown as **Unavailable**, as displayed in Figure 5-37.

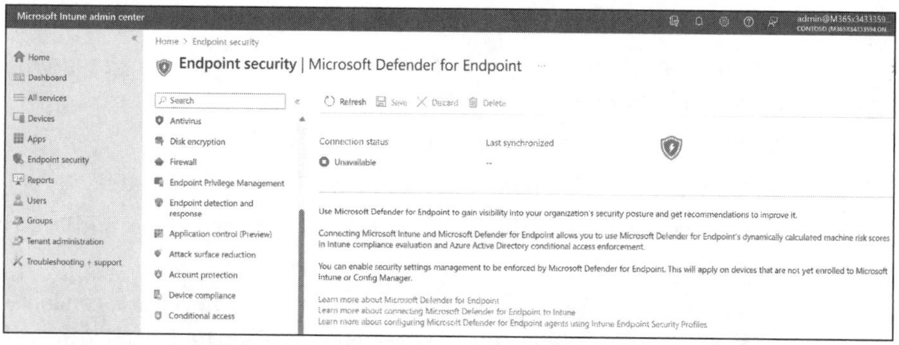

FIGURE 5-37 Microsoft Defender for Endpoint

2. Select **Connect Microsoft Defender For Endpoint To Microsoft Intune In Microsoft Defender Security Center**. This will open the Microsoft 365 Defender portal.

3. Select **Settings** > **Endpoints** > **Advanced Features**. Set the **Microsoft Intune Connection** to **On**, as shown in Figure 5-38, and then select **Save Preferences**.

4. Once the connection is established, services will sync approximately every 24 hours.

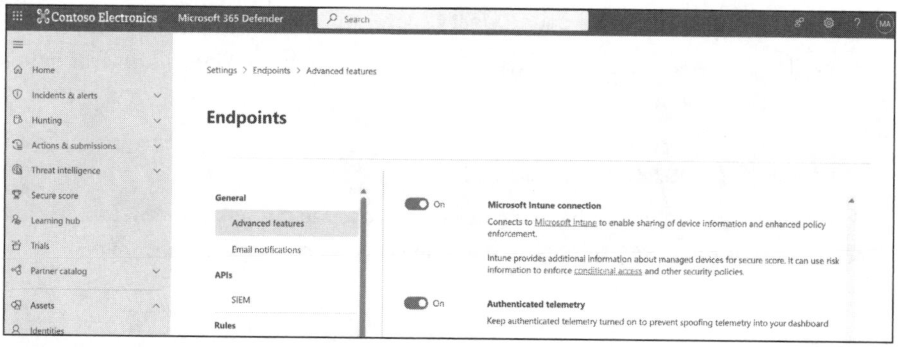

FIGURE 5-38 Configure Intune connection

Once the connection between Intune and Defender for Endpoint is configured, Intune will receive an onboarding configuration package. Using a device configuration profile, you can deploy this configuration package to Windows Devices from Intune. When you deploy a configuration package, the device will be configured to communicate with Defender for Endpoint services and can scan local files and detect security threats. The enrolled device will forward risk-level telemetry to Microsoft Defender for Endpoint using settings defined in compliance policies.

In addition to using configuration packages to onboard devices using Intune, you can also configure an endpoint detection and response policy. Intune endpoint detection and response policies allow you to configure device security without using the larger set of settings available in a device configuration profile. Endpoint detection and response policies might also be used with Configuration Manager.

Follow these steps to create a device configuration profile to onboard a device already enrolled in Intune to Defender for Endpoint:

1. From the Microsoft Intune admin center, choose **Endpoint Security** >**Endpoint Detection And Response** > **Create Policy**.

2. For **Platform**, choose **Windows 10 And Later**.

3. For **Profile Type**, select **Endpoint Detection And Response** > **Create**.

4. On the **Basics** page of the **Profile Creation Wizard**, provide a **Name** and **Description** and select **Next**.

5. On the **Configuration Settings** page of the **Profile Creation Wizard**, configure sample sharing for all files and expedite telemetry reporting frequency. Sample sharing allows suspicious files to be collected from a device. You enable expedited telemetry if a device is at high-risk and you want rapid notification if Defender for Endpoint suspects the device is compromised.

6. On the **Scope Tags** page, select **Scope Tags** to select a set of tagged devices. Select **Next**.

7. On the **Assignments** page, choose which groups of user and device profiles will be assigned this device configuration profile. Choose **Next**.

8. On the **Review + Create** page, select **Create**.

You will need the Microsoft Defender ATP permission to view Windows devices onboarded to Microsoft Defender for Endpoint using Intune.

> **MORE INFO** **ONBOARD USING INTUNE**
> You can learn more about onboarding devices attached to Intune at *https://learn.microsoft.com/en-us/microsoft-365/security/defender-endpoint/configure-endpoints-mdm.*

Onboard using Configuration Manager

You can use System Center Configuration Manager 2012 R2 or Microsoft Configuration Manager current branch to onboard managed endpoint clients to Microsoft Defender for Endpoint. You should install the Configuration Manager Endpoint Protection site system role when preparing to use Defender for Endpoint with Configuration Manager.

Defender for Endpoint does not support being deployed through a client's Out-Of-Box Experience (OOBE) deployment phase. You can create a Configuration Manager detection rule that polls the client frequently to determine if it has been onboarded to Defender for Endpoint. Configuration Manager can be configured to retry onboarding the client until the detection rule determines that Defender for Endpoint has been deployed. This detection rule should check if the OnboardingState registry value is set to DWORD 1 in the HKLM\SOFTWARE\Microsoft\Windows Advanced Threat Protection\Status area of the client computer's registry.

To enable Endpoint Protection and manage custom client settings, perform the following steps:

1. In the **Configuration Manager** console, select **Administration**; in the **Administration** workspace, select **Client Settings**.

2. In the **Home** section, select **Create** > **Create Custom Client Device Settings**. In the **Create Custom Client Device Settings** dialog, enter a name and description for the settings you will be configuring and choose **Endpoint Protection**.

3. Configure the following Endpoint Protection client settings and choose **OK**:

   - **Manage Endpoint Protection client on client computers**   Choose this option when you want to manage Defender for Endpoint through Configuration Manager.

   - **Install Endpoint Protection client on client computers**   Choose this option if you want to deploy Defender for Endpoint through Configuration Manager.

   - **Allow Endpoint Protection client installation and restarts outside maintenance windows**   Enable this option to override behavior so that installation and restarts can occur outside designated maintenance windows.

   - **Suppress any required computer restarts after the Endpoint Protection client is installed**   Allows you to block clients from restarting after the Defender for Endpoint client is installed. The computer will wait until the next maintenance window to restart.

   - **Allowed period of time users can postpone a required restart to complete Endpoint Protection installation**   If a restart is required, allows you to configure how long a user can postpone the restart.

   - **Disable alternate sources for initial definition update on client computers**   If you enable this setting, the client will only use Configuration Manager to obtain the initial definition update.

4. Deploy the custom client device settings to a Configuration Manager collection.

You can install Defender for Endpoint from the command prompt on a client computer connected to a Configuration Manager instance by performing the following steps:

1. Locate the `scepinstall.exe` executable file from the Client folder of the Configuration Manager installation folder to the client computer on which you want to deploy Defender for Endpoint.

2. Open an elevated command prompt, switch to the directory with the executable file, and execute the file. The command line argument /s can run the installer silently.

3. After the installer completes, Windows Defender for Endpoint will automatically perform a definition update check.

> **MORE INFO** **ONBOARDING USING CONFIGURATION MANAGER**
>
> You can learn more about onboarding devices using Configuration Manager at *https://learn. microsoft.com/microsoft-365/security/defender-endpoint/configure-endpoints-sccm.*

Onboard using Group Policy

The first step you must take is to download the Group Policy configuration package from the Microsoft 365 Defender portal. You can do this by performing the following steps:

1. In the navigation panel, select **Settings** > **Endpoints** > **Device Management** > **Onboarding**.

2. Choose **Windows 10** or **Windows 11** as the target operating system.

3. In the **Deployment Method** section, choose **Group Policy**.

4. Select **Download Package** and save the zip file.

Extract the zip file to a shared folder configured with read-only permissions. The extracted files should have a folder named `OptionalParamsPolicy` and a `WindowsDefenderATPOnboarding Script.cmd` file, and then you must perform the following steps:

1. In the **Group Policy** management console on a computer with the Remote Server Administration Tools Group Policy installed, create a new Group Policy Object.

2. Edit the new Group Policy object. In the Group Policy Management Editor, navigate to **Computer Configuration** > **Preferences** and select **Control Panel Settings**.

3. Right-click **Scheduled Tasks** and select **New** > **Immediate Task**.

4. In the **Task** window, select the **General** tab. Under **Security Options**, choose **Change User Or Group**, enter **SYSTEM**, and then click **Check Names To Assign NT AUTHORITY\SYSTEM** and choose **OK**.

5. Choose **Run Whether User Is Logged On Or Not** and select the **Run With Highest Privileges** checkbox.

6. Set the name field to **Defender for Endpoint Deployment**.

7. On the **Actions** tab, choose **New** and ensure that **Start A Program** is chosen in the **Action** field. Provide the UNC path to the `WindowsDefenderATPOnboardingScript.cmd` file, being careful to use the file server's fully qualified domain name in the UNC address.

8. Close the **Group Policy Management Editor** and link the **Group Policy Object** at the group policy scope to which you want to install the Defender for Endpoint client.

You can link the GPO to an OU that hosts computer accounts and use security group filtering to limit the application of the policy to computer accounts that are group members.

MORE INFO **ONBOARDING USING GROUP POLICY**

You can learn more about onboarding devices using Group Policy at *https://learn.microsoft. com/microsoft-365/security/defender-endpoint/configure-endpoints-gp*.

Onboard using script

You can download a packaged zip file from the Microsoft 365 Defender Portal by performing the following steps:

1. In the navigation panel, select **Settings** > **Endpoints**. Select **Device Management** > **Onboarding**.

2. Choose **Windows 10** or **Windows 11** as the target operating system.

3. In the **Deployment Method** section, choose **Local Script**.

4. Select Download Package and save the zip file.

Once you have downloaded the zip file, you can extract the file, resulting in a script named `WindowsDefenderATPLocalOnboardingScript.cmd` being present in the folder in which you extracted the files. Run this script using an elevated command prompt.

MORE INFO **ONBOARDING USING A LOCAL SCRIPT**

You can learn more about onboarding devices using Configuration Manager at *https://learn. microsoft.com/en-us/microsoft-365/security/defender-endpoint/configure-endpoints-script*.

Manage Defender for Endpoint settings

You can configure the following Defender for Endpoint settings by navigating to **Settings** > **Endpoints** in the Microsoft 365 Defender portal.

- **General Settings**   Allows you to configure general settings.

- **Rules**   Configuration of automation settings and suppression rules.

- **Configuration Management**   Configure how security settings are applied to endpoint clients managed by Intune or Configuration Manager.

- **Device Management**   Manage the onboarding and offboarding of endpoint devices.

General settings

In the **General** section of Defender for Cloud's Endpoints settings, you can configure the following items:

- **Advanced Features** Advanced features allow integration with other products and services. Table 5-1 lists the advanced features you can enable for Endpoints in Microsoft 365 Defender. The **Advanced Features** page is shown in Figure 5-39.

- **Licenses** Allows you to manage the utilization and availability of client licenses.

- **Email Notifications** Allows you to create rules that determine device and alert sensitivities that will trigger email notifications. Also allows you to configure the properties of the email notifications. Also allows you to configure notifications for detected vulnerabilities.

- **Auto Remediation** Allows you to remediate potentially unwanted applications (PUA) even when PUA detection is not configured on devices. Enabling this option will restrict users from installing PUA on their devices.

TABLE 5-1 Advanced Features

Feature	Description
Enable EDR in block mode	Enables behavioral blocking and containment capabilities by blocking malicious artifacts or behaviors observed through post-breach endpoint detection and response (EDR) capabilities.
Allow or block file	Allow or block specific files.
Hide potential duplicate device records	When enabled, hides duplications that occur because the device was discovered multiple times or unintentionally onboarded.
Custom network indicators	Configures endpoint devices to allow or block connections to IP addresses, domains, or URLs in the custom indicator lists.
Tamper protection	Malicious apps are prevented from disabling security features, including virus and threat protection and behavior monitoring.
Show user details	Displays information about users retrieved from Microsoft Entra ID.
Skype for Business integration	Allows communication with users through Skype for Business.
Office 365 Threat Intelligence connection	Connects Microsoft 365 Defender to Office 365 Threat Intelligence to enable security investigations across Office 365 mailboxes and Windows devices.
Microsoft Defender for Cloud Apps	Forwards Microsoft Defender for Endpoint signals to Defender for Cloud Apps. This provides deeper visibility into sanctioned and unsanctioned cloud apps (also known as *shadow IT*).
Web content filtering	Restrict access to websites containing undesirable content and track web activity across all domains.
Device discovery	Allows onboarded devices to discover unmanaged devices on connected networks.

Live Response	Allows users assigned Live Response privileges to connect remotely to connected endpoint clients they are authorized to access using a remote shell connection.
Live Response for Servers	Allows users assigned Live Response privileges to connect remotely to connected servers they are authorized to access.
Live Response unsigned script execution	Allows technicians to use unsigned PowerShell scripts when responding in Live Response scenarios.
Share endpoint alerts with Microsoft Compliance Center	Allows endpoint security alerts to be forwarded to Microsoft Compliance Center. This allows for more comprehensive insider risk management policies.
Microsoft Intune connection	Allows for a connection to Intune for sharing of device information and policy enforcement.
Authenticated telemetry	Configures authentication for telemetry to block spoofed telemetry being injected into Microsoft 365 Defender dashboards.
Preview features	Allows for preview features to be accessed and integrated with Defender for Endpoint before they become generally available.

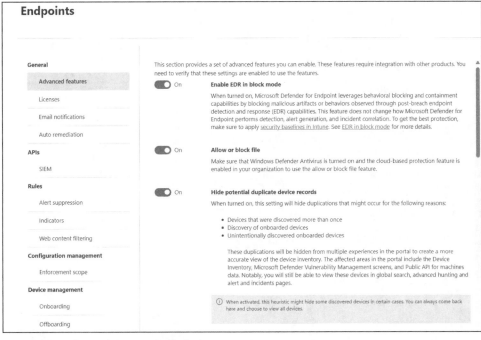

FIGURE 5-39 Advanced Features for endpoints

Rules

In the **Rules** section of Defender for Cloud's Endpoints, you can configure **Indicator** and **Web Content Filtering Rules**.

Indicators, also called *indicators of compromise (IoC)*, are forensic artifacts identified on a host network. Detection of an IoC indicates that a computer or network intrusion has likely occurred. IoCs can include

- File hashes of known malware
- Signatures of malicious network traffic
- URLs or domain names of known malware sources

Microsoft uses a library of IoCs with products such as Defender for Endpoint. You would use the Indicator functionality of Defender for Endpoint to create exclusions, such as when you know a specific file is safe or a specific IP address or URL is not malicious. You would provide that information in this area of Defender for Endpoint settings so that these files or network locations are not restricted for your organization.

Web Content Filtering allows you to create policies to block the following web content categories:

- Adult Content
  - Cults
  - Gambling
  - Nudity
  - Pornography/Sexually Explicit
  - Sex Education
  - Tasteless
  - Violence
- High Bandwidth
  - Download Sites
  - Image Sharing
  - Peer-to-Peer
  - Streaming Media & Downloads
- Legal Liability
  - Child Abuse Images
  - Criminal Activity
  - Hacking
  - Hate & Intolerance
  - Illegal Drug
  - Illegal Software
  - School Cheating
  - Self-Harm
  - Weapons

- Leisure
  - Chat
  - Games
  - Instant Messaging
  - Professional Networking
  - Web-based Email
  - Social Networking
- Uncategorized
  - Parked Domains
  - Newly Registered Domains

When creating the policy, specify which content categories you want to block. Figure 5-40 shows a policy where websites categorized as related to Professional Networking will be blocked, but other content will be allowed.

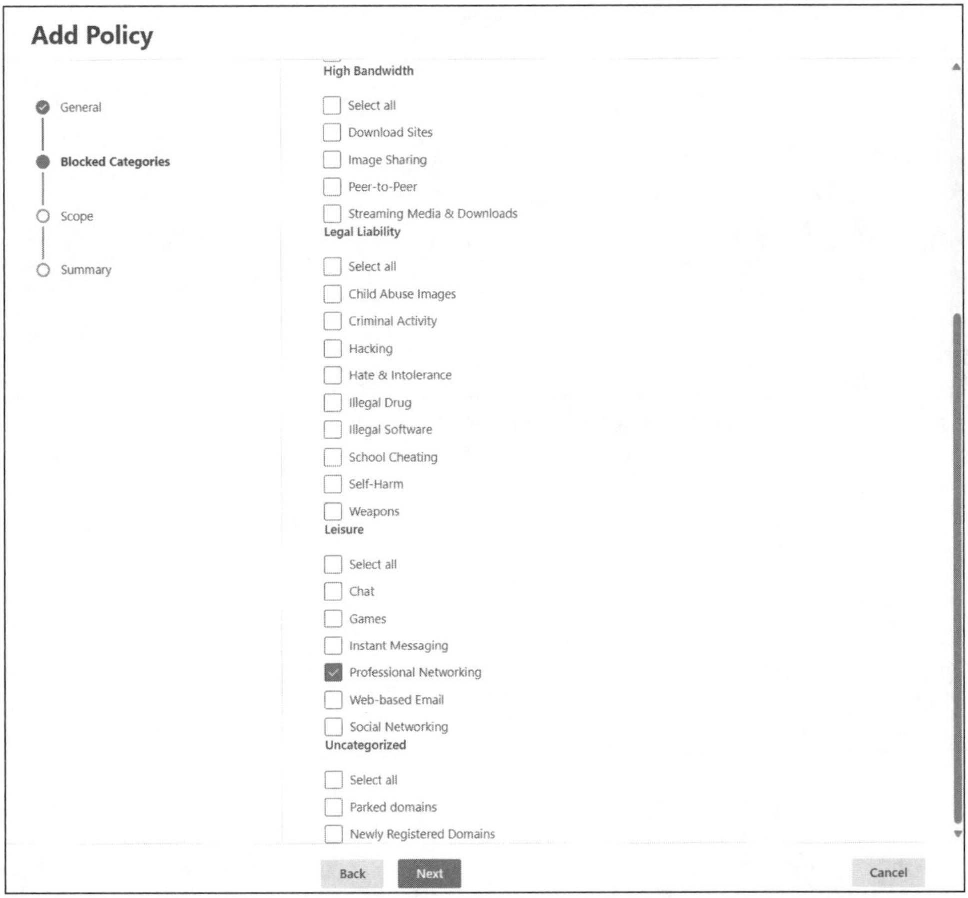

FIGURE 5-40 Category blocking

Configuration Management

The Configuration Management section of Microsoft Defender for Endpoint settings allows you to configure security settings in Intune to be enforced by Microsoft Defender for Endpoint. To do this, you must enable integration for Microsoft Defender for Endpoint under Intune. Figure 5-41 shows configuration management enabled for both Windows Client and Windows Server devices.

Security setting management

Allow security setting in Intune to be enforced by Microsoft Defender for Endpoint (MDE). This configuration setting will apply to devices that are not yet enrolled to Intune.

You'll need to turn on the integration in Microsoft Defender for Endpoint connector settings under Intune. For more information and pre-requisites, see Security settings management for Microsoft Defender for Endpoint.

Use MDE to enforce security configuration settings from Intune

On

Enable configuration management

Choose which OS platforms to apply the settings on.

☑ Windows Client devices

☑ Windows Server devices

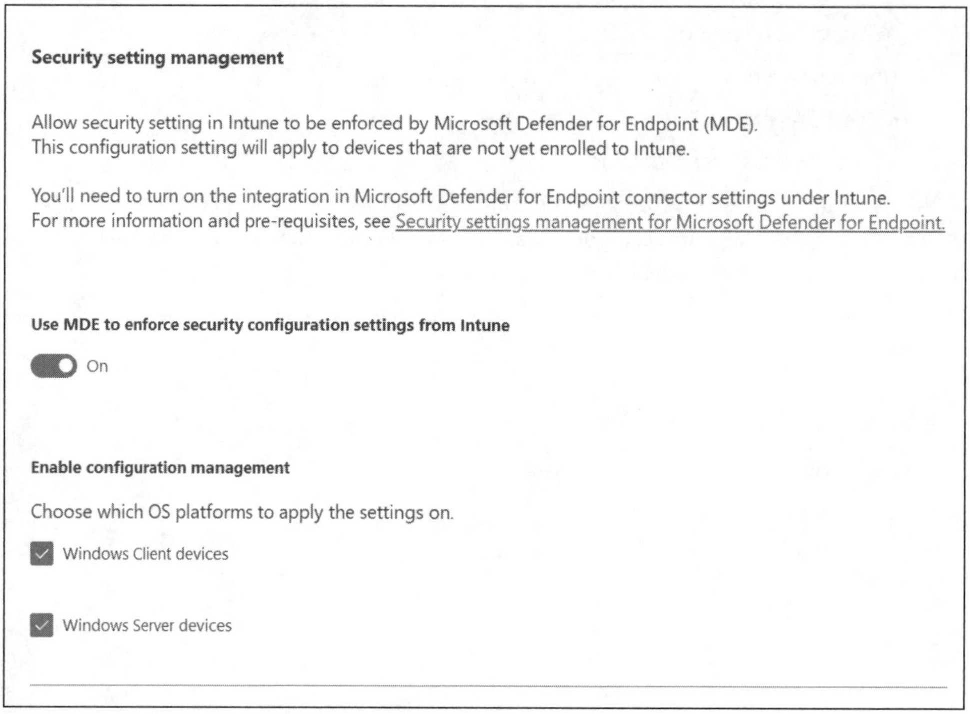

FIGURE 5-41 Configure security to be enforced by MDE

Device Management

The Onboarding section of Device Management provides you with a deployment tool to obtain onboarding packages. You choose the operating system and the method of onboarding. You can then choose which deployment method to use to onboard, as shown in Figure 5-42. Onboarding using Intune, Configuration Manager, Group Policy, and Scripts was detailed earlier in this chapter in the "Onboarding devices Endpoint" section.

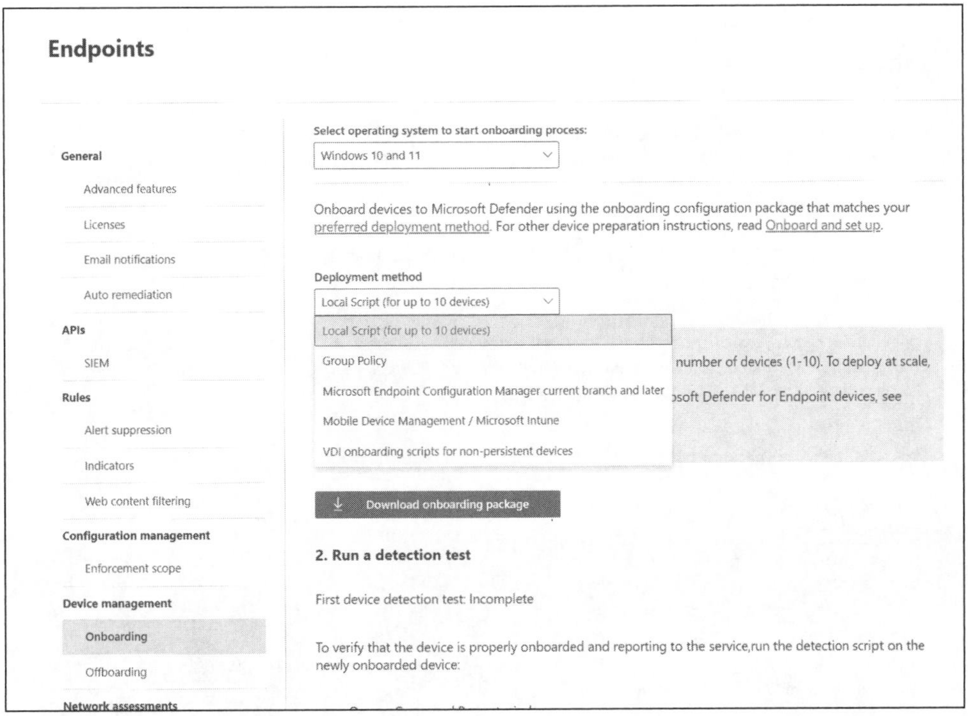

FIGURE 5-42 Onboarding devices

The **Offboarding** section is presented similarly to the **Onboarding** section, except that you choose the method you want to use to remove Microsoft Defender for Endpoint and then download a package allowing you to do this. Figure 5-43 shows that you can offboard a device using a local script, group policy, Configuration Manager, or Microsoft Intune.

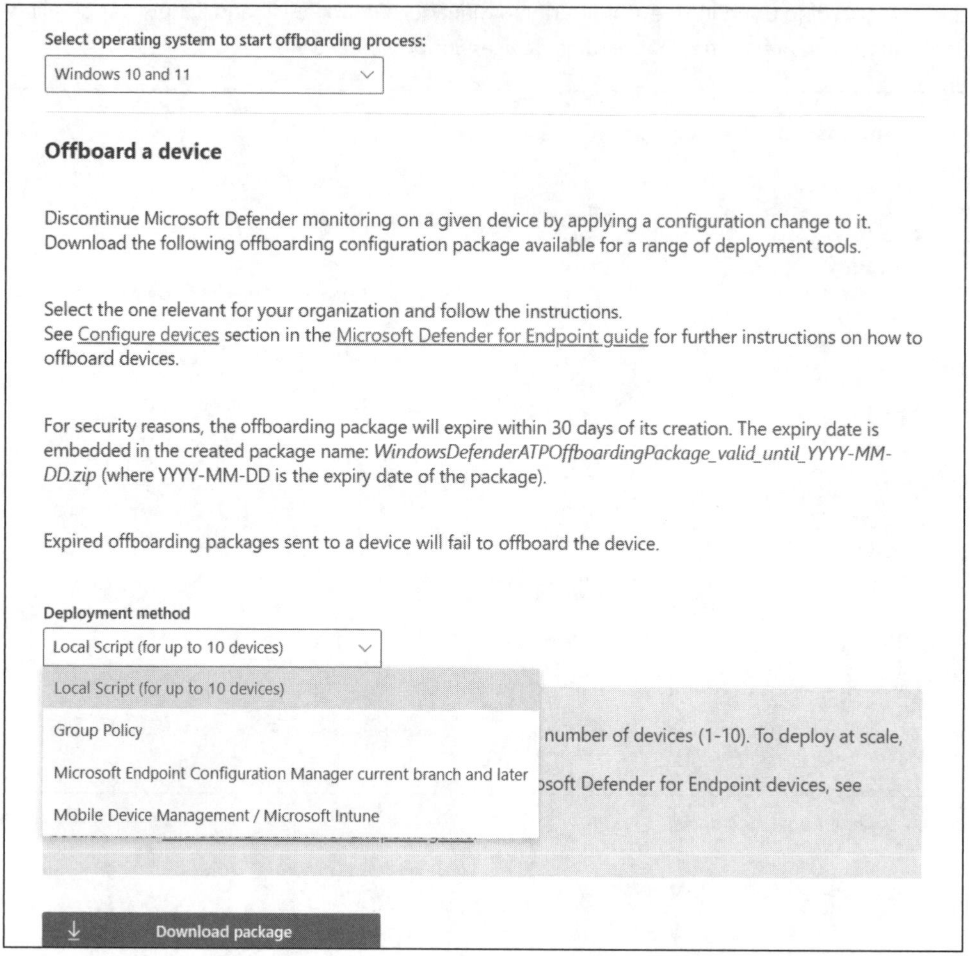

FIGURE 5-43 Offboard options

MORE INFO   **DEFENDER FOR ENDPOINT SETTINGS**

You can learn more about configuring general Defender for Endpoint settings at *https://learn.microsoft.com/en-us/microsoft-365/security/defender-endpoint/preferences-setup*.

EXAM TIP

Remember the different methods you can use to deploy Defender for Endpoint.

Chapter summary

- Secure Score allows you to assess the current security posture of your Microsoft 365 tenancy against all the actions you could take to secure that tenancy.

- Incidents are collections of related entities relevant to a security problem.

- Threat analytics allow you to view information about prominent threats and how your organization's digital estate might be vulnerable to them.

- Defender for Office allows you to protect content transmitted through Exchange, SharePoint, and Teams.

- Attack simulations allow you to run trial phishing campaigns against users in your organization to determine whether they need further security training.

- Defender for Endpoint allows you to use Microsoft 365 tools to manage the security of the endpoint devices in your organization.

Thought experiment

In this thought experiment, demonstrate your skills and knowledge of the topics covered in this chapter. You can find answers to this thought experiment in the next section.

Configuring Microsoft 365 Defender settings and policies

You are in the process of configuring Microsoft 365 Defender settings for your organization. One of the challenges you face is that while you want to block people in your organization from sending messages that Microsoft 365 recognizes as spam, most of the messages sent by people in your organization's Sales department are being identified as spam.

As other policies evolve at your organization, you want to ensure you can audit and track changes to Defender for Office policy over time. You also have a number of Windows 11 clients at your organization that are not managed by Intune or Configuration Manager but are members of your organization's Active Directory Domain Services domain. You want to ensure that Defender for Endpoint is deployed on these client computers.

With this information, answer the following questions:

1. What steps can you take to prevent Sales team members from being tripped up by the outbound spam filter while keeping the rules in place for everyone else?

2. What tool can you use to audit and track Defender for Office policy changes over time?

3. How can you deploy Defender for Endpoint to the domain-joined Windows 11 clients not managed by Intune?

Thought experiment answers

This section contains the solution to the thought experiment. Each answer explains why the answer choice is correct.

1. Create a custom anti-spam policy for the Sales team that exempts them from the outbound spam rules. This policy will only apply to the Sales team, so everyone else who sends a message that looks like spam will have it trigger the default policies.

2. You can use the Configuration analyzer to audit and track policy changes over time.

3. You can use a Group Policy Object to deploy Defender for Endpoint to Windows 11 clients that are members of an Active Directory Domain Services domain.

CHAPTER 6

Manage Microsoft Purview compliance

Managing Microsoft 365 involves more than just the traditional IT Professional task of ensuring that everyone can write documents in Word and Excel, access their email, and meet with colleagues over Microsoft Teams. Not only must you ensure that the data generated by your organization is secure and available, but it must be managed to comply with the regulations to which your organization is subject.

Skills in this chapter:

- Skill 6.1: Sensitive information types
- Skill 6.2: Sensitivity labels and policies
- Skill 6.3: Retention labels and policies
- Skill 6.4: Data Loss Prevention (DLP)

Skill 6.1: Sensitive information types

Sensitive information is data that regulation specifies requires special treatment. The specific information that would be classified as sensitive will depend on the legislation your organization is subject to, but in general, personally identifiable information and information that is confidential to your organization would fall under the term *sensitive information*.

> **This section covers the following skills:**
> - Data lifecycle management
> - Managing sensitive information
> - Compliance-related roles

Data Lifecycle Management

Microsoft Purview Data Lifecycle Management allows you to retain the information you are required to store and dispose of content that does not need to be kept. Removing information that does not need to be kept for compliance reasons reduces your storage costs and limits risk and liability. Automating the process reduces the amount of time administrators need to spend "spring cleaning" different data stores. Data lifecycle management uses tools including retention policies, retention labels, mailbox archiving, archive policies, and inactive mailbox policies.

When designing a Data Lifecycle Management strategy, you should take into account the following factors:

- **Understand Microsoft 365 retention and deletion functionality** These topics are covered throughout this chapter, but it's important to understand how the deletion and modification of content items function when an item is subject to retention. You should also understand why you use retention policies and the differences with retention labels.

- **Identify which workloads have retention requirements** Making this determination might require consultation with your organization's legal department because retention requirements are not just determined by the organization's business goals. Instead, retention requirements are determined by its responsibilities as defined by compliance regulations.

- **Design retention policies for the identified workloads** These policies should meet regulatory and organizational requirements.

You should also consider implementing archive mailboxes in Exchange and retention tags and retention policies in messaging records management to automatically transfer messages from an individual's primary mailbox to their archive mailbox.

> **MORE INFO   DATA LIFECYCLE MANAGEMENT**
>
> You can learn more about Data Lifecycle Management at *https://learn.microsoft.com/en-us/purview/data-lifecycle-management*.

Manage sensitive information types

Sensitive Information Types (SIT) are classifiers that identify sensitive information based on the pattern of the information. For example, credit card numbers, passport numbers, and tax identification numbers all have a specific format that can be detected by automated classifiers that recognize the type of information by its format. Microsoft Purview has many built-in SITs to identify common sensitive information types. Creating your own SIT or training one using artificial intelligence is also possible.

> **MORE INFO   SENSITIVE INFORMATION TYPES**
>
> You can learn more about sensitive information types at *https://learn.microsoft.com/en-us/purview/sensitive-information-type-learn-about*.

Trainable classifiers

Trainable classifiers examine content locations in your Microsoft 365 tenancy to understand the nature of the data that you store. Trainable classifiers use machine learning to determine what SITs are present and used by your organization. Content is located by:

- Keywords or metadata values
- Using previously identified patterns of sensitive information like social security, credit card, or bank account numbers
- Recognizing an item because it's a variation on a template
- Using the presence of exact strings and exact data match

Microsoft 365 includes several pre-trained classifiers that are ready to use. You can also train a custom classifier by providing data examples conforming to the pattern you want the categorizer to recognize. You can then provide positive and negative examples and use reinforcement learning to allow the model to understand how to recognize the SIT pattern correctly.

> **MORE INFO   TRAINABLE CLASSIFIERS**
>
> You can learn more about sensitive information types at *https://learn.microsoft.com/en-us/purview/classifier-learn-about*.

Create custom SIT

Rather than feed an artificial intelligence model data, you can definite a custom SIT programmatically. This is an especially fun way of approaching the topic if you lie awake at night thinking about how to compose satisfying regular expressions.

To create your own SIT, you can identify sensitive information using

- Regular expressions
- Keyword lists
- A keyword dictionary
- Sensitive information type functions
- Confidence levels

Sensitive information–type functions allow you to identify sensitive information programmatically. In an SIT definition, confidence level reflects how much supporting evidence is detected in addition to the primary element. The more supporting evidence an item contains, the higher the confidence that a matched item contains the sensitive info you're looking for.

To create a custom SIT, perform the following steps:

1. In the **Microsoft Purview** portal, go to **Data Classification**, select **Classifiers**, and then select **Sensitive Info Types**. Choose **Create Sensitive Info Type**.

2. On the **Name Your Sensitive Info Type** page, provide values for **Name** and **Description** and choose **Next**.

3. On the **Define Patterns For This Sensitive Info Type** page, select **Create Pattern**.

4. On the **New Pattern** page shown in Figure 6-1

   - Choose the default **Confidence Level** for the pattern. The values are **Low Confidence**, **Medium Confidence**, and **High Confidence**.

   - Choose and define the **Primary Element**. The primary element can be a **Regular Expression With An Optional Validator**, a **Keyword List**, a **Keyword Dictionary**, or one of the preconfigured **Functions**.

   - Provide a numerical value for **Character Proximity**.

   - Add **Supporting Elements**. These can be regular expressions with an optional validator, a keyword list, a keyword dictionary, or one of the predefined functions.

   - Add any additional checks from the list of available checks.

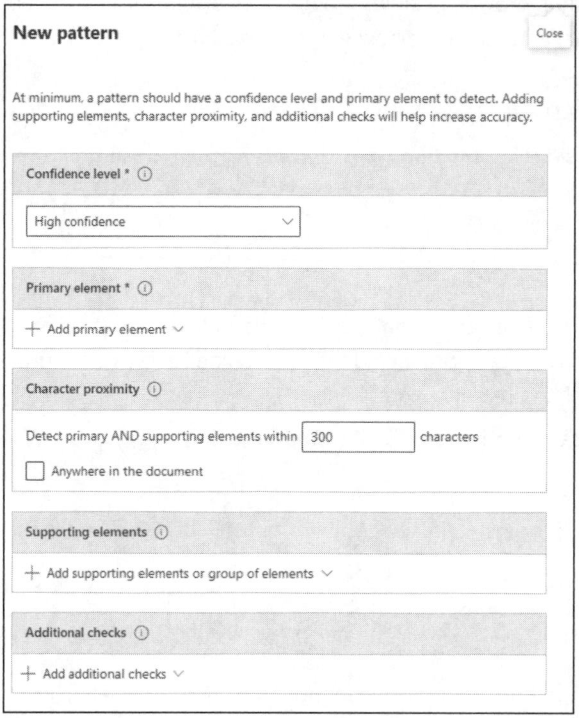

FIGURE 6-1   Content retention options

5. Choose **Create** and select **Next**.

6. Choose the recommended confidence level for this sensitive information type.

7. Check your settings and choose **Save**.

Compliance-related roles

A user must be assigned a compliance role to perform compliance-related tasks in Microsoft Purview. Remember to assign only the least privileges necessary when assigning a compliance-related role. The role groups listed in Table 6-1 are related to Microsoft Purview role assignments:

TABLE 6-1 Microsoft Purview role groups

Role group	Function
Audit Manager	Manage audit log settings and search, view, and export audit logs.
Audit Reader	Search, view, and export audit Logs.
Communication Compliance	Provides permission to all the communication compliance roles: Administrator, Analyst, Investigator, and Viewer.
Communication Compliance Administrators	Create/edit policies and define global communication compliance settings.
Communication Compliance Analysts	Communication compliance analysts can investigate policy matches, view message metadata, and take remediation actions.
Communication Compliance Investigators	Communication compliance analysts can investigate policy matches, view message content, and take remediation actions.
Communication Compliance Viewers	Communication compliance viewers can access the available reports and widgets.
Compliance Administrator	Members can manage settings for device management, data loss prevention, reports, and preservation.
Compliance Data Administrator	Members can manage settings for device management, data protection, data loss prevention, reports, and preservation.
Compliance Manager Administrators	Manage template creation and modification.
Compliance Manager Assessors	Create assessments, implement improvement actions, and update test status for improvement actions.
Compliance Manager Contributors	Create assessments and perform work to implement improvement actions.
Compliance Manager Readers	View all Compliance Manager content except for administrator functions.
Content Explorer Content Viewer	View the contents files in Content Explorer.
Content Explorer List Viewer	View all items in Content Explorer in list format only.
Data Catalog Curators	Allows you to perform create, read, modify, and delete actions on catalog data objects and establish relationships between objects.
Data Estate Insights Readers	Provides read-only access to all Insights Reports across platforms and providers.

Data Investigator	Perform searches on mailboxes, SharePoint Online sites, and OneDrive for Business locations.
Data Source Administrators	Manage data sources and data scans.
eDiscovery Manager	Members can perform searches and place holds on mailboxes, SharePoint Online sites, and OneDrive for Business locations. Members can also create and manage eDiscovery cases, add and remove members to a case, create and edit Content Searches associated with a case, and access case data in eDiscovery (Premium).
Global Reader	Members have read-only access to reports and alerts and can see all the configuration and settings.
Information Protection	Provides full control over all information-protection features, including sensitivity labels and their policies, DLP, all classifier types, Activity Explorer and Content Explorer, and all related reports.
Information Protection Admins	Create, edit, and delete DLP policies, sensitivity labels and their policies, and all classifier types. Manage endpoint DLP settings and simulation mode for auto-labeling policies.
Information Protection Analysts	Access and manage DLP alerts and activity explorer. Grants view-only access to DLP policies, sensitivity labels and their policies, and all classifier types.
Information Protection Investigators	Access and manage DLP alerts, Activity Explorer, and Content Explorer. View-only access to DLP policies, sensitivity labels and their policies, and all classifier types.
Information Protection Readers	View-only access to reports for DLP policies and sensitivity labels and their policies.
Organization Management	Members can control permissions for accessing features in these portals and manage settings for device management, data loss prevention, reports, and preservation.
Privacy Management	Manage access control for Privacy Management solutions in the Microsoft Purview compliance portal.
Privacy Management Administrators	Privacy management solution administrators can create/edit policies and define global settings.
Privacy Management Analysts	Privacy management solution analysts can investigate policy matches, view messages and metadata, and take remediation actions.
Privacy Management Contributors	Manage contributor access for privacy management cases.
Privacy Management Investigators	Privacy management solution investigators can investigate policy matches, view message content, and take remediation actions.
Privacy Management Viewers	Privacy management solution viewers can access the available dashboards and widgets.
Records Management	Members can configure all records-management aspects, including retention labels and disposition reviews.
Supervisory Review	Members can create and manage the policies defining which communications are subject to review in an organization.

MORE INFO   **COMPLIANCE-RELATED ROLE GROUPS**

You can learn more about compliance-related roles at *https://learn.microsoft.com/en-us/ microsoft-365/security/office-365-security/scc-permissions.*

Skill 6.2: Sensitivity labels and policies

Sensitivity labels allow you to classify and protect data. A label can be attached to a content item, and the policies applied by that label determine what actions can and cannot be performed on that content.

> **This section covers the following skills:**
> - Sensitivity labels
> - Sensitivity label policies

Sensitivity labels

Sensitivity labels are persistent and stored in file and email message metadata, meaning the label will be stored with the content. You can apply a single sensitivity label to a file or email message. Files and email messages can have both sensitivity and retention labels applied concurrently.

Sensitivity labels allow you to do the following:

- **Configure protection settings that include content markings** You can create a label that, when applied to a document or email, applies a watermark to the content. For example, a "Top Secret" watermark could be applied to each document page.

- **Configure content encryption** Encryption settings can restrict where and how the content can be accessed. Encryption settings allow you to select which users or groups have permission to perform specific actions and the duration over which those actions can be performed. For example, you can allow one group of users in your organization to modify a document while users in another group in another organization can only view it.

- **Limit which applications can access the content** You can use a sensitivity label to restrict which applications can open the content and what actions can be taken within that content.

- **Use Microsoft Defender for Cloud Apps to protect content in third-party apps** With Defender for Cloud Apps, you can detect, classify, label, and protect content in third-party apps and services, such as Salesforce, Box, or Dropbox, even if the third-party app or service doesn't directly support sensitivity labels.

- **Protect containers that include Microsoft Teams, Microsoft 365 Groups, and SharePoint sites** This allows you to block access to content with a specially configured label applied from unmanaged devices or locations external to the perimeter network firewall.

- **Protect meetings and chat by labeling and encrypting meeting invites**
You can also use sensitivity labels to enforce Microsoft Teams–specific options for
the meeting and chat.

- **Protect data saved outside the service**   Use sensitivity labels in Power BI to protect
data when it's saved outside the service.

You can also use sensitivity labels to label content without using any protection settings.
This allows you to generate usage reports and activity data for data based on the label applied
to the data, even if the label does nothing to protect the data. For example, you can use reports to determine how files related to a specific project are accessed throughout the organization without restricting that access.

Label scope

When configuring sensitivity labels, you specify the label's scope, which determines which settings can be configured for the label and which apps and services the label will be available to.
Figure 6-2 shows the scope label page.

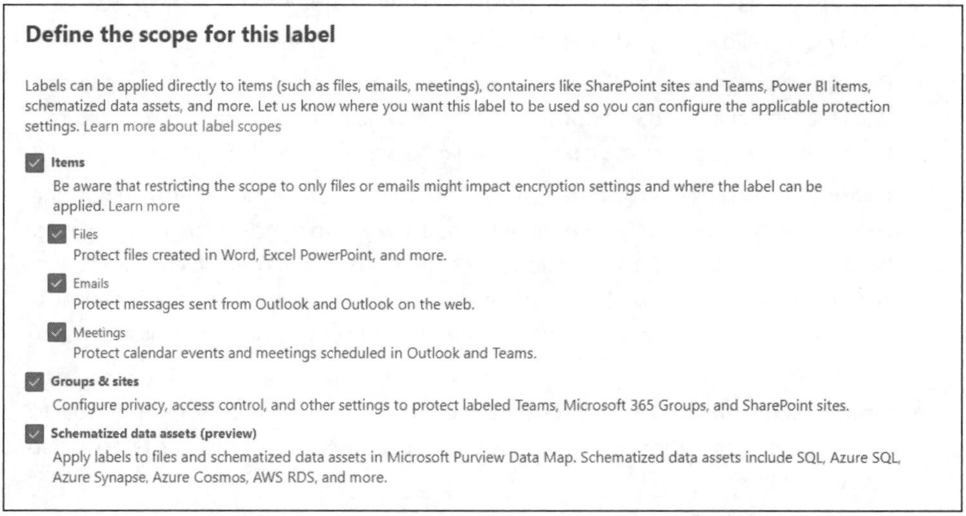

Define the scope for this label

Labels can be applied directly to items (such as files, emails, meetings), containers like SharePoint sites and Teams, Power BI items, schematized data assets, and more. Let us know where you want this label to be used so you can configure the applicable protection settings. Learn more about label scopes

☑ **Items**
Be aware that restricting the scope to only files or emails might impact encryption settings and where the label can be applied. Learn more

  ☑ Files
  Protect files created in Word, Excel PowerPoint, and more.

  ☑ Emails
  Protect messages sent from Outlook and Outlook on the web.

  ☑ Meetings
  Protect calendar events and meetings scheduled in Outlook and Teams.

☑ **Groups & sites**
Configure privacy, access control, and other settings to protect labeled Teams, Microsoft 365 Groups, and SharePoint sites.

☑ **Schematized data assets (preview)**
Apply labels to files and schematized data assets in Microsoft Purview Data Map. Schematized data assets include SQL, Azure SQL, Azure Synapse, Azure Cosmos, AWS RDS, and more.

FIGURE 6-2   Label scope options

The available scopes are as follows:

- **Items**   Items include files, emails, and meetings. You can allow the label to be used for
all three or restrict the label to specific items such as email messages or Microsoft Teams
meetings.

- **Groups & Sites**   Allows Microsoft Teams, Microsoft 365 Groups, and SharePoint sites
to have labels attached.

- **Schematized Data Assets**   Allows you to apply labels to files and special data assets
in Microsoft Purview Data Map. This includes applying labels to SQL, Azure SQL, Azure
Synapse, and Azure Cosmos data assets.

By default, using the **Groups & Sites** and **Schematized Data Assets** scopes is not available unless you enable it for your Microsoft 365 tenancy.

Label priority

Only one label can apply to a file, email message, or container, such as a SharePoint site. Label priority determines which labels apply. The list of labels configured is shown on the **Labels** page under **Information Protection** in the Microsoft Purview compliance portal, as shown in Figure 6-3.

Labels

Sensitivity labels are used to classify email messages, documents, sites, and more. When a label is applied (automatically or by the user), the content or site is protected based on the settings you choose. For example, you can create labels that encrypt files, add content marking, and control user access to specific sites.
Learn more about sensitivity labels

+ Create label   💬 Labels for your users   ↓ Export   ○ Refresh   6 items

		Name	Order	Scope	Created by	Last modified
☐	⋮	Personal	0 - lowest	File, Email		Jul 24, 2023 9:57:28 AM
☐	⋮	Public	1	File, Email		Jul 24, 2023 9:57:28 AM
☐ ˃	⋮	General	2	File, Email		Jul 24, 2023 9:57:29 AM
☐ ˃	⋮	Confidential	5	File, Email		Jul 24, 2023 9:57:31 AM
☐ ˃	⋮	Highly Confidential	9	File, Email		Jul 24, 2023 9:57:37 AM
☐	⋮	Confidential - Finance	13 - highest	File, Email	Megan Bowen	Jul 27, 2023 4:16:44 AM

FIGURE 6-3 Labels

The most restrictive labels should have the highest priority value. When labels are automatically applied, the last in the list of applicable labels will be applied—the label or sublabel furthest down the list from the top.

Create a sensitivity label

To create a sensitivity label, perform the following steps:

1. In the Microsoft Purview compliance portal,, select **Information Protection** > **Labels** > **Create Label**.

2. On the **Name And Tooltip** page of the **New Sensitivity Label** wizard, provide the following information:

    ■ **Name**   The label's name.

    ■ **Display Name**   This is the name users will see in their applications once you publish the label.

    ■ **Description For Users**   This explains to the user how the label functions.

    ■ **Description For Admins**   This provides extra context for administrators who might need to manage the label.

    ■ **Label Color**   Applies a color to a parent label and all sublabels.

3. On the **Define The Scope Of This Label** page, choose the scope in which the label can be used: **Items**, **Groups & Sites**, and **Schematized Data Assets**. You can select **Files**, **Emails**, and/or **Meetings** within the **Items** scope.

4. On the **Choose Protection Settings For Labeled Items** page, choose whether the label will enable the following options:

   ■ **Apply Or Remove Encryption**   Determines who can access items with this label.

   ■ **Apply Content Marking**   Allows you to configure watermark settings.

   ■ **Protect Microsoft Teams Meetings And Chats**   Allows you to configure protection for Microsoft Teams meetings and chats. A Teams Premium license is required.

5. On the **Encryption** page shown in Figure 6-4, configure the following options:

Encryption

Control who can access items that have this label applied. Items include emails, Office files, Power BI files, and meeting invites (if you chose to configure meeting settings for this label). Learn more about encryption settings

○ Remove encryption if the file or email or calendar event is encrypted

◉ Configure encryption settings

ⓘ Turn on co-authoring Office desktop apps so multiple users can simultaneously edit documents that are labeled and encrypted by sensitivity labels. Learn more about this setting

[Go to co-authoring setting]

Assign permissions now or let users decide?

| Assign permissions now | ∨ |

The encryption settings you choose will be automatically enforced when the label is applied to email and Office files.

User access to content expires ⓘ

| Never | ∨ |

Allow offline access ⓘ

| Always | ∨ |

Assign permissions to specific users and groups * ⓘ

Assign permissions

			0 items
Users and groups	**Permissions**	**Edit**	**Delete**

No data available

☐ Use Double Key Encryption ⓘ

FIGURE 6-4 Encryption options

- **Remove Encryption If The File Or Email Or Calendar Event Is Encrypted**   Allows the user to remove encryption on an encrypted item.
- **Configure Encryption Settings**   You can choose to assign permissions or allow users to assign permissions.
- **User Access To Content Expires**   Allows you to specify a date or period after the label is applied when access to the content expires.
- **Allow Offline Access**   Allows you to specify whether offline access is allowed. You can also allow offline access for a configurable number of days.
- **Users And Groups**   Allows you to apply different permissions based on Microsoft 365 group membership.
- **Use Double Key Encryption**   This allows you to store an additional key in the double-key encryption service for decrypting content. Required by some compliance legislation.
- **Permissions**   You can assign the following permissions, shown in Figure 6-5, on a per-user, group, email address, or email address domain basis:
  - **View Rights**
  - **Edit Content**
  - **Save**
  - **Print**
  - **Copy And Extract Content**
  - **Reply**
  - **Reply All**
  - **Forward**
  - **Edit Rights**
  - **Export Content**
  - **Allow Macros**
  - **Full Control**

FIGURE 6-5 Permissions options

6. On the **Content Marking** page, choose
   - Whether you want to add a watermark and what text it will use
   - Whether you want to add a header and what text it will use
   - Whether you want to have a footer and what text it will use

7. On the **Auto-Labeling For Files And Emails** page, you can configure whether this label is applied automatically when the specified content conditions are met.

8. On the **Define Protection Settings For Groups And Sites** page, choose whether you want to configure privacy and external user access settings and whether you want to enable external sharing and conditional access.

9. On the **Schematized Data Assets** page, specify whether you want to configure automatic labeling for schematized data assets and the conditions under which that labeling occurs.

Sensitivity label policies

Sensitivity label policies allow you to publish sensitivity labels to users or groups and specify a default label for unlabeled documents, emails, meeting invites, and new containers (SharePoint Sites, Microsoft Teams groups, and Microsoft 365 groups). A sensitivity label policy also allows you to require a justification for changing an existing assigned label to a lower level of sensitivity.

Multiple sensitivity label policies can be applied according to the order listed in the Microsoft Purview compliance portal. Label policies lower down the list have a higher priority than those toward the top. The **Label Policies** page is shown in Figure 6-6.

Label policies

Create sensitivity label policies to publish one or more labels to your users' Office apps (like Outlook and Word), SharePoint sites, and Office 365 groups. Once published, users can apply the labels to protect their content. Learn more about sensitivity label policies

🖵 Publish label   ○ Refresh   3 items

Name	Order	Created by	Last modified
☐ Global sensitivity label policy	⋮ 0 - lowest		Jul 24, 2023 9:57 AM
☐ Confidential-Finance Policy	⋮ 1	Megan Bowen	Jul 27, 2023 4:16 AM
☐ Highly Confidential Policy	⋮ 2 - highest	Megan Bowen	Jul 27, 2023 4:17 AM

FIGURE 6-6   Label policies

> **MORE INFO**   **SENSITIVITY LABELS AND POLICIES**
>
> You can learn more about sensitivity labels and policies at *https://learn.microsoft.com/en-us/purview/sensitivity-labels*.

Skill 6.3: Retention labels and policies

As the volume of data that organizations generate increases over time, it becomes more difficult to manage that information manually. Retention policies allow you to automate the process of keeping information that you are required to keep as long as you need to keep it and to delete information when it is no longer required by the organization or due to compliance regulations. Retention policies are assigned at a site or mailbox level. Retention labels allow retention settings to be applied at an item level, such as to a specific folder, document, or email message.

> **This section covers the following skills:**
> - Retention policies
> - Retention labels
> - Preservation locks
> - Inactive mailbox retention

Retention policies

Retention policies allow you to assign retention settings to locations such as Exchange Mailboxes, SharePoint sites, OneDrive, and Microsoft Teams. A single Microsoft 365 tenancy can have up to 10,000 policies. This maximum number includes the policies for retention, policies for DLP, information barriers, eDiscovery holds, In-Place Holds, and sensitivity labels. You should add users responsible for managing retention policies and labels to the Compliance Administrator administrative role group.

The most basic retention actions are:

- **Retain Content**   Ensure that the content is not permanently deleted and is available for eDiscovery searches.
- **Delete Content**   Permanently delete content without it being archived in any internal or external location.
- **Retain And Then Delete**   Retain content for a specific period, usually defined by compliance regulation, and then permanently delete it once the retention period specified by compliance rules expires.

When you assign retention policies to content, the content remains where it is, be it a file share, an Exchange mailbox, or a SharePoint site. If a person edits or deletes content that is subject to a retention policy, a copy of the content is automatically retained in one of the following locations:

- **SharePoint and OneDrive sites**   The copy is retained in the Preservation Hold library.
- **Exchange mailboxes**   The copy is retained in the Recoverable Items folder.
- **Microsoft Teams and Viva Engage messages**   The copy is retained in a hidden **SubstrateHolds** subfolder in the Exchange **Recoverable Items** folder.

These locations are not visible to end users unless they have been assigned compliance roles. A user with the Compliance Administrator role group permissions or equivalent eDiscovery permissions can identify and restore content from these locations.

Settings for retaining and deleting content

Retention policies allow you to retain items for a specific period, define when you want the retention time to be measured, and decide what action to take when the retention period expires. These options are shown in Figure 6-7.

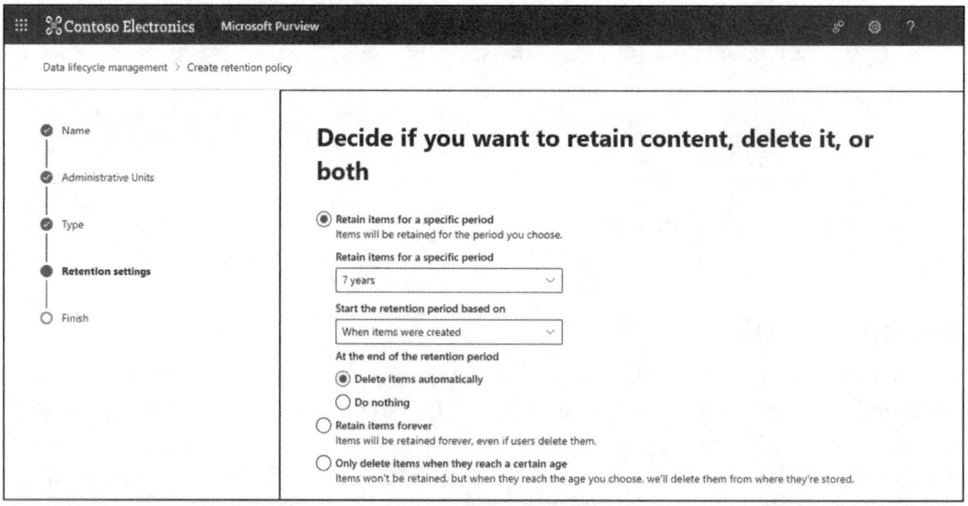

FIGURE 6-7   Content retention options

You have the following retention options:

- **Specify a retention period**   The default values are **5 Years**, **7 Years**, and **10 Years**, but you can also specify a custom value in years, months, and days.

- **When to start calculating the retention period**   The options are from when the item was created or when the item was last modified.

- **What to do when the retention period expires**   You can choose between deleting the items automatically or performing no action.

- **Choose to retain the items forever**   When you choose this option, users can delete the items, but they will remain stored in one of the locations discussed earlier in this chapter in the section on retention policies where a user with administrative privileges can recover them.

- **Delete items when they reach a certain age**   When you choose this option, a user can delete an item not retained in one of the locations discussed earlier in this chapter. The item is automatically deleted once the age limit you specify is reached.

Adaptive and static retention policies

There are two options when defining a retention policy scope: **Adaptive** and **Static**. See Figure 6-8.

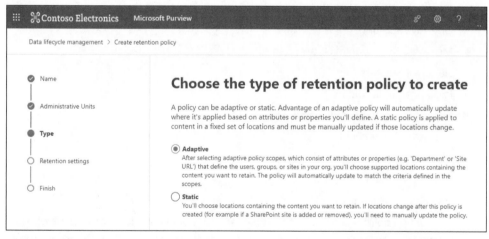

FIGURE 6-8   Retention policy types

- **Adaptive**   The policy scope is defined by a query. The query runs daily using the attributes or properties you specify for the selected location. A single policy can have multiple adaptive scopes. For example, a retention policy with an adaptive scope that uses the Entra ID attribute job title "Manager" will apply different retention settings to users with the Manager job title. There are no limits on the number of items per policy. Exchange public folders do not support retention policies that use adaptive scopes.

- **Static**   Applies to all instances for a specified location and can use inclusions and exclusions for that location. You can use retention policies with static scopes to manage the retention settings of items in Exchange public folders. Policies with static scopes have the following item limits:

    - **Exchange mailboxes**   1,000
    - **Microsoft 365 groups**   1,000
    - **Microsoft Teams channel messages**   1,000
    - **Microsoft Teams chats**   1,000
    - **Viva Engage community messages**   1,000
    - **Viva Engage user messages**   1,000
    - **SharePoint sites**   100
    - **OneDrive accounts**   100

Adaptive scopes allow you to apply a separate retention policy to inactive mailboxes.

Creating retention policies

You can create retention policies for the following locations:

- Exchange mailboxes
- SharePoint sites or SharePoint classic and communication sites
- OneDrive accounts
- Microsoft 365 Group mailboxes and sites
- Skype for Business
- Exchange public folders
- Microsoft Teams channel messages
- Microsoft Teams chats
- Microsoft Teams private channel messages
- Viva Engage community messages
- Viva Engage user messages

While retention policies can support multiple services identified as locations, creating a single retention policy that supports all supported locations is impossible. If you choose Microsoft Teams or Viva Engage as locations when you create a retention policy, all other locations will be excluded. If you want to create a retention policy for Microsoft Teams and Viva Engage, it must be separate from the retention policy you use for all other locations.

To create a retention policy, perform the following steps:

1. In the Microsoft Purview compliance portal shown in Figure 6-9, select **Data Lifecycle Management** > **Microsoft 365** > **Retention Policies**.

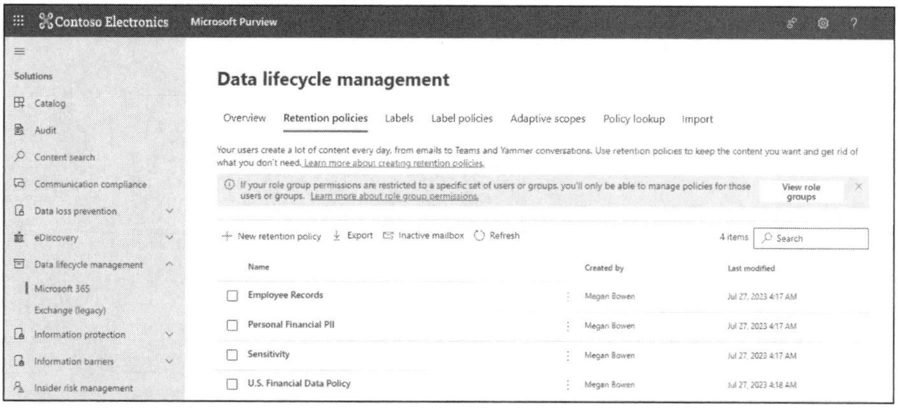

FIGURE 6-9 Retention policies

2. Select **New Retention Policy** to start the **Create Retention Policy Configuration** wizard and name your new retention policy.

3. You can add **Microsoft Entra ID Administrative Units** on the **Policy Scope** page. If your organization uses administrative units with Entra ID, a retention policy that doesn't include SharePoint sites or Exchange public folders can be automatically restricted to specific users by selecting administrative units. If your account has been assigned to an Entra ID administrative unit, you must choose one or more administrative units. The default selection of **Full Directory** should be chosen if you don't want to restrict the policy by using administrative units or your organization hasn't configured administrative units. You must also choose **Full Directory** for a policy to include the locations for SharePoint sites and Exchange public folders.

4. On the **Choose The Type Of Retention Policy To Create** page, select **Adaptive** or **Static**.

   - **Adaptive** If you use an **Adaptive** scope, it must exist before running the **New Retention Policy** wizard. On the **Choose Adaptive Policy Scopes And Locations** page, select **Add Scopes** and select one or more adaptive scopes that have been created. Then, select one or more locations. The locations you can select depend on the scope types added.

   - **Static** If you chose **Static** on the **Choose Locations** page, toggle **On** or **Off** any locations except those for Microsoft Teams and Viva Engage. You can leave it set to the default to apply the policy to the entire location or specify **Included** and **Excluded**. Figure 6-10 shows choosing where to apply locations for the **Static** option.

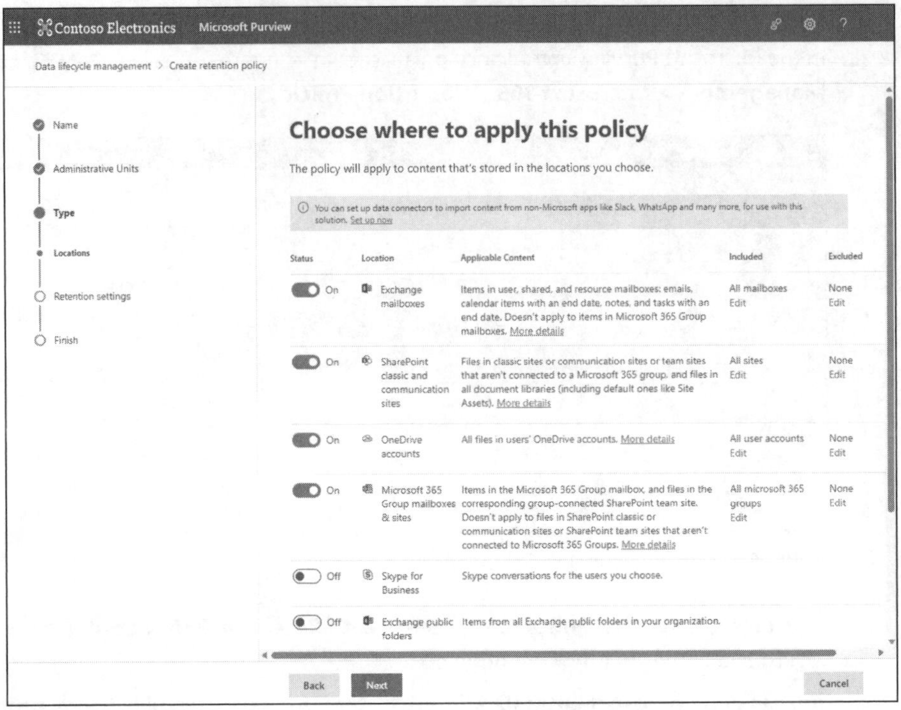

FIGURE 6-10 Retention policy locations

5. On the **Decide If You Want To Retain Content, Delete It, Or Both** page, specify the configuration options for retaining and deleting content.

6. Complete the configuration and save your settings.

Multiple retention policies can apply to the same content. When multiple retention policies apply, a calculation is performed by comparing the policies to determine how long the item is retained and, if the item is deleted, when the period expires. When comparing multiple policies, the longest retention period applies. When it comes to deletion, the shortest deletion period wins. So, if one policy is set to **Do Nothing** when the retention period expires, and another is set to **Delete**, the item will be deleted when the longer of the retention periods expires.

Retention labels

Retention labels allow retention settings to be applied at the item level rather than based on the content's location. You can use retention labels with retention policies or by themselves. Only a single retention label can be applied to an item at a time. Retention settings from retention labels differ from retention policies in that they travel with the content if it's moved to a different location within your Microsoft 365 tenant.

Retention labels have the following additional differences to retention policies:

- Users can manually apply retention labels to Outlook, OneDrive, and SharePoint content.
- You can use trainable classifiers to apply retention labels automatically. You can also use Power Automate compliance actions to apply retention labels to items.
- The retention period can be measured from when the content was labeled, based on an event, as well as the period since the content was created or when the content was last modified.
- You can configure default labels for SharePoint items and Exchange messages.
- When the retention period ends, you can configure a disposition review to determine whether the content should be permanently deleted. You can also automatically apply a different retention table.
- You can configure a proof of disposition record to be generated when content is deleted at the end of its retention period.
- You can use retention labels as a condition in Microsoft Purview Data Loss Prevention policies. For example, you could create a DLP policy that blocks documents from being emailed outside the organization if a specific retention label is applied.
- Retention labels override retention policies as they are applied at the item level. For example, if a retention policy says an item should be retained for **8 Years** and a retention label specifies it should be deleted after **5 Years**, the item will be deleted after **5 Years**.

To create a retention label, perform the following steps:

1. In the Microsoft Purview compliance portal shown in Figure 6-11, select **Data Lifecycle Management** > **Microsoft 365** > **Labels** and choose **Create A Label**.

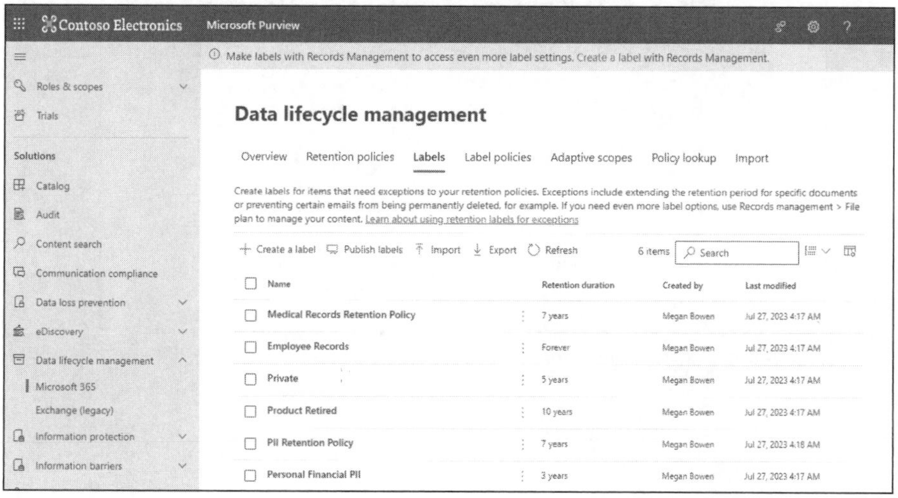

FIGURE 6-11 List of retention labels

2. On the **Name Your Retention Label** page, specify the label name users will see. You can also provide a description for users and a description for administrators. It's helpful to enter information about the retention period that will be applied.

3. On the **Define Label Settings** page, choose between the following options:

   - **Retain Items Forever Or For A Specific Period**   Labeled items cannot be permanently deleted during this period. Allows you to specify what happens to an item once the retention period expires.

   - **Enforce Actions After A Specific Period**   Allows you to configure a set of actions to occur after a specific period.

   - **Just Label Items**   Applies a label to the item, which is useful for sorting items or which can be used with DLP policies.

4. On the **Define The Retention Period** page shown in Figure 6-12, specify the retention period and how the retention period should be measured.

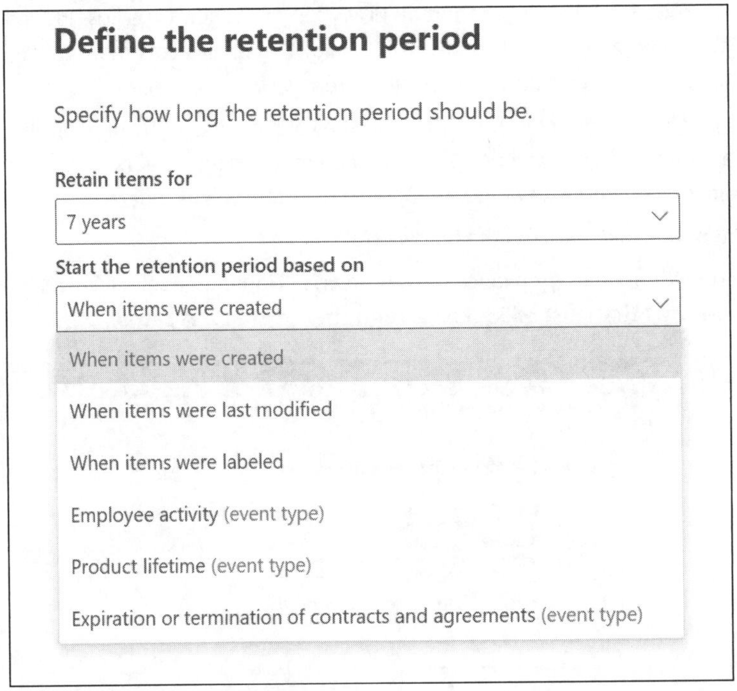

Define the retention period

Specify how long the retention period should be.

Retain items for

7 years   ⌄

Start the retention period based on

When items were created   ⌄

When items were created

When items were last modified

When items were labeled

Employee activity (event type)

Product lifetime (event type)

Expiration or termination of contracts and agreements (event type)

FIGURE 6-12   Label retention period options

5. On the **Choose What Happens After The Retention Period** page shown in Figure 6-13, choose what occurs when the retention period expires.

Choose what happens after the retention period

These settings determine what happens to items when the retention period ends.

◉ **Delete items automatically**
We'll permanently remove labeled items from wherever they're stored.

○ **Start a disposition review**
Let the disposition reviewers you assign in the next step decide if items can be safely deleted or whether other actions (such as changing the retention period) should be taken. Learn more

○ **Change the label**
You can extend the period by choosing an existing label to replace this one with. Learn more about relabeling items

○ **Deactivate retention settings**
Labeled items won't be retained or deleted when their retention settings are deactivated. You'll have to manually remove any items that you want deleted.

FIGURE 6-13   Label retention expiration options

Once you've created a label, you need to publish it using a retention label policy so users can apply it. Retention label policies can be adaptive or static, just like retention policies. A retention label policy's scope determines where your publication's retention labels will be available. To publish labels using a retention label policy, perform the following steps:

1. In the Microsoft Purview compliance portal shown in Figure 6-14, select **Data Lifecycle Management** > **Microsoft 365** > **Label Policies**. Click **Create A Label**.

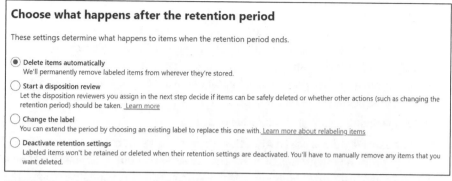

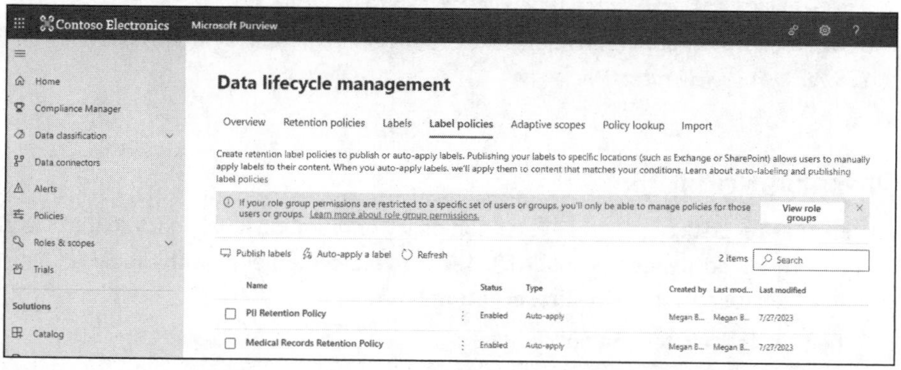

FIGURE 6-14   Label policies

2. Select **Publish Labels**. You will be asked which labels to publish. Make your selection and select **Next**.

3. On the **Administrative Units** page, you can add **Microsoft Entra ID Administrative Units.** If your organization uses administrative units with Entra ID, a retention policy that doesn't include SharePoint sites or Exchange public folders can be automatically restricted to specific users by selecting administrative units. If your account has been assigned to an Entra ID administrative unit, you must choose one or more administrative units. Choose the default **Full Directory** option if you don't want to restrict the policy using administrative units or your organization hasn't configured administrative units. You must also choose **Full Directory** for a policy to include SharePoint sites and Exchange public folder locations.

4. On the **Scope** page, select **Adaptive** or **Static**.

   - **Adaptive**   If you use an **Adaptive** scope, it must exist before running the **New Retention Policy** wizard. On the **Choose Adaptive Policy Scopes And Locations** page, select **Add Scopes** and select one or more existing adaptive scopes. Then, select one or more locations. The locations you can select depend on the scope types you've added.

   - **Static**   If you choose **Static** on the **Choose Locations** page, toggle **On** or **Off** any of the locations. You can leave it at the default Full Directory setting to apply the policy to the entire location or specify **Included** and **Excluded**.

5. Provide a policy **Name** and click **Finish** to publish the retention labels to the chosen scope.

> **MORE INFO**   **RETENTION POLICIES AND RETENTION LABELS**
>
> You can learn more about retention policies and retention labels at *https://learn.microsoft.com/en-us/purview/retention*.

Preservation locks

A **Preservation Lock** configures a retention policy or retention label policy so that the policy cannot be disabled, deleted, or made less restrictive. Even someone with Global Administrator privileges cannot overcome the **Preservation Lock**.

When you lock a retention policy

- No one can disable or delete the policy.
- Locations can be added but not removed.
- You can extend the retention period but not decrease it.

When you lock a retention label policy

- No one can disable or delete the policy.
- Locations can be added but not removed.
- Labels can be added but not removed.

You configure Preservation Locks using the `Set-RetentionCompliancePolicy` PowerShell cmdlet with the `RestrictiveRetention` parameter set to true.

Inactive mailbox retention

If the Microsoft 365 user account associated with a mailbox subject to a retention policy or containing items with retention labels applied is deleted, the mailbox is converted to an inactive mailbox. Inactive mailboxes provide a location to store the email messages of former employees. These mailboxes can be accessed by users assigned eDiscovery permissions who can use content search to search and export the contents of inactive mailboxes during eDiscovery investigations.

You can view a list of inactive mailboxes in your organization by performing the following steps:

1. In the Microsoft Purview compliance portal, select **Data Lifecycle Management** under **Solutions**, and then choose **Microsoft 365** > **Retention Policies** > **Inactive Mailboxes** (see Figure 6-15).

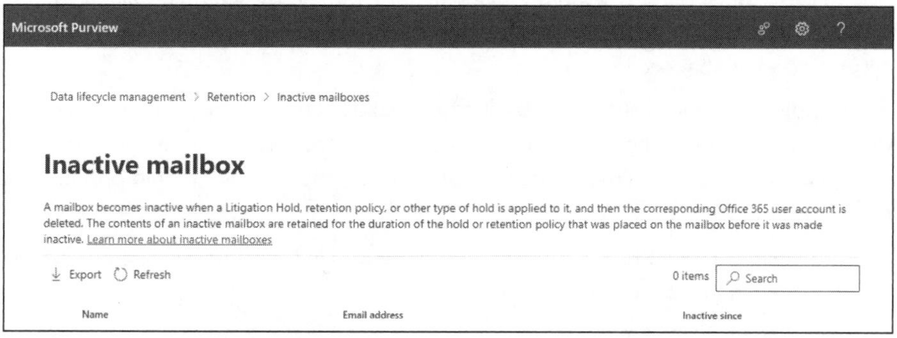

FIGURE 6-15   Inactive mailboxes page

2. From this page, you can view the details of inactive mailboxes, including whether the mailbox is subject to a **Litigation Hold**.

You can restore an inactive mailbox should it be necessary to provide a new employee access to the contents of the previous employee's mailbox. When you do this, the contents are copied to a new mailbox, and the original inactive mailbox is retained according to the applied retention policies and labels.

Skill 6.4: Data Loss Prevention

Data Loss Prevention (DLP) is a feature of Microsoft 365 that allows you to restrict the sharing of information based on the nature of that information. For example, you can use DLP to block people in your organization from sending email messages outside the organization if the emails or attachments contain sensitive words, phrases, or data patterns. DLP in Microsoft 365 also provides functionality that will generate alerts when an event occurs, and you can also examine DLP reports to determine whether DLP is functioning as intended.

> **This section covers the following skills:**
> - DLP policies
> - DLP alerts

DLP policies

DLP policies consist of rules, conditions, and actions. DLP policies may contain one or more rules, and each rule consists of the conditions that trigger the rule and the actions that are performed when that occurs.

DLP policy conditions allow you to specify the content the rule looks for and the context in which that content is being used. For example, the content might be a person's government identification number, and the context might be an attempt to share that information outside the organization.

You can apply DLP policies to data at rest, in use, and in transit. You can apply DLP policies to data stored in the following locations:

- Exchange Online email
- SharePoint Online sites
- OneDrive accounts
- Microsoft Teams chat and channel messages
- Windows 10 and Windows 11 client devices
- macOS (Catalina 10.15 and higher) client devices
- On-premises repositories, such as file shares
- Power BI sites

DLP policy actions are what happens once the condition is met. Actions include:

- **Block Access To The Content**   For email content, this would prevent a person from sending the message. Depending on the rule configuration, this might prompt a non-delivery report, a policy tip, or an email notification. For content in a SharePoint site, it would restrict access to the content to all security principals except the site collection administrator, document owner, and the person who last modified the document.

- **Send A Notification**   You can configure notifications to be sent to the person who shared, emailed, or last modified the content. For example, if Sarah wrote the initial email that was protected, and Grayson tried to forward it to an external address, you can have Sarah notified.

Creating policies

To create a DLP policy, perform the following steps:

1. In the Microsoft Purview compliance portal, select **Data Loss Prevention** under **Solutions** and select **Policies**. On the **Policies** page shown in Figure 6-16, select **Create Policy**.

Policies

Use data loss prevention (DLP) policies to help identify and protect your organization's sensitive info. For example you can set up policies to help make sure information in email and docs isn't shared with the wrong people. Learn more about DLP

+ Create policy   ↓ Export   ○ Refresh   5 items   🔍 Search

	Name	Order	Last modified	Status
☐	Default Office 365 DLP policy	⋮ 0	Jul 24, 2023 9:57 AM	On
☐	Default policy for Teams	⋮ 1	Jul 24, 2023 9:57 AM	On
☐	Default policy for devices	⋮ 2	Jul 25, 2023 9:58 AM	On
☐	U.S. Financial Data	⋮ 3	Jul 26, 2023 9:26 PM	On
☐	General Data Protection Regulation (GDPR)	⋮ 4	Jul 26, 2023 9:27 PM	On

FIGURE 6-16   DLP policies

2. On the **Start With A Template Or Create A Custom Policy** page, select **Custom** from the **Categories** list and then select **Custom Policy** from the **Templates** list. Select **Next**.

3. Give the policy a **Name** and **Description**. Policies cannot be renamed. Select **Next**.

4. Select **Full Directory** under **Admin Units**.

5. On the **Choose Locations To Apply The Policy** page shown in Figure 6-17, select all the locations to which you want to apply the policy. Select **Next**.

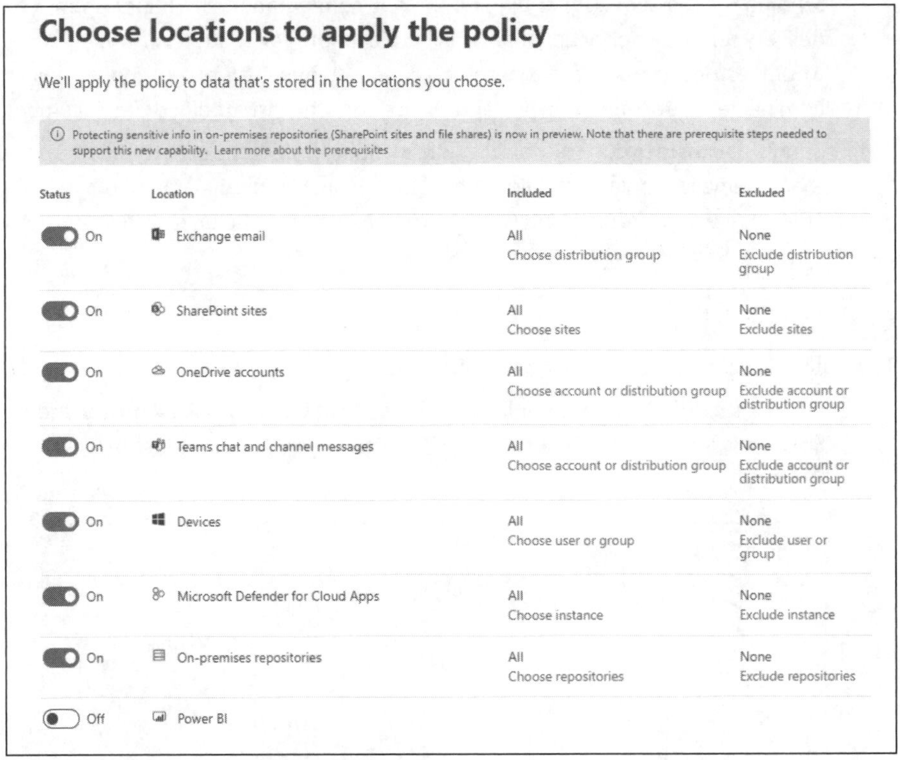

Choose locations to apply the policy

We'll apply the policy to data that's stored in the locations you choose.

ⓘ Protecting sensitive info in on-premises repositories (SharePoint sites and file shares) is now in preview. Note that there are prerequisite steps needed to support this new capability. Learn more about the prerequisites

Status	Location	Included	Excluded
⬤ On	📧 Exchange email	All Choose distribution group	None Exclude distribution group
⬤ On	🌐 SharePoint sites	All Choose sites	None Exclude sites
⬤ On	☁ OneDrive accounts	All Choose account or distribution group	None Exclude account or distribution group
⬤ On	🗂 Teams chat and channel messages	All Choose account or distribution group	None Exclude account or distribution group
⬤ On	🪟 Devices	All Choose user or group	None Exclude user or group
⬤ On	𝄢 Microsoft Defender for Cloud Apps	All Choose instance	None Exclude instance
⬤ On	🗄 On-premises repositories	All Choose repositories	None Exclude repositories
◯ Off	📊 Power BI		

FIGURE 6-17 DLP policy locations

6. Ensure that the **Create Or Customize Advanced DLP Rules** option is selected on the **Define Policy Settings** page. Select **Next**.

7. On the **Customize Advanced DLP Rules** page, Select **Create Rule**. **Name** the rule, provide a **Description**, and select the **Conditions**, **Exceptions**, **Actions**, **User Notifications**, **User Overrides**, **Incident Reports**, and whether to stop processing additional DLP policies and rules if the policy is triggered (**If There's A Match For This Rule, Stop Processing Additional DLP Policies And Rules**). Figure 6-18 shows this page.

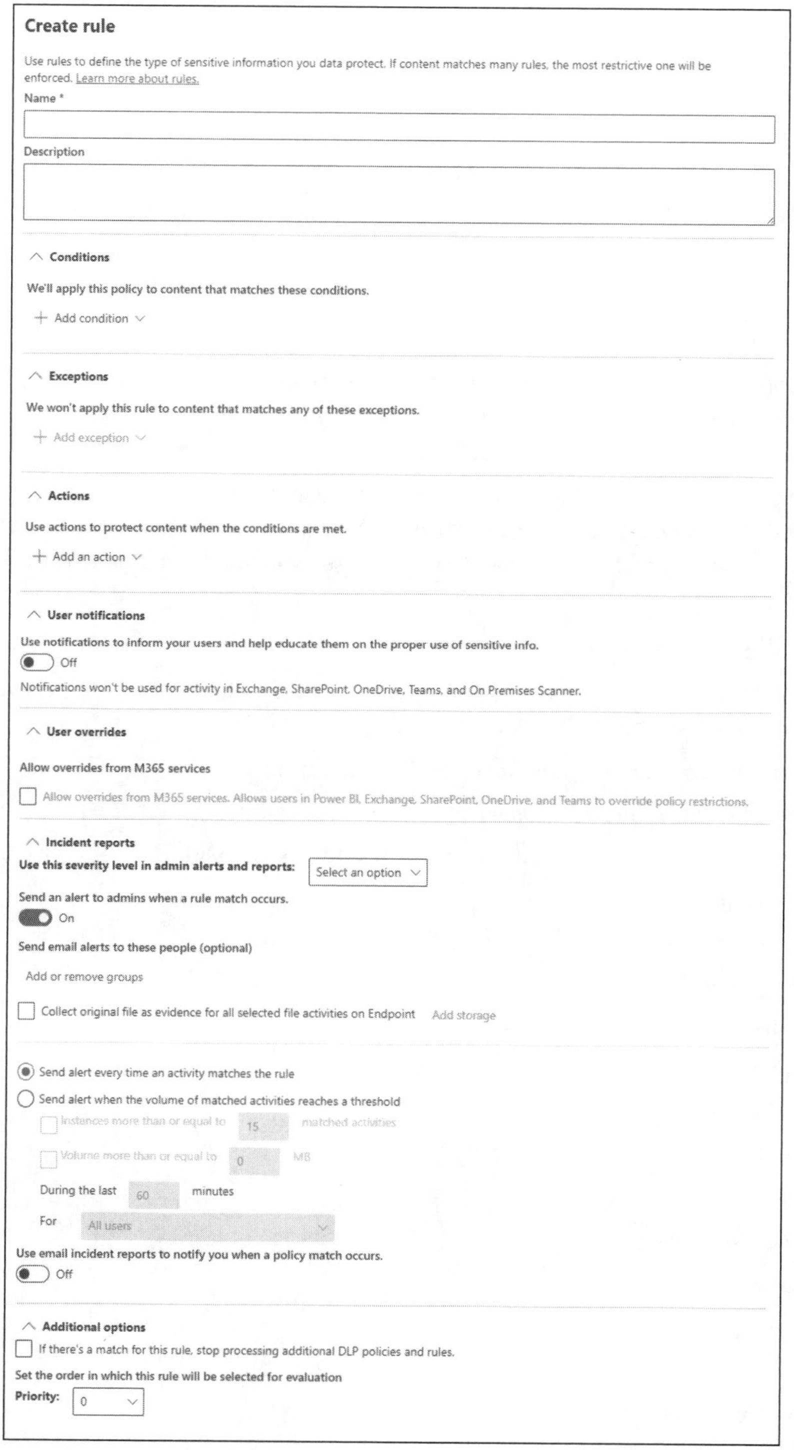

Create rule

Use rules to define the type of sensitive information you data protect. If content matches many rules, the most restrictive one will be enforced. Learn more about rules.

Name *

[   ]

Description

[   ]
[   ]

∧ **Conditions**

We'll apply this policy to content that matches these conditions.

+ Add condition ∨

∧ **Exceptions**

We won't apply this rule to content that matches any of these exceptions.

+ Add exception ∨

∧ **Actions**

Use actions to protect content when the conditions are met.

+ Add an action ∨

∧ **User notifications**

Use notifications to inform your users and help educate them on the proper use of sensitive info.

(●) Off

Notifications won't be used for activity in Exchange, SharePoint, OneDrive, Teams, and On Premises Scanner.

∧ **User overrides**

Allow overrides from M365 services

☐ Allow overrides from M365 services. Allows users in Power BI, Exchange, SharePoint, OneDrive, and Teams to override policy restrictions.

∧ **Incident reports**

Use this severity level in admin alerts and reports: [Select an option ∨]

Send an alert to admins when a rule match occurs.
(●) On

Send email alerts to these people (optional)

Add or remove groups

☐ Collect original file as evidence for all selected file activities on Endpoint   Add storage

(●) Send alert every time an activity matches the rule
(○) Send alert when the volume of matched activities reaches a threshold

☐ Instances more than or equal to   [15]   matched activities

☐ Volume more than or equal to   [0]   MB

During the last   [60]   minutes

For   [All users   ∨]

Use email incident reports to notify you when a policy match occurs.
(●) Off

∧ **Additional options**

☐ If there's a match for this rule, stop processing additional DLP policies and rules.

Set the order in which this rule will be selected for evaluation

Priority: [0   ∨]

FIGURE 6-18   DLP policy rule

8. On the **Policy Mode** page, choose whether to test the policy first, turn the policy on, or keep the policy off after the policy is created.

9. Complete the policy setup wizard by selecting **Submit**.

> **MORE INFO** **CREATING AND DEPLOYING DLP POLICIES**
>
> You can learn more about creating and deploying DLP policies at *https://learn.microsoft. com/en-us/purview/dlp-create-deploy-policy*.

Testing policies

Implementing a DLP policy in test mode allows you to evaluate the effect of the controls by implementing them in a manner that will not adversely impact them. Test mode allows you to evaluate the effectiveness of DLP policies without enforcing them.

While in test mode, an organization should monitor the policy's outcomes and fine-tune it to meet the company's control objectives. While fine-tuning, the organization should ensure that it doesn't adversely or inadvertently impact valid user workflows and productivity.

DLP alerts

By default, Microsoft Purview DLP audits activity with the following file types, irrespective of whether they are subject to a DLP policy:

- Word files (.doc, .docx, .docm, .dot, .dotx, .dotm, .docb)
- PowerPoint files (.ppt, .pptx, .pos, .pps, .pptm, .potx, .potm, .ppam, .ppsx)
- Excel files (.xls, .xlsx, .xlt, .xlm, .xlsm, .xltx, .xltm, .xlsb, .xlw)
- Outlook (.pst, .ost, .msg)
- Archive (.zip, .zipx, .rar, .7z, .tar, .gz)
- PDF files (.pdf)
- .csv files (.csv)
- .tsv files (.tsv)
- .txt files (.txt)
- .rtf files (.rtf)
- .c files (.c)
- .class files (.class)
- .cpp files (.cpp)
- .cs files (.cs)
- .h files (.h)
- .java files (.java)

You can also add custom file extensions as a condition in a policy if one of the existing sets does not meet your organization's needs.

The following activities can be audited and managed through Endpoint DLP policies:

- **Upload To Cloud Service, Or Access By Unallowed Browsers**   Allows you to detect upload attempts of protected data to restricted service domains if the uploader is using Edge. To stop users from simply opening another browser, you can detect if a user attempts to interact with a protected item using an unauthorized browser. When you enable this functionality, DLP blocks the upload activity and redirects the user to use Microsoft Edge, which will allow or block the upload or access based on DLP policy configuration.

- **Copy To Another App, Process, Or Item**   Allows you to detect if a user tries to copy information from a protected item into another app, process, or item (such as copying from a protected email into Notepad). This specific activity will not detect copying and pasting within the same app, process, or item.

- **Copy To USB Removable Media**   Detects user attempts to copy items or information to removable media such as a flash card or USB device.

- **Copy To A Network Share**   Detects if a user attempts to copy a protected item to a network location, including a mapped network drive.

- **Print A Document**   Allows you to detect if a user attempts to print a protected item to a locally attached or network printer.

- **Copy To A Remote Session**   Allows you to detect if a user attempts to copy an item to a remote desktop session.

- **Copy To A Bluetooth Device**   Triggered when a user attempts to copy an item to an unauthorized Bluetooth app. These apps must be defined in the Endpoint DLP settings.

- **Create An Item**   Detects when a user attempts to create an item.

- **Rename An Item**   Detects when a user attempts to rename an item.

The options shown on the Microsoft Purview **Alerts** dashboard in Figure 6-19 allow you to create alert policies and then view data about the alerts those policies generate. You can use an Alert policy to apply a category to alerts triggered by a policy, determine which users the alert policy applies to, configure a threshold for the policy to trigger an alert, and determine what notification level occurs when an alert is triggered. You can use the **Alerts** page to view and filter alerts, set an alert status to help you manage alerts, and dismiss alerts after you've resolved the incident that triggered the alert.

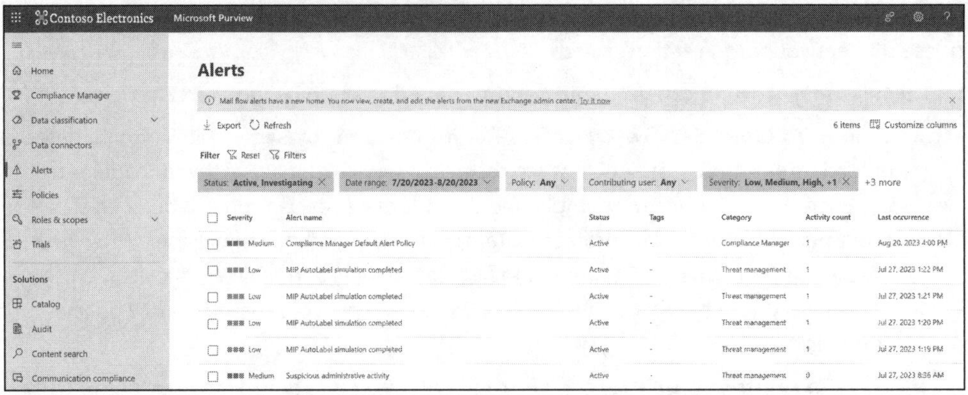

FIGURE 6-19 Microsoft Purview Alerts

The DLP Alerts Management dashboard allows you to view alert notifications. This dashboard also allows you to:

- Configure DLP alert settings
- Review DLP alerts
- Triage DLP alerts
- Track DLP alert resolution

> **MORE INFO** **ALERT POLICIES**
>
> You can learn more about Alert Policies at *https://learn.microsoft.com/en-us/purview/alert-policies*.

Chapter summary

- Data Lifecycle Management is a framework through which you determine how much time you need to retain different types of information.
- Configuring a sensitive information type (SIT) allows you to detect and classify special types of information.
- There are many compliance roles that allow discrete tasks to be performed within Microsoft Purview. You should use the principle of least privilege when assigning users to role groups and rarely assign the more privileged roles.

- Retention policies allow you to apply retention settings to data stores. Retention labels allow retention settings to be applied to specific content items.
- The user can delete items subject to a retention policy but are retained in special locations.
- DLP policies allow you to control who can access specific information and what types of access they have. You can use DLP policies to block the printing of content items or stop them from being shared outside the organization.

Thought experiment

In this thought experiment, demonstrate your skills and knowledge of the topics covered in this chapter. You can find answers to this thought experiment in the next section.

Compliance at Tailwind Traders

You are responsible for implementing Microsoft Purview's compliance functionality at Tailwind Traders. You are interested in configuring appropriate role group assignments, retention policies, and sensitivity settings. Part of your implementation plan should address the following scenarios:

- One of your legal staff, Lynette, should be able to search and view DLP events in the audit logs but should not be able to manage the settings of the audit log.
- Inactive Exchange mailboxes should have a different retention policy applied to them. This policy should apply to Exchange mailboxes that are currently inactive and any mailboxes that become inactive in the future.

With this information, answer the following questions:

1. Which role group should you assign to Lynette?
2. What scope should you use when creating a retention policy for the inactive Exchange mailboxes?
3. Sensitivity label Alpha has a priority of 1, and sensitivity label Beta has a priority of 10. Which label will apply if automatic labeling attempts to apply both labels to the same content item?

Thought experiment answers

This section contains the solution to the thought experiment. Each answer explains why the answer choice is correct.

1. The Audit Reader role group allows a user assigned to the role group the ability to Search, View, and Export Audit Logs but does not allow them to manage Audit Log Settings.

2. You should create a retention policy with an adaptive scope. Only policies with an adaptive scope can apply to current and future inactive mailboxes because the policies work based on the properties of the location. A static retention policy would require you to constantly specify which mailboxes are inactive.

3. Because sensitivity label Beta has a higher priority value, it will be applied through automatic labeling.

CHAPTER 7

MS-102 Microsoft 365 Administrator exam updates

The purpose of this chapter

This chapter will be updated over time, and a PDF will be posted online so that you can access the latest information about exam changes, even after you purchase this book.

Why do we need a chapter that updates over time? For three reasons:

1. To add more technical content to the book before it's time to replace the current book edition with the next edition. This chapter will include additional technology content and possibly additional PDFs containing more content.

2. To communicate details about the next version of the exam, to tell you about our publishing plans for that edition, and to help you understand what that means to you.

3. To accurately map the current exam objectives to existing chapter content. While exam objectives evolve and products are renamed, much of the content in this book will remain accurate and relevant. In addition to covering any content gaps that appear through additions to the objectives, this chapter notes how the new objectives map to the current text.

After the initial publication of this book, supplemental updates will be provided as digital downloads for minor exam updates. If an exam has major changes or accumulates enough minor changes, we may announce a new edition. We will do our best to provide any updates to you free of charge before we release a new edition. However, if the updates are significant enough between editions, we may release the updates as a low-priced standalone eBook.

If we produce a free updated version of this chapter, you will be able to access it on the book's companion website. Simply visit the companion website and see the "Exam updates" section.

If you have not yet accessed the companion website, follow these steps:

1. Browse to *microsoftpressstore.com/register*.

2. Enter the print book ISBN (even if you purchased an eBook).

3. After registering the book, go to your account page and select the **Registered Products** tab.

4. Click the Access Bonus Content link to access the companion website. Select the Exam Updates link or scroll down to that section to check for updates.

About possible exam updates

Microsoft reviews exam content periodically to ensure that it aligns with the technology and job role associated with the exam. This includes but is not limited to incorporating functionality and features related to technology changes, changing skills needed for success within a job role, and revisions to product names. Microsoft updates the exam details page to notify candidates when changes occur. Once you register this book, you will be notified when updates are made and the updated chapter is available.

Impact on you and your study plan

Microsoft's information helps you plan, but it also means that the exam might change before you pass the current exam. That impacts you, affecting how we deliver this book to you. This chapter gives us a way to communicate in detail about those changes as they occur, but you should watch the following sites for news:

- **Microsoft Learn**   Check the main source for up-to-date information: *learn.microsoft.com*. Make sure to sign up for automatic notifications.

- **Microsoft Press**   Find information about products, offers, discounts, and free downloads: *microsoftpressstore.com. Make sure you register your purchased products*.

As changes to the MS-102 exam occur, we will publish an updated version of this chapter that will likely include the following:

- **The content that has been removed**   If you plan to take the new exam version, you can ignore the removed content when studying for the exam.

- **New content planned per new exam topics**   This will tell you what's coming.

Exam objective updates

You can find the current study guide for Exam MS-102 at

learn.microsoft.com/en-us/certifications/resources/study-guides/ms-102

It contains the most recent version of the exam objective domain.

Updated technical content

The current version of this chapter has no additional technical content.

Objective mapping

This *Exam Ref* is structured by the author based on the topics and technologies covered on the exam and is not structured based on the specific order of topics in the exam objectives. Table 7-1 maps the current version of the exam objectives to chapter content, allowing you to locate where a specific exam objective item is covered without consulting the index.

TABLE 7-1 Exam objectives mapped to chapters

EXAM OBJECTIVE	CHAPTER
Deploy and manage a Microsoft 365 tenant	
Implement and manage a Microsoft 365 tenant ■ Create a tenant ■ Implement and manage domains ■ Configure organizational settings, including security, privacy, and profile ■ Identify and respond to service health issues ■ Configure notifications in service health ■ Monitor adoption and usage	1
Manage users and groups ■ Create and manage users ■ Create and manage guest users ■ Create and manage contacts ■ Create and manage groups, including Microsoft 365 groups ■ Manage and monitor Microsoft 365 license allocations ■ Perform bulk user management, including PowerShell	2
Manage roles in Microsoft 365 ■ Manage roles in Microsoft 365 and Azure AD ■ Manage role groups for Microsoft Defender, Microsoft Purview, and Microsoft 365 workloads ■ Manage delegation by using administrative units ■ Implement privileged identity management for Azure AD roles	3
Implement and manage identity and access in Azure AD	
Implement and manage identity synchronization with Azure AD ■ Prepare for identity synchronization by using IdFix ■ Implement and manage directory synchronization by using Azure AD Connect cloud sync ■ Implement and manage directory synchronization by using Azure AD Connect ■ Monitor synchronization by using Azure AD Connect Health ■ Troubleshoot synchronization, including Azure AD Connect and Azure AD Connect cloud sync	2
Implement and manage authentication ■ Implement and manage authentication methods, including Windows Hello for Business, passwordless, tokens, and the Microsoft Authenticator app ■ Implement and manage self-service password reset (SSPR) ■ Implement and manage Azure AD password protection ■ Implement and manage multifactor authentication (MFA) ■ Investigate and resolve authentication issues	4
Implement and manage secure access ■ Plan for identity protection ■ Implement and manage Azure AD Identity Protection ■ Plan Conditional Access policies ■ Implement and manage Conditional Access policies	4

continues

EXAM OBJECTIVE	CHAPTER
Manage security and threats by using Microsoft 365 Defender	
Manage security reports and alerts by using the Microsoft 365 Defender portal ■ Review and take actions to improve the Microsoft Secure Score in the Microsoft 365 Defender portal ■ Review and respond to security incidents and alerts in Microsoft 365 Defender ■ Review and respond to issues identified in security and compliance reports in Microsoft 365 Defender ■ Review and respond to threats identified in threat analytics	5
Implement and manage email and collaboration protection by using Microsoft Defender for Office 365 ■ Implement policies and rules in Defender for Office 365 ■ Review and respond to threats identified in Defender for Office 365, including threats and investigations ■ Create and run campaigns, such as attack simulation ■ Unblock users	5
Implement and manage endpoint protection by using Microsoft Defender for Endpoint ■ Onboard devices to Defender for Endpoint ■ Configure Defender for Endpoint settings ■ Review and respond to endpoint vulnerabilities ■ Review and respond to risks identified in the Microsoft Defender Vulnerability Management dashboard	5
Manage compliance by using Microsoft Purview	
Implement Microsoft Purview information protection and data lifecycle management ■ Implement and manage sensitive info types by using keywords, keyword lists, or regular expressions ■ Implement retention labels, retention label policies, and retention policies ■ Implement sensitivity labels and sensitivity label policies	6
Implement Microsoft Purview data loss prevention (DLP) ■ Implement DLP for workloads ■ Implement Endpoint DLP ■ Review and respond to DLP alerts, events, and reports	6

Index

B

B2C IEF Keyset Administrator role, 104

B2C IEF Policy Administrator role, 104

banned password lists, configuring, 153

basic authentication, 142–143

Billing Administrator role, 104

Bing Data Collection setting, 30

.biz domain, 11

blocked users, 225

Bookings setting, 28

Briefing Email setting, 28

C

Calendar setting, 28

certificate-based authentication, 146–147

Cloud App Security Administrator role, 104

Cloud Application Administrator role, 104

Cloud Device Administrator role, 104

Cloud Discovery Global Admin role, 126

CNAME records, 11, 23–26

collaboration protection, 191

Collection Administrators role, Microsoft Purview, 132

.com domain, 11

Compliance Administrator role, 105, 126, 138

compliance and security roles, 138–139

Compliance Data Administrator role, 105

compliance reports, scheduling and reviewing, 40–42

compliance-related roles, Microsoft Entra ID, 245–246

Conditional Access Administrator role, 105

conditional access policies, 167–171

configuration analyzer tool, 212–213

Configuration Manager, using with Defender for Endpoint, 229–230

contoso.com domain, 10

Cortana setting, 28

.co.uk domain, 11

Credential Harvest scenario, 216

Custom App Launcher Tiles setting, 31

custom domain names, configuring, 12–13. *See also* domain names

custom domain, verifying, 13–14

Custom Themes setting, 31

Customer Lockbox Access Approver role, 105

Customer Lockbox setting, 30

D

Data Curators role, Microsoft Purview, 132

Data Lifecycle Management, Microsoft Purview, 242

Data Location setting, 31

data loss prevention reports, 149–115

Data Readers role, Microsoft Purview, 132

Data Source Administrator role, Microsoft Purview, 132

default domain, setting, 15–16. *See also* domains

Defender for Cloud Apps, 125–126

Defender for Endpoint

    Configuration Management, 236

    Device Management, 237–238

    features, 226

    General settings, 232–233

    onboarding devices, 226–231

    rules, 233–235

Defender for Office, threat management, 214–215

Defender for Office Policies, EOP (Exchange Online Protection), 191

Delegated Administrator partner type, 33

S

T